BULLY

MW00610906

by

Anthony Lospinoso

TABLE OF CONTENTS

Introduction..5

Section One: The Early Years 11

Section Two: Reaching New Highs, The High School Years

Part 1: A Bully Is Born.. 41

Part 2: A Bully's Rise And Potential Reformation 71

Section Three: Collegiate Awakenings

Part 1: Passing Judgement 105

Part 2: The Point Of No Return.. 146

Section Four: Early Manhood: Realization And Change

Part 1: Seeking Forgiveness.. 177

Part 2: Repairing Relationships 193

Section Five: Bullying In Our Current Social Climate

Part 1: Victims Of An Unrelenting Epidemic.............................. 223

Part 2: Finding A Voice 258

Section Six: Anti-Bullying Resources

Important Anti-Bullying Organizations 279

Important Anti-Bullying Advocates.............................. 299

Other Celebrity Anti-Bullying Activists.............................. 305

LGBTQ Youth And Bullying 316

Mental Health And Bullying 318

Cyberbullying 321

Rethink Anti-Cyber Bullying Application............................ 325

Important Information For Adults 328

Say Goodbye To Bullying 331

Acknowledgements 333

Author Bio 346

Mission Statement.. 347

BULLY COMPLEX

*The True-Life Story of a
Victim-Turned-Bully-Turned-Advocate*

INTRODUCTION

The blood on the carpet and the walls would only be a small part of the story. My victim shaking uncontrollably, bleeding and crying would tell the rest. My sick sense of fulfillment afterwards, only proved that I had mentally gone off the rails. The alpha male bully had finally satisfied his never-ending appetite.

Bravado is only a small part of having a Bully Complex. There are many factors and reasons that can contribute to having this complex. You will read for yourself what goes into this mental condition. I will first enlighten you to some extent.

Bully Complex is the blood-thirsty need to force power or will over others and make them feel inferior in order to satisfy one's own insecurities. Bully Complex is a mental condition that many people have developed. Some people seem to be born with it, as they possess an innate mean streak. For me, I developed my Bully Complex over time, due to certain experiences that left an indelible impression on me. I was victimized at an early age by ruthless bullies. This had catastrophic consequences for me, because all the victimizations I was subject to eventually caused me to become a bully.

Bully Complex is also the name of my story which is an intense emotional journey. It's the life-altering transformation of one man who proved that change, no matter when it comes in your life, can happen if you let it. It's the awareness of your actions and making amends to all those you hurt along your journey. My story is about realizing ultimate change and trying to become the best form of yourself that you can possibly be.

My name is Anthony Lospinoso, and I was once the biggest bully you could have ever known. My complex was cultivated over time, as I started out as the victim experiencing innumerable encounters where I was tormented as a child. I lived in perpetual fear, and I avoided going to school where I was continuously bullied. Eventually, I went through an unlikely transformation from hapless victim to becoming the biggest bully on the block. This life-altering metamorphosis is how I developed my Bully Complex.

I became addicted to the power and popularity that came with being a bully. I was so ecstatic to break away from being the victim that I reveled in being the bully. This complex had literally taken over my existence. I had an insatiable need to overpower others, because for the first time since my childhood, I had finally become the one with the power. I felt like I was in command, and finally broke free from the restraints that were shackling me. This feeling was glorious, and I wasn't going to relinquish my newfound power. I used this power not only to target prey on my own, but I incorporated group bullying into the mix. I was the ringleader, and I gathered others to join me in my cruel crusade. I had others stand behind and watch me as I victimized others. I was a coward who needed protection. My weak-minded nature led me and my followers down a dark path.

My Bully Complex continued to amplify with time. My popularity ascended from year to year during high school. My newfound prominence went to my head until I was taken finally down a peg during my senior prom. I thought for sure that I'd be a shoo-in to become prom king. After all, I thought I had become so popular that in my delusional mind, I was some type of a king, and the king needed a crown, didn't he? I didn't get voted prom king during that senior prom. I may not have received my crowning moment in high school, but my popularity culminated in a shining moment during my college years. I was indeed crowned Homecoming King and all it did was accelerate my ever-growing Bully Complex. The moment the crown was put on my head, all it did was validate my unending need for popularity. I had an unquenchable thirst for popularity, and I was determined to maintain my throne. That crown fueled an already raging fire. My Bully Complex had become an uncontrollable problem. This was one wildfire that would prove tough to put out.

The crowning led me to think that I was *the man*. I thought I could do what I pleased. My head was bloated and had gotten so big that the crown shouldn't have been able to fit any longer. My inflated ego led me to hurt others in extreme ways. I always took my victimizations to the limits, and one time, I took it to the breaking point. I went way over the line. I went over the edge, as I did something I should have never done.

This was the culmination of the coronation that had gone to my head. This was the final act of a coward who preyed on the weak. Or was it? Did almost destroying this victim finally lead me to change my heinous ways?

I am not proud of my deplorable actions and all the countless people I have hurt in my life. All I can say is that believing in change and making it happen is a part of the journey to making amends with both myself and those who I have victimized.

Many factors went into my Bully Complex. My built-up anger and aggression from being mocked and ridiculed as a child fueled my tyrannical ways. Once I gathered the confidence and popularity I needed, I unleashed my rage onto anyone I perceived to be a weaker individual. If you were not a confident person, you did not want to cross my path. I preyed on the weak. I bullied people for any reason I could, and primarily for reasons they could not control. I found their weaknesses and I exploited them. I was relentless, and my harshness knew no bounds. I bullied people for their ethnicity, their religion, their social status, intelligence levels, their looks, physical deformities, and countless other reasons I cannot even begin to name.

Part of my prejudices had accrued from growing up in a small east coast town. I grew up in a tiny New Jersey town called Kenilworth. Also known as "K-Town," this small suburban area is a tight-knit community that sticks together. Now, in my early forties, I have lived most of my life in this primarily Italian-American town. You will hear about my hometown often, because it helped shape me into the man I have become. To me, Kenilworth is the greatest town, because everyone seems to know one another, and we all have each other's backs.

Growing up in a small town certainly had its benefits, but it also had some major negatives. I grew up without much cultural diversity around me, which will be frequently addressed. Kenilworth is certainly not racist, as I may seem to depict at times. I refer to the town as sheltered, as there were few minorities living there. "Sheltered" is definitely the best word to describe the town. People moved to Kenilworth, grew up there and many of them never leave. The same families have been there for generations. With the same people inhabiting the town for so long, this made the town more like one big family. This made for a unique setting, as most people don't have the relationships that we have.

Because of the lack of turnover and cultural diversity, I grew up with many misconceptions of the world. I don't know if I was totally racist, but I was certainly ignorant. I feel I was this way because I was not exposed to other races and cultures. According to a 2010 United States census, Kenilworth was populated with close to 8,000 people and 88% of that was white. The next highest race was African American at almost 3%, therefore, I am not exaggerating when I talk about the lack of cultural diversity. Because of this, I was slightly prejudiced, and it would take life experiences to open my eyes to see the world for what it really is.

Living a sheltered adolescence aided in fostering my closed-minded mentality. I couldn't break away from these barriers until I broke away from the town. It was then that I learned about other cultures and finally made friends with different types of people from all different races. I am proud to say I have broken away from my racism, judgmental attitude, and stereotypes of other people.

As I recount my life, there will be graphic language used throughout this book. There will be racial, homophobic, and offensive terms used. Some of the recollections will be quite disturbing and will be hard to read. What I did to my victims can be horrifying at times. I did not hold back in writing these accounts, and everything that I have written here is factual. I felt it was absolutely necessary to tell my story and tell it in its truest form.

The anecdotes and nicknames you will hear are factually accurate. I have changed some of the real names of people to protect them or protect myself. Some of the events may have some slight details that have been changed. All the bullying incidents described were either administered to me or I performed them to others, with a few minor exceptions. There are one or two times that I take the blame for a friend who victimized somebody in my presence. I did not want to put any of my friends in harm's way by naming them as a perpetrator. I was always the ringleader, and I most likely pressured my friends into the bullying they engaged in. I would always have other kids aiding me with my incessant bullying.

I am not proud of my actions in this book. However, these stories are powerful, and I am hoping to catch your attention. I feel this is necessary as the bullying epidemic needs everyone's full attention. I hope we can all join efforts to fight together and finally end the bullying epidemic. We can all fight to make this a bully free world.

I decided to write this book because we can all connect to it. Everyone has either been bullied, been a bully, or been a witness to bullying. We have all encountered bullying one way or another in our lives. No matter where you stand on this spectrum, I want you to see how you can affect other people's lives. Most of the time, the actions we take—or more importantly do not take—will cause negative effects. I have been someone who has been on the receiving end of these effects.

I, of course, have been on all sides of the bullying spectrum, thus I offer up a unique perspective from all sides. Considering the landscape of our society, and how prevalent bullying has become, I felt like this is the most important piece of knowledge that I could lend to this world. I am trying to empower those who have been bullied and bossed around. I want to give the victimized a voice and a feeling of hope. Additionally, I want the bullies to realize there is a point of going too far. I have included explicit details on how I was bullied and how I then bullied others. I am not encouraging kids to read this and follow suit. I rather want them to realize how much pain I was in and how much pain I then inflicted. I am not proud of my actions and I want anyone to know that if you read this and try to replicate my despicable actions, that you are not a good human being. Nobody should be subjected to the things I did to others and the way I victimized them. I've realized that nobody is better than another person. All the bullying I was a part of wasn't right in any way. Bullying others is never the right thing to do.

For those who are being broken down, beaten, and bullied, I want you to realize that it's OK to fight back, but to an extent. I talk about several tragedies that have ended in death or near death because bullying had gone too far. Many children have sought retribution by killing their classmates. I have never thought about killing anyone in retribution for victimizing me, and neither should you. I say yes to standing up for yourself, using your voice, and if absolutely necessary, your fists. The last one I only advocate if you feel that is the only possible recourse. You should always try to talk things out first. If someone is beating you, then yes, you have a right to defend yourself, but you should never initiate the physicality. Violence is never the answer.

I am hoping to illustrate how violence has become a common theme in bullying. Whether it is the bully administering the physicality or it is the victims retaliating, extreme violence has become far too prevalent. Many victims are fighting back in deadly ways, and this needs to stop immediately. I advocate fighting back, but not to injure or kill the bullies. In some instances, the victims are inflicting pain upon themselves. Some of these victims go as far as killing themselves. Suicide is never the answer and is a serious matter that we all need to have on our radar. Unfortunately, this has become a serious trend in bullying situations. This will hopefully be an educational exploration for many of you, as I aim to enlighten you and shed some light on our ever-growing bully epidemic.

SECTION ONE

THE EARLY YEARS

"There I lay covered in sand, drooling, blood dripping from my forehead. I lay in the sand pit on the playground, broken, beaten, and bloodied."

I have been either a victim or a bully almost my entire life. I have changed my bullying ways over the last ten years, because I finally realized that I've hurt people, and never realized the extent of those scars. My time spent as a bully was rather significant, and it took hard doses of reality to change that. When you're the one being bullied, it's rough, unpleasant, and often excruciating. You feel like a victim and you feel helpless. When you're the one doing the bullying, you feel like you have power over someone. In reality, you are just displaying immense insecurities from deep within.

I remember hating school from a young age, but looking back, it wasn't the actual school part I hated. I hated getting picked on and beat up. I was one of the few Asian kids in my school. Even before I knew what a "Chink" was, other kids would yell the racially charged slur right in my face. Not only would they yell the hurtful, derogatory slur at me, but they would shout it with such venom that I wanted to cry. Sometimes I *would* cry, and somehow that only accelerated the teasing. Besides being Asian, I was one of the heaviest kids in my class from an early age. I was known as the fat kid growing up. The combination rolled together to form my nickname, and I became known as the "Fat Chink."

When I was in first grade, in the very beginning of the bullying, I wouldn't fight back. I would start a scene and cry, throw a fit, and then yell at my teacher and the principal, screaming that I wanted to go home. I remember my mom or dad carrying me out of school kicking, screaming, and crying. I spent most days of the first grade crying and sulking in front of the entire class. I wasn't only crying physical tears, but I was crying out emotionally and praying for help. I wanted

11

someone to help me and save me from all the bullying I had to endure. However, I didn't know how to communicate to the school authorities or my parents that I was being tormented daily. I was embarrassed to reach out for help. I didn't want anyone to know that I was being teased to that extent. Consequently, I held all of the pain and hideous feelings inside. My parents would ask me what was wrong, and I just said that I hated school. The fact was that I didn't hate school, I just hated being bullied.

As time went on, there were more and more things to ridicule me about. Since I was overweight at a young age, I had some early medical problems. I had high blood pressure and high cholesterol. This was all a bit overwhelming for a child in the first grade. Due to my health issues, the doctor ordered I be put on a special diet. I was not able to be a normal kid. I couldn't eat candy or drink soda like the other kids. Some of my favorite things to eat to this day are cakes, cookies, and ice cream. But the young, overweight me was not allowed to eat any of these sweet treats. Well, once other kids realized I didn't eat candy and other childish delights like everyone else, it became more fodder to badger me about. I became a "weirdo," or kids would say, "Maybe he's retarded?" Meanwhile, even if I was able to explain why, young children wouldn't understand, nor have sympathy. As a matter of fact, more fat jokes would probably ensue.

Imagine being the kid who couldn't eat candy on Halloween. After being diagnosed with these medical problems, I couldn't eat any candy at all. This was like torture and further fuel used by the bullies to torment me. Prior to learning about my medical conditions, I was obsessed with Reese's Pieces candies. I still am to this day, as I periodically gorge myself on those little pieces of peanut butter bliss. Today eating Reese's is just a guilty pleasure, but as a kid it's supposed to be a rite of passage. For me, it was anything but. Not being able to eat them was flat out torturous for me. Torture because I wanted to be normal like all the other kids and be able to eat candy. Torture because all the other kids perceived me to be weird for not eating candy. I was made to be an outcast as other kids laughed that I couldn't indulge in all the sweet, chocolaty treats that they were feasting away on.

Halloween went from my favorite holiday to my least favorite in an instant. I remember kids asking me questions in an insensitive manner, "Why don't you have a piece of chocolate, weirdo? What's wrong with you? Why won't you have candy with the rest of us? What are you, some kind of a freak?"

Kids can be flat out mean. It's as simple as that. They have no filter and the insults they hurl can be shocking. Kids often don't think about their actions especially when bullying others. They don't realize the legitimate damage that they can cause others. The bullies make their victims feel alienated. The victims are often isolated and in turn keep to themselves.

Kids all want to be popular and they have a need to be perceived as "cool." Many times, kids want to look cool in front of the crowd. This need to be cool drives them to bully others. Kids often form groups to bully other kids that are perceived to be weaklings or outcasts. This is a mob mentality that is consistent in bullying. Bullies team up to victimize, and this gives them a false sense of empowerment. These kids have a habitual need to fit in. Forming these groups consisting of bullies makes them feel like they are a part of something. We need to break this persistent and pesky mentality.

I was made to be an outsider when I couldn't act as what was perceived to be a normal child. When I couldn't eat ice cream, this made me a weirdo in other kids' eyes. So, there I was: detached, labeled as an outcast. Nobody accepted me. I felt lost and alone. I was a loner, beaten and broken down at a young, impressionable age. Something made me different from the other kids and this polarized me from the group.

Now I look back and I realize that I received absurd amounts of ridicule for a serious medical condition. This was a condition that ultimately could have threatened my life if I had not adhered to this special diet. Most young kids wouldn't understand special diets; therefore, they just didn't understand me and my unusual eating habits.

When I was really young and I had that special diet, my parents used some odd techniques to try and deter me from eating so much. They brought me to see the movie *Fatso* starring Dom DeLuise. Dom DeLuise was an American actor and comedian who was known as the "fat guy." In the movie, DeLuise struggles with his obesity and eating habits. He can never seem to get his eating under control. In one particular scene, DeLuise dunks his bread into Italian red sauce, and that's something that I absolutely loved to do in my youth.

My parents said, "See? Keep doing that, and you're gonna be like Fatso!" My parents were just trying to help and were trying to inject some humor in the situation. It was pretty visible that I was upset with this new diet. They were trying to brighten what was a gloomy situation for me. All I wanted to do was dunk my bread, but I couldn't. That perturbed me and made me significantly upset. I didn't want to be like Fatso! My parents were only trying to help, but at the time their eccentric tactics only added to my deflating confidence.

Although my parents had good intentions, the kids at school did not. They would yell "Fatso" and "Fat Chink" at me with malice and hate in their eyes. But that's what bullying is all about, picking off other's weaknesses. Years later, I would bully people for similar reasons, ones they couldn't control. Facial features, being poor, listening to styles of music, being too smart, being dumb, the list goes on and on, but nothing was off limits when it came to my victimizations. I also say that I bullied "people" because once I was old enough, I not only bullied other kids, but I bullied teachers, janitors, college-age students, and I went as far as to bully certain authority figures who were supposed to be the ones with the power. If I sensed weakness and I felt I could bully you, then I would. I bullied anyone I felt superior to. I never stopped until one specific day when everything changed, and I had an epiphany.

On that day, I ran into someone I had previously bullied and I didn't even remember him from high school. But he sure remembered me, and he loathed me. I could feel the hate seething from every fiber of his being. The feelings were emanating off his enraged aura. His eyes pierced through my soul as he struck and splintered my nerves. I could tell he wanted to pulverize me. I thought, *What could I have possibly done that was so atrocious to this guy?* I was dumbfounded as to why he seemingly wanted to leave me lying in a pool of my own blood. I will get to what happened with me and the young man as there is so much more of what led me to this life-altering moment. I underwent an inordinate amount of change. I went from being the one who was bullied to the ultimate bully.

From the first grade all the way until high school, I felt like I was completely powerless and defenseless. Early on, I was only name-called and mocked verbally, but the victimizations would only accelerate over time. The mental abuse would soon be complemented by physical torment. When I reached the fifth and sixth grades, that's when I endured the worst of it. Here is some of what I can recall:

There I lay covered in sand, drooling, blood dripping from my forehead. I lay in the sand pit on the playground, broken, beaten, and bloodied. This was almost a daily occurrence on our playground after school. I was constantly beaten and humiliated.

There was a tire park on our playground, where we made all our professional wrestling heroes come to life. We would emulate the most popular wrestlers of the time like The Ultimate Warrior, Macho Man Randy Savage, and Ric Flair. I couldn't perform anywhere near my idols' levels. Every day, I was tossed over the side of the tires. I was then humiliated as the boys would gather around me and spit and drool all over my face. I would cry from the humiliation and the emotional agony. The spit and tears would combine into a disgusting river of liquid pouring off my beaten face.

Each day, there was a battle in a circular pit of sand surrounded by half tires. We would have what is known as a "battle royal," just like the professional wrestling match held in the WWE. The match has between ten and thirty men in the ring at one time. In order to be victorious, you must throw your opponents over the top rope. The last man standing would be the victor. In our twisted rendition, we had to throw each other over the tires and out of the circle. Most days, I was eliminated quickly. Usually, I was punched a few times and then thrown over rather easily, like a sack of potatoes. However, there was this one special day that I would not give up.

I had been beaten down over and over. I was exhausted, dripping sweat, and my face was bloody to a pulp. I remember laying there, sand covering my eyes, blinded, but I was not mentally beaten this time. Suddenly, several of my "opponents" started coming towards me, as only a few gladiators remained. A sea of crimson red was flowing over my face like a red river. Through blood-covered eyes, I could see there were three cretins hovering over my gory body, which was covered in my own drool, with sand covering my carcass like breading on fried chicken.

One boy yelled, "Let's beat him up some more!"

I was ready for it that day, as I would not give up.

Then one of the weary combatants said with empathy, "He's had enough, let's just throw him over."

With that, the three boys picked me up and threw me over the tires. As the year went by, I continued to fight harder and harder. I stood up to these cretins. I was never the last man standing; thus, I never won a battle royal match, but I gained a little respect as I took beating after beating. They kept knocking me down, but I kept getting back up.

There was no denying my enduring heart. Unlike most who are bullied, I did not cry, and I did not run. Not anymore anyway. I used to run and cry, but I came to learn that this only fueled the bully's fire. I now knew that standing my ground would earn me some amount of respect. I would still get picked on, but the beatings became shorter, and more times than not, the antagonizer would move on to easier prey. I was becoming less of the hunted as some bullies don't always want to deal with someone who actually fights back.

These were the daily beatings I took as a fifth and sixth grader. Even though I fought back, I was not good at it, hence why I was still picked on. I was certainly good at taking a beating, but I would get my butt kicked day after day. I often had to hide my wounds from my parents because I was never going to divulge what was really happening to me. If I had a bruise on my face, I would lie about where it came from. I would have frequent "falls off of my bicycle." I was ashamed of the ceaseless victimizations and I didn't want my parents to know the pain I was in. I wish I could have opened up to them, but I just didn't know how. I just kept my parents in the dark when it came to my anguish.

I was the public whipping boy for a bevy of bullies. There wasn't a day that went by that I was left alone. I would be harassed in some form and there was nobody there to stop it. My psyche was fragile and with each passing day at school, my spirit wilted. All the constant abuse shattered my soul like a splintered piece of glass. Mentally, I was beaten down and dejected. My joy for being a kid had been dampened. I became somewhat of an introvert. I never wanted to give up, but I certainly had thoughts of hurting the ones who hurt me. I never reached the point that retaliation became a reality. Thankfully, I didn't want to hurt anyone, especially myself. I wasn't suicidal or anything, but I did want the pain to end. I wanted to escape and run away. The happiness of being a little boy was stripped away and I was consumed with fear and sadness.

Enduring this mental abuse daily wore on me. I never wanted to go to school and when I was there, I tried to fake being sick. I took frequent trips to the nurse's office, but most days I was denied from being sent home. The nurse was fed up with seeing me, but maybe she could have recognized that something was going awry in my life. Maybe she could have seen the anguish in my eyes and maybe she could have helped me.

I would have rather been in the nurse's office than engage with the other kids. Every trip to the playground would just end in agony for me. Everywhere I went, there were bullies waiting to prey on my weakened spirit. My fragile mental state made me try to steer away from social activities. I was tired of the constant abuse, and I did everything I could to avoid the bullies.

Despite being the punching bag for most of the alpha boys, I did actually have a couple of friends. Even though I had friends, most of them would not stick up for me in fear of being beaten or made fun of themselves. Had any of them stuck up for me, they would become the subject of ridicule. Most of my friends weren't the "cool" kids, but they also weren't the ones being bullied. Even though I was upset about the situation, I understood it. Why put yourself in the line of fire? Would I have done it for them? I doubt it, as I hated being beaten up, ridiculed, and tormented.

As a matter of fact, I had chances to help others who were being bullied. My cousin, Joe, was one year above me in school and he was bullied relentlessly. I remember Joe being somewhat different. Since he was a year older than me, we pretty much went through schooling together.

My cousin endured a lot of verbal harassment. Kids discovered new words that would hurt him deeply. We all discover bad words for the first time. I remember when somebody at school found out what "being gay" meant and then started calling people "gay." Of course, this was mainly the boys calling each other gay. That's what happened that day at recess when all the boys branded my cousin Joe as gay. Girls didn't usually engage in such juvenile banter at the time. Times have changed when it comes to girls and bullying, so I have heard. I hear they can be just as sinister as boys now. But back when I grew up, the girls would bully on occasion, but in general from my experiences, they did not engage like the boys. This is why women were always considered to be more mature than men. This is probably true for the most part. However, if little girls are bullying just as much as little boys nowadays, this is quite a scary development. Considering the new times we live in, boys and girls both need to recognize that bullying is wrong and stop this infantile behavior. We need to be more aware of how immature bullying really is.

The immature boys continued to harass my cousin Joe. More words were being spread around school about being gay. The word "faggot" became a term that we threw around. If you did something perceived as being gay, you'd be called a "fag." This was the first time that I had seen my cousin harassed on the playground. This was a place where you were supposed to let loose and have fun, but instead this became a breeding ground for bullies. I remember one specific afternoon during lunch recess when a bunch of kids were calling Joe a "fag" and saying he was "gay." The sanctity of the playground was desecrated that day. After that day, these homophobic slurs and other forms of bullying became commonplace on the playground. As my cousin was pelted with a verbal assault, I just stood there silently. I stayed off to the side, hoping the harassment would not come my way, and I just watched as the kids pelted my cousin with this offensive onslaught. I mostly did nothing but kept coy and stood idly by as my cousin was ridiculed day after day, until one day I decided to do something.

I joined in.

See, when you are the one being bullied, sometimes you revert to bullying others. This may seem like a way to cope, but it is not in any way. Even though others may have bullied you and made you feel a certain way, doing it to others is still explicitly wrong. Why did I want to make Joe feel the way that I was often made to feel? I joined in with the other bullies and called him a "fag" for as long as I could remember. It was rare that I was not being bullied, so if someone else was going to get ridiculed and I could be a part of it, then, *count me in!* I thought.

When the other boys weren't around, Joe would say that I was his cousin and should not join the others. He would say that we are family and that blood is thicker than water, therefore we should stick together. But that did not matter to me. What mattered to me was when he was around, I was mostly left alone. So, I was not letting up on the "fag." Joe was someone that took the onus off me and I yearned to be out of the spotlight for good.

I remember one day after weeks of these victimizations, my cousin finally decided to report the hounding torment to a lunch aid during recess. The aid did nothing and said that she had not heard any of the bruising insults. The only advice the aid offered was for Joe to stay away from the bullies, and to go in another direction on the playground.

The aid was no help to Joe, just as I had been no help to him. He was probably starting to feel helpless. The aid made a definite impact on Joe's behavior, as he must have felt like there was nobody who would help him with the bullying that he was enduring on a daily basis.

The fact that the aid did nothing to help is extremely distressing. This was in a different time, as this occurred over thirty years ago, but we are still dealing with similar problems in our current time. There are still adults who witness bullying and do not intervene. This is a dangerous trend when it comes to bullying, and something that we all need to recognize. If the adults aren't getting involved, then we are in trouble when it comes to the bullying epidemic. When adults witness bullying or hear about it and don't help, this makes kids like Joe act out. These kids may even harm themselves or others if they do not get the assistance that they need. Joe acted out when he didn't receive help. I obviously cannot speak for Joe and the behavior he displayed. I can only speak about what I witnessed and what I believe.

I remember Joe displaying similar behaviors to me in school, except I had displayed these behaviors in the first grade. I am sure the aid had something to do with his outlandish behavior as he used to scream, cry, and yell at his teachers, the principal, and anybody that would listen. Looking back, I now realize he was doing the same exact thing I was doing: looking for a way to escape. He, too, wanted to get out of school any way he could. Joe wanted refuge from the nonstop bullying.

Joe had recurrent outbursts in school which actually perpetuated the bullying. Kids would see him unleash his temper and they would laugh at him. One day I remember Joe was in the classroom across the hall. Our class could hear the whole incident as he erupted with rage. Joe was berating and barking at the teacher. I was in the back of the classroom where I could see clearly across the hall. I was able to see Joe vehemently run out of the classroom and the teacher chase after him. The teacher grabbed Joe, but he spun around in a tizzy and in one sweeping motion, he ripped the bewildered instructor's shirt right off his body. Everyone in the back of my class and several others who had followed the action in the other class now exploded with laughter.

Joe was removed from school and suspended. Joe is a great guy with an even more amazing heart. I'm sorry he had to go through what he endured. I'm sorry that I joined in at times and I can never fix that. I know we are well beyond it, but I still harbor unresolved feelings. I betrayed Joe when he needed me and for that I can never be forgiven, I can only move forward and continue to make my amends.

After Joe ripped the teacher's shirt, the incident opened my eyes and made me realize that I could unleash some of my pent-up rage on my teachers as well. Because I was the punching bag for countless bullies, I needed a way to vent and find an outlet for all my built-up emotions. The way I coped was being rebellious and outlandish during class. I soon became a menace to the teachers, counselors, principals, and any authority figure at the schools I attended. I wreaked havoc and bulldozed a path of destruction.

In the fifth grade, one of our assignments was to bring in a piece of poetry that moved us and to recite it in front of the class. Here's part of what I recited one blistery winter afternoon:

"Hey, Satan, payin' my dues

Playin' in a rockin' band

Hey, mamma, look at me

I'm on the way to the promised land

I'm on the highway to hell

Highway to hell

I'm on the highway to hell

Highway to hell"

These are famed lyrics to the AC/DC song, "Highway to Hell." That was poetry to me. But when I said, "Hey Satan," the teacher's jaw dropped along with a few of my classmates who weren't ready for such lewdness. This was in the late 1980s and the world was a vastly different place. Yes, the world is a more sensitive place now, but back then we lived in a world where we recited the Pledge of Allegiance and boldly proclaimed to be "One Nation Under God." Christianity and the belief in God were widely talked about subjects, especially in our town. Talking about God was not considered taboo. So, when I uttered phrases about Satan and a Highway to Hell, surely there would be hell to pay.

The teacher immediately sent me to the principal's office. I was asked where I learned such outrageous terms as "Satan" and "Hell" and why did I utter them in my fifth-grade classroom?

My response to the principal was, "I don't have to tell you shit, and you can go to hell, too!"

The principal couldn't believe that I had hurled such profanity in his direction. Curse words were highly rebellious to say when I was at that age. This was the start of me pushing boundaries and challenging adult authority figures.

Do you remember when you were young and the first time you discovered curse words? I remember the first time I heard someone say the word "cock" and the look on my mom's face because she knew I had heard. One of my cousins probably uttered the word at a family event. But nonetheless, the first time the "forbidden" word hit my eight-year-old ears, I was ready to unleash its glory upon everyone. But I had to wait, because I knew this was a bad word judging by my mom's reaction. So I waited for what I thought to be the perfect day. We were on a family drive. My dad was driving, my mom was in the passenger seat, and my little sister and I were in the back seat. There was a popular song playing on the radio called "Solid as a Rock." This was the time I was going to drop the word and see how my parents would react. I was always one to push boundaries. Hence, here came the chorus and I sang aloud clear as day, "And I'm solid, solid as my cock!" That didn't go so well, as it brought about a deserved tongue lashing. My mom exclaimed, "Anthony! Don't you ever say that again! That's a bad word!"

I didn't realize at the time exactly what I had said. I just wanted to use the word cock. I not only used it, but to me, I had used it magnificently. That song was almost meant to use the word cock! But it was not meant for an eight-year-old boy to blubber out of his naive young mouth. Even worse, this was not something my six-year-old sister should have heard with her innocent young ears! Bottom line, that shouldn't have come out of my mouth. The same goes for the verbal assault I sent towards the principal.

Cursing at him landed me in a month's worth of detention. But to this point, I was already used to detention. It just didn't faze me anymore. It had become a regular part of my school day just as heavy metal had. I mean, I was a defiant young boy who rebelled against authority. What do you think I was gonna listen to? I blasted all my favorite bands including Metallica, Black Sabbath, Anthrax and AC/DC. I thought I was such a little badass. I had a penchant for heavy guitars, and I reveled in the harsh vocal bliss of the hardest rock. Well, the hardest rock that I could find at that time in my life, anyway. I discovered heavy metal in the fifth grade at my friend Laz's house. Laz put on Metallica's mighty "Master of Puppets" album and it blew my doors off. The first chords reeled me in and soon after I was addicted. I have never looked back, and to this day, I am still in love with heavy metal and madly obsessed with Metallica.

The music I loved certainly didn't attract many girls back in those days. Nowadays there are plenty of "metal chicks" that not only like the music, but they go to concerts, too. Girls my age found metal music repulsive. People considered you a misfit, an outcast, a burnout, for listening to metal. I was definitely on my way to becoming a burnout, and tried to live my life as one. By eighth grade, I succeeded. I cut class, I had a bad attitude, and of course, I listened to heavy metal. The only thing keeping me from becoming the stereotypical burnout was the fact that I didn't have long hair like some of my friends did. I just never looked good with long hair, and my mother was strict with appearances, so I probably would have gotten grounded if I had grown my hair out. Most of all I respected her wishes, therefore heavy metal hair was not happening.

Needless to say, I had many early troubles with girls. It was in the seventh grade that I first remember seeing young boys and girls making out. They would do it all the time, in the school yard, on the bus, and in the hallways. I was so jealous as I knew I would never get a kiss. I was a misfit heavy metal listening derelict. Add that to my huge self-esteem issues I had at the time and it was a recipe for repulsiveness. My perpetual negativity led to repetitive repugnant thoughts of myself and the way that I looked. I considered myself to be extremely ugly. I likened myself to Eddie Munster, but without the pointy ears. For those of you who didn't grow up watching 80s sitcoms, Eddie Munster was a character on an old sitcom called "The Munsters." Eddie was a werewolf with pointy ears, and had god awful looking hair. If you've never seen him, please Google him in order to see the image that I saw when I looked in the mirror. Forget self-esteem issues, I had no self-esteem.

That year in seventh grade, we would have the first school dance of our young lives. It was a big deal to ask a girl to dance, and I had zero self-confidence. I just watched as many of the other boys with self-esteem asked for dances with pretty girls. I sat in the corner with a few other kids and I stewed. We were perceived as the "losers" and we knew it.

I wasn't sad; the situation actually made me quite angry. Not only was I a beaten-down, bullied kid, but I had no skills when it came to flirting with girls. After all, I was branded the "fat chink," so how could I possibly have any skills with pretty girls?

Everyone could see me brooding in the corner. Then a girl who I was friendly with walked over to me and ever so sweetly asked, "Anthony, would you like to dance?"

I should have happily accepted and went out onto the dance floor with her. But years of anger and anguish had built up inside of me. I convinced myself that she was taking pity on me and that's not what I wanted. Certainly, this angel did not want to dance with me, Eddie Munster! Either she was taking pity on me or she was playing a joke on me. This could not be sincere. My mind twisted all these repugnant thoughts around until my head was spinning like a washer on spin cycle. Suddenly, all my feelings welled up and I erupted. I yelled in her sweet angelic face, "FUCK YOU!"

She looked startled and scurried back over to her friends. I have been mad at myself to this day for acting in such a foul manner. She had no ill intentions and was being 100% sweet, but I couldn't help myself, and I took my mounting anger and self-pity out on her. Her name was Maria, and we had been in classes together since Kindergarten. We were pretty close, and I considered her a friend at that point in life. That's how I know she was being genuine, and her intentions were pure. So, Maria, if you're reading this, I'm sorry. I know it was a long time ago and we have gotten past it, but it's something that has stayed with me. Maria didn't deserve that, and I wish I wasn't such an angry little boy.

My insecurities with women would last for a long time. It wasn't until college that I began to think I was somewhat decent-looking, and grew out of my Eddie Munster phase. I did have one girlfriend in high school, so I guess I wasn't a complete failure with the ladies. But I certainly was no Zach Efron at the time.

My lack of self-esteem only accelerated my ever-growing Bully Complex. There were many reasons for my self-esteem issues, but the main reason was being overweight. I caught infinite amounts of ridicule for being bigger than most of my classmates. The worst of the victimizations would come during gym class. I was always amongst the last ones to be picked in gym class, as nobody wanted the fat kid on their team. Anyone that gets picked last in gym class will tell you that it's a blow to your confidence. This is something that stays with you, as it affects your self-esteem. Even today, this causes a fire to burn in my belly, as I work extra hard in the gym to avoid being the fat kid who is picked last in gym class.

Another trouble in gym class was doing push-ups. In fact, I couldn't even do one. When it came time to do the dreaded activity, the cackling and catcalling would begin. The kids would yell, "Come on Fatso, push yourself up!" "Look at Fatty, he can't even do one push-up!"

Push-ups weren't my only Achilles heel, since I also had trouble running. We were forced to do physical fitness tests and that always involved running a mile around the track. I would endure extreme torment and name calling as I "ran" around that unforgiving track. I had to make frequent stops to catch my breath and I walked more than I was able to run. I could never actually *run* a full mile and I was always the last one in my class to cross the finish line. The other children were unrelenting with their verbal assault. "Come on Fatso, run faster! Catch up Fat Ass! Fat Boy looks like he's gonna pass out on the track!" Even the physical education instructor would put me down. He would say that if I ran faster maybe I would lose some weight. Instead of motivating me, he made me feel even worse about myself. Talk about kicking someone when they are down.

All the ridicule and bullying made me want to find a way to release my rage. I decided to take my escalating anger out on my teachers, especially after the treatment from my gym instructor. I was more than ready to unleash my torture upon any and all educators.

I would ask around and find out which classes had a shaky commander that I could go in and abuse. There were certain teachers with the reputation that you could act up in their classes. I would always target these classes, so I could harass someone else in an attempt to take the pain away from my own constant harassments.

I heard that band class was one of the most mischievous classes in school. I couldn't even play an instrument, but I heard that it didn't matter. Could I pound on a giant drum occasionally? Yes, I certainly could! That was how I was allowed into band class. I was the guy in the back that pounded the oversized drum. After all, this was all a ruse; I was not taking band to play or learn an instrument. I was there to torture Mr. Tuplinsky, a.k.a. "Mr. Toupee," who earned his nickname for his off-kilter hairpiece flopping from his tilted head.

Now, going into this class, I had heard that Mr. Toupee had a penchant to lose his temper and blow his top. Well, my plan was to have him blow his top so badly that his toupee came flying off!

This class was generally a hornet's nest for class clowns to come together. Most people in band class were just there to fool around and have a grand old time. I almost felt bad for the students that were there to actually learn an instrument and take this circus of a class seriously. My presence would dash all hope of any normality in that class.

I engaged in general clownish behavior in the beginning. Banging the drum when I wasn't supposed to, catcalling at Mr. Toupee, and going so far as wearing a wig to class, in order to further mock Mr. Toupee. This was all generally routine. But so far, I hadn't been able to get this man to explode and show this famous temper that I had heard so much about.

Then one day, I finally found a way to get under his skin and his toupee. Mr. Tuplinsky was proudly playing classical records for us on his record player. All the famous composers, which included Bach, Mozart, and Beethoven. Now, as I told you already, I was and always will be a metal head. Back then, I was a *stubborn* metal head, and I did not want to hear that type of music or any other type for that matter. To me, the rest of it was all garbage. I wanted the classical music to stop. I came up with a devious plan.

I whispered to a fellow class-clown next to me. He repeated my mischievous plan to another perpetrator, and soon I could see the word go around the entire band room. My clowning classmates' faces lit up with my light bulb of an idea. Now it was time to light up Mr. Toupee's classroom by implementing the madness.

I made eye contact with my more than willing accomplices. Everyone was ready. I looked around and counted aloud, "One, two, three!" At that moment, all of us troublemakers jumped up and stomped on the floor. Yahtzee! The record skipped as I had planned.

Mr. Tuplinsky glared around the room looking for a perpetrator. He seemed unsure that I had orchestrated this, but I wouldn't stop until he did.

Again, I barked, "One, two, three!" We all jumped once more making the record skip even worse than the first go around.

This time, Mr. Toupee was visibly rattled. He looked around and said, "Cut it out! Stop this immediately! If you don't stop, you will suffer the consequences!"

Of course, I didn't stop, I wanted to see a full-blown explosion. I was now the commander of the entire room. After each subsequent *one, two, three* count, most of the room jumped and stomped in unison. Before I knew it, after the fifth time of rapid-fire jumping, the record came off the player which proved to be quite symbolic.

Mr. Toupee turned fire engine red and screamed at the top of his lungs, "CUT THE SHIT!" By now, he had seen me as the lead conductor, which prompted him to dart towards me and look directly into my eyes as he screamed, "I'll kill you! You friggin' little shit!"

He then continued dashing towards me and I could see the ominous intentions in his eyes. I really thought he might harm me. I ran down the aisle as fast as I could and bolted into the hallway. I could hear Mr. Toupee scampering behind me. I ran into the boy's bathroom down the hall. I couldn't tell you why I did this, because now I was trapped.

Mr. Tuplinsky ran in and grabbed me by the shirt. He pounded me into the wall with a great thud. He looked at me and then something strange happened. He broke down. In near tears, he looked at me and said, "Why? Why? Why must you disrupt the class and disrespect me like that? Everyone in that class thinks I'm a fool! You little shit!"

The class next door must have heard the disturbance because the next thing I know, their teacher came in and separated us. That was my last hurrah in Mr. Toupee's class, as I was quickly removed from band. It wouldn't be the first time I was taken out of a class for my foolish shenanigans and it certainly wouldn't be the last.

You see, early on I learned a little trick that helped to enable my bad behavior in the classroom. I was always tall for my age, therefore my unsuspecting educators usually sat me in the back of the classroom. I came to learn over the years that you can get away with much, much more in the back of the class. I would yell out degrading nicknames towards my teachers or other students. I could throw objects when the teacher turned to write on the chalkboard. Being in the back of the class went a long way in developing the menace that I would become.

My behavior towards my educators only worsened with time. Shortly after band class, I found myself in a class that I would disrupt relentlessly. One of my earliest memories of lashing out started with a teacher named Miss Pisto. She had a reputation of being a teacher that you could basically screw around with. She, like Mr. Toupee, had a reputation of blowing up at students. Despite her blow ups, students loved her class because you could fool around and not do much work. Needless to say, when I drew one of her classes, I was excited. I couldn't wait to start my unending and unnerving harassment.

I remember one time as clear as the beautiful spring day it occurred on. The windows were open because, as I said, the weather was glorious. I had been brewing my idea for a while now, but that glorious day was the day I had picked to implement my mayhem. The sunny day was about to get gloomy and turn into a hailstorm.

As Miss Pisto wrote a lesson plan for our day on the blackboard, I sprang into action. I lunged at a group of books that were lined upright directly next to the open windows. With one triumphant and quick pounce, I managed to heave the entire row of books off the second floor. I took a quick second to watch the books crash down onto the asphalt below. I then sprang back into my seat as if nothing happened. Of course, this made some noise and Miss Pisto turned around to see what had occurred.

Her face was horrified as she walked towards the window and saw a dozen books sprawled across the asphalt below. She began screaming at the top of her lungs, "Who did this? Who did it? Someone tell me, now!"

Nobody owned up to it of course, and this further enraged the unhinged educator. She went off on a tirade which she was famous for. She glared one by one at the known troublemakers of the class and announced each name consecutively. She bellowed, "Donald! Robert! Matthew!" Then she screamed my name next, "Anthony!" However, every name she bellowed and each subsequent stare only elicited one response: laughter. As a matter of fact, at this point, the entire class was laughing relentlessly as she then wilted and began to cry. This, too, was another Miss Pisto trademark.

I would continue to torture Miss Pisto throughout the year. I made her cry on several occasions, and I never once felt bad. I was flat out cruel. Kids can be cruel and especially mean to others, however I was plain ruthless. Making her break down in tears wasn't enough for me, I had something bigger in mind for the embattled educator. My crowning achievement was yet to come. I had been planning something big for Miss Pisto. But I needed to goad her into believing that I was not a troublemaker any longer, that I had changed, and I was now a sweet little angel. Needless to say, this plan took a few weeks to implement. Good thing for me, this lady was beyond gullible.

For several weeks, I acted like a suck up and I was extra nice to the clueless teacher. I would answer with "Yes, Ma'am," and I made sure to thank her for the wonderful lesson that day. A couple of my fellow troublemaker classmates were suspicious and asked me on the playground what was up. They thought I had gone soft. I assured them that it was all part of a master plan, and to stay tuned for the grand finale of my expertly planned tomfoolery. I could tell they all were anxious for what I had in store.

The day finally arrived. The day I had been pining for.

Miss Pisto would always have one of the students go fill up her coffee cup with fountain water. Well, I had gained enough trust and kissed up enough, that on that day she finally asked me to go fill her cup. This was the day I was anxiously awaiting. I said, "Well surely Miss Pisto, I will be right back."

It just so happens that the water fountain was right next to the boy's bathroom. I ran in and quickly scooped toilet water into the coffee cup. I now know it was despicable, but at the time, I thought it was ingenious. I returned with a big shit-eating grin on my face, but I played it off as best I could, as not to alert her to my foul play. I quickly rearranged my smirk into a polite smile and handed her the coffee cup. "Here you go Miss Pisto." She replied in kind, "Thank you."

I sat down and waited a few minutes. I let her take a few sips. She turned to start putting notes on the chalkboard. I then said, "Excuse me, Miss Pisto." As she turned to look at me, I looked her dead in the eye, with the devil in my eyes, and said, "How does the toilet taste?"

Her face went blank at first, then she grew white as an albino ghost. She peered over at her coveted coffee cup, and looked back at me in horror.

I gave her a wry smile as if to say, "*Yup.*"

Her ghostly appearance quickly changed to a fiery, crimson red. Then something happened that nobody expected. She dashed at me with rage in her eyes. She scratched my neck with her long, witch-like nails. Then she got behind me and choked me, while her nails dug into my skin.

It was all very surreal, but to be honest, it didn't hurt one bit. I had gotten my ass beat countless times at this point. Even this crazed lady trying to choke me with all her strength couldn't damage me. I was almost immune to the pain from all the beatings I had taken over the years. The fact that I felt nothing made me begin to laugh incessantly.

The class went from mortified silence to outrageous laughter when I began laughing. Finally, another teacher ran in, as he must have heard the ruckus from across the hall. He hollered, "Miss Pisto, stop! Miss Pisto!"

She finally relented and at that moment realized what she had done. She was instantly apologetic. "I am so sorry, sweetie."

In true pre-teen fashion, I muttered, "Yeah OK, whatever."

I was immediately sent to the principal's office and my mom was called in.

Now, I wasn't sure which way this was going to go. Yes, I gave the teacher toilet water (allegedly), but I also had red marks all over my neck. I had some time with my mother alone as the principal took Miss Pisto's account of what had happened.

My mom looked at me and said, "What happened? I want the truth." She was obviously infuriated at the sight of her boy with scalding nail marks that had clearly drawn blood across his neck.

I told her pretty much the whole story, except I told her that I had not given Miss Pisto toilet water, and that after I said, "How does the toilet taste?" I quickly added, "Only kidding."

My mom immediately took my side if only because my neck looked like a beaten piece of butcher's meat. When we went into the office, the principal immediately tried to say that I had instigated the beating by giving the teacher toilet water. My mother would have none of it. She stared at the unstable teacher and said, "I don't care what he did, look at his neck." My mother then looked right at Miss Pisto and said, "Listen bitch, if you ever touch my son again, I will come here and tear you limb from limb."

The principal's face was priceless. I had a slight smirk on my face that I couldn't hold back.

After the meeting mercifully came to an end, the principal sent us away and said he would get back to us with any punishments. I think he was afraid of my mother since he would not hand out any punishments in her presence. I later received a three-day suspension, which was like a vacation for me, so I was thrilled.

My elation would soon turn to disappointment. I was no longer allowed to have Miss Pisto as my teacher. So, my crowning achievement, although remarkable, was doused with the fact that I could no longer have this outlandish psycho to torment. Understandably so, I mean the lady did put an MMA choke hold on a boy not yet a teenager.

There would be plenty of dirty deeds ahead of me, as this was only the beginning. I had just started to unleash all of my pent-up rage and this was the calm before the storm. I would soon explode and release a torrential downpour on all those in my way. This path of destruction would spare few and would go way beyond the grammar school hallways.

My mischievous ways even spilled over into Sunday school. I hated going to church and I hated waking up early on Sunday mornings even more. Sunday school was inside a classroom and I didn't want to be at yet another day of school, even if it only lasted an hour or two. I found it completely monotonous and boring, but my parents insisted I go. They wanted me to make my confirmation, so that I could be married in a church one day. I was a young kid and that really didn't register in my mind. I couldn't comprehend marriage or love or even having a girlfriend at that age, so going to Sunday school didn't mean anything to me.

Obviously, my feelings about going to class on Sunday mornings led to me be a nuisance. I certainly wasn't what the church considers to be a "good Christian." I questioned what I was taught in the Bible. I didn't understand how three people were supposed to be one. The nuns definitely didn't care for my divisive nature and they often told me that I'd be punished. Every Sunday, I'd endure a verbal lashing. I openly defied them, questioned their beliefs, and talked back with my wise mouth. Other kids were astonished with my outlandish behavior.

One cold, blistery Sunday morning, I pushed my misconduct to the limits. Every Sunday, the nun leading our class would hang her jacket in the closet. I was tired of being berated in front of my classmates at this point. I ran over as the nun was hanging her coat and I shut the closet door behind her and locked it.

The nun began screaming and yelling through the closed closet door. She said that I would go to hell if I didn't release her. At this point, some of the class was laughing and others had their mouths agape in awe. I refused to release her. Several minutes later, another nun from a different class came over and let her out. I was sent to the head nun's office.

My parents were called in and were shocked to hear about my newest act of disobedience. The head nun wanted to throw me out of Sunday school, but my parents implored her to let me stay in the class. The head nun begrudgingly gave me a second chance, as I suppose part of the teachings were to forgive. I was hoping to get thrown out, but I would have no such luck. My parents put their foot down that I was to behave in Sunday school from now on, or I would be punished. I hated being punished when I was that young, so I adhered to their desire.

I probably could have used another way to vent my emotions than to torture teachers and nuns. Maybe if I fought the kids who bullied me, that would have helped me release some of this rage. However, I was not a fighter. Even though I had been in many "fights," none of them could be considered a real fight. A fight consists of two people trading blows back and forth. I was always the recipient of an ass kicking and I never could fight back. Hence the reason these were not actually fights.

In the seventh grade, one of my best friends decided it was time for me to learn how to fight. Donny and I were riding bikes. I always followed behind him. One day, he pulled over to the side of the road. He ran up onto an abandoned grass field and he put his fists up in a fighting stance.

I said, "What are you doing?"

He replied, "Today, you are going to learn how to fight!"

I was dumbfounded. I did not want to fight my friend. I steadfastly refused.

He told me that I did not have a choice in the matter. He proceeded to punch me right in my unsuspecting grill.

I fell to the ground in agony.

"Get up and fight back!" he barked.

I stood up with impetus and he told me to get in his face. "I don't want to fight you! You're my friend!"

He snarled and plowed his iron fist into my skull once more.

I again dropped to the ground.

"Get up and fight."

Now I was enraged. I went after him with fury in my eyes. I started to punch back. He would let me hit him a few times, but he was much stronger than me. He would laugh the punches off and then knock me down again and again.

Donny then proclaimed something that would stick with me to this very day: "I don't care how many times I knock you down! If I knock you down six times, you get back up and fight me seven times!"

And so, the fight kept going and going for what seemed like a lifetime. I kept hitting the ground, but I would continually bounce off the grassy knoll. I started to channel my ferocity into my clenched fists. I started wailing back at Donny. He looked surprised by my aggression. The fight started to become competitive. Finally, after brawling for several grueling minutes, Donny knocked me down and pinned me into the grass. He stared into my fiery eyes and said, "Good job! That's enough for today."

As that year went on, Donny and I grew closer and my fighting skills became sharper and sharper. He was my best friend and now my fighting mentor. I started to feel emboldened. At this point, I hadn't been picked on in a while. I was gaining respect just by hanging with Donny, or as many referred to him, "The Don." The Don is a mafia reference to somebody who is in charge. The Don was frequently in charge and because I was his friend, I was transforming into someone that was liked. Donny was my very first friend who was respected and was somewhat popular. He was never bullied. Our friendship lessened my victimizations, to a degree. Hanging with The Don didn't totally alleviate me from the pain, as I was still bullied when he wasn't around. Even though I was becoming more liked due to our friendship, I still had to endure many physical beatings. The mental punishment was something that still haunted me as well.

"Duh-duh, duh-duh, duh-duh Fat Chink! Duh-duh, duh-duh, duh-duh Fat Chink!" The chorus of that oppressing song would ring out from several menacing kids. The song stung my inner being and I loathed its very existence. The kicker was that Donny and his older siblings had made the song up. Even though we were good friends, Donny did often make fun of me. It was always in the presence of his older siblings as they constantly bashed me. His siblings would initiate the song, but Donny would join in with them. I guess I was an easy target.

I was tortured by that song, as it would not escape me. Once other kids heard the racially laced jingle, they too joined in and sang it at me. I'm half Italian and half Korean, but our town was mostly inhabited by Italians, prompting me to get mocked for being half Asian.

That ominous song haunted me and I can hear it ringing in my ears to this very day. I was already mentally drained from all the bullies that took a piece of my soul on a daily basis. Now I had what was supposed to be one of my best friends mocking me. I just stood there and took the abuse. I had no mental strength to fight back and tell them to stop. I don't think they would have stopped, but I could have tried. I could have stuck up for myself, but my mental state would not allow that. I was severely beaten down and I had no tenacity to fight back.

That song and all the bullying culminated in the most embarrassing moment of my life. At eighth grade graduation, as my name was called out, the song and chant began. "Duh-duh, duh-duh, duh-duh Fat Chink!" Over and over, it seemed to never end. The vicious chants incessantly rang throughout the horrified auditorium.

I sheepishly looked over at my parents, holding back my tears. I was about to burst especially when I saw my mom's face turning beet red. She is full Korean and I could see her blood boiling. She looked like she wanted to crush every single audience member that was chanting. However, my mother was seated towards the front and the menacing chants were emanating from the back of the auditorium. This ceremony had become a highly combustible state of affairs.

It took everything inside of me, but I managed a small smile and a nod to my mother as if to say, "I'm OK Mom." The chant finally subsided as I walked back to my seat, demoralized, and more beaten down than ever. This was supposed to be a joyous occasion, but I was left melting in a pile of what was left of my humanity.

Afterwards, my mom tried to bring it up, but I shut her down. I became visibly agitated and said that I didn't want to talk about it. That was always my answer to being bullied, hiding it and afraid to speak of it. This was my way of pushing the feelings down. In retrospect, I should have talked to my mom about all the bullying, but I was too ashamed. I was just a kid and I didn't want my parents to defend me. I wanted to stand up for myself. That day was coming soon.

One day that summer, we were playing football in the schoolyard. One kid who I despised started singing the "Fat Chink" song to me. On the next play, I lined up against him and I started calling him a "Dirty Jew." He was the only Jewish person that I had ever known. He was different just as I was. Who was he to call me the "Fat Chink"? He was the only Jewish person in our whole town (that I knew of at the time).

The jabbering went back and forth for a few plays. The other kids began antagonizing me. They got in my face saying, "Are you gonna let this Jew talk to you like that?" They were pouring gasoline on an already raging fire, and I was about to explode.

On the very next hike, I just lunged forward, and I plowed my shoulder into the boy's knee. I then body slammed him onto the unforgiving concrete. All the kids surrounded us and started to cheer. Specifically, they were cheering for me, and that fueled me as I ferociously began to pummel him. They chanted in unison, "Pound that Jew!" The chants grew louder, and my inner wrath grew exponentially. Everything was suddenly in slow motion. I took a mental snapshot to capture the moment and take everything in. I was engulfed by the cheers and I felt self-worth for the first time ever. I was invigorated as I beat down my arch nemesis. I felt a power that I had never felt before. I never wanted to relish that feeling.

Then, after several minutes, a few of the surrounding kids decided to mercifully end the beating for my first victim. But for me, that was my first triumph and I felt on top of the world. For the first time in my life, I had beaten somebody else up. I was no longer the one that took the beating, because I was the one delivering the punches. I had administered my first beat down and it made me feel exhilarated. This was the start of something; I wanted to feel empowered like that more often.

Later in life, I would have another run in with this boy. We dislike each other to this day. He was indeed my arch nemesis. I do have to state that my current dislike for him has nothing to do with him being Jewish, I just dislike the person he is. At the time of this beating, however, my ignorance hindered me from seeing the truth. The fact was that we just didn't mesh. My disdain for him had nothing to do with him being Jewish.

Over the years, I've learned something about disliking people. I have realized that there are bad people in every race or group. Just because this boy was Jewish did not make him a bad person. Bad people will never be defined by a whole race, nationality, or religion. Bad people are bad because that's who they are. This is something we all need to realize. Many of us project our hate on groups of people, whether it's Muslims, Jews, African Americans, or Asians. Many groups of people are targeted and receive unwarranted hate. This hate spreads, and spreading hate only makes this world a dreadful and unpleasant place to live. Spreading hate is the cancer of our society.

That day when I fought and beat up the Jewish boy was just the beginning of my hateful ways. Beating him up jumpstarted my bullying ways. My Bully Complex was beginning to form and would only flourish in the coming years. I was intoxicated with the high of beating him up and I wanted to feel that high more and more. High school was on the horizon and a monster would soon be unleashed.

SECTION TWO

REACHING NEW HIGHS,

THE HIGH SCHOOL YEARS

PART 1: A BULLY IS BORN

"My body flailed around like a fish out of water as they continued to choke and suffocate me."

My freshman year in high school was a strange time for me. I straddled the line between being the "cool" bully and the beaten down overweight Asian kid that was out of place. I was a burnout, and I ran with the metal heads. We would listen to heavy metal, drink beer, and smoke cigarettes. I didn't even like smoking cigarettes, but it was all a part of the image. I didn't even inhale most of the time as I only wanted to look the part. Sometimes, we would even pound beers in the woods before school. Those I actually slugged down because I wanted to explore how getting buzzed would make me feel. We thought we were so cool, but looking back we were just big losers. Smoking cigarettes and drinking beer before school is immature and nothing I condone now.

Most of my burnout friends had long hair. I was the lone exception because as previously mentioned my mom would not allow such blasphemy. I probably would have looked funny with long hair anyway. We all donned T-shirts of our favorite bands spanning the heavy metal gamut at the time. The most popular bands were Anthrax, Judas Priest, Iron Maiden and Ozzy Osbourne, and of course, my personal favorite, Metallica, who to me are the greatest metal band of all time.

Ozzy Osbourne, of course was famously in Black Sabbath. However, at the time, Ozzy had his own solo band and he had an immensely bad reputation. He had bitten the head off a live bat accidentally, and his music was often interlaced with Satanic imagery. Most of us had to hide the fact that we listened to Ozzy from our parents. My parents were used to my heavy metal musical choices by that point, at least. My parents were pretty smart; they recognized I didn't worship Satan or anything. Sure, I was a menace in school, and I had started to drink. That was a battle between child and parents that went strong for my four years of high school. Ultimately, I would win because I would sneak away and drink whenever I could. At first it was to uphold my metal head, burnout image. But I eventually enjoyed the buzz and the drunk feelings evoked by a six pack of beer and soon after vodka.

Us metal heads used to think we were so cool and that our music was the best. We would make fun of the kids who liked "pussified rock". Our biggest targets were Bon Jovi, Poison, and Stryper. We considered these bands "fag" bands, and if you liked them, in turn, *you'd* be a "fag". *How could anyone like such pussy sounding rock music?* we inanely thought. Anyone who wore the T-shirts of these bands would get spit on and howled at by our group of misfits. We'd laugh at them and call them fags. We told them to stop listening to pussy music. They were afraid of us and usually scurried away after we heckled them. This was a form of hazing as well as the ultimate form of bullying.

I remember secretly liking a few pop songs like George Michael's "Faith" and another particular song that would have gotten me mocked. That song was by a pop diva named Tiffany and the song was "I Think We're Alone Now." I knew all the words and I enjoyed it, but I had to hide it. I was ashamed and afraid of the ridicule I was sure to receive. I probably even liked a song or two from the "fag" bands. But I could never admit to that, as I knew my friends would mock me, and who knows, I could even get kicked out of the group for such heresy!

It's funny, because nowadays I have no shame about what music I like or anything else for that matter. Now I listen to Bon Jovi or Poison, those very bands that I blackballed years ago. I know it's hard when you are young, and you think you will get made fun of if you like certain music or television shows or movies or whatever it is. But don't let others bring you down. You like what you like with pride. Our individual likes and differing tastes are what make all of us different. What makes you different is what makes you special.

I will tell you to stand tall and be an individual. Don't concern yourself with how others will perceive the things you like. Be proud and stand by your personal tastes. You don't have to follow the crowd. We should all practice individuality. Don't become a part of the herd and follow like a sheep. I know it's hard, because we all want to be a part of the crowd. We all crave acceptance, but sometimes carving your own path can be gratifying. You don't always need to justify your wants, needs, and likes to others. All the approval you need is your own self approval. If you're happy with who you are, then nothing else matters! Life is all about finding who we are and being happy with that person. Don't ever let others diminish your self-worth.

If you are a bully and bringing others down because they are different and like something perceived to be "uncool," just leave them be. What you are doing is completely unnecessary. Don't be like me and bully people who like something that is perceived to be different. If something is perceived as nerdy or soft or whatever, who cares? You're not the one who is listening to it or watching it. Hazing others over our differences is childish and immature.

As a freshman, I learned all about being hazed. Freshmen were supposed to get hazed by the upperclassmen, and it happened on an almost daily basis. You would usually see a line of freshmen doing jumping jacks in the hallway. In the lunchroom, freshmen would carry the upperclassmen's trays for them. Depending on who you were, or how cooperative you were, would depend on the degree of hazing. Carrying books was pretty normal, but some seniors took their torment to another level. Some of them had the neophytes shine shoes and even eat raunchy, unappetizing things like bugs and dirt. Luckily, my last name carried a little clout in our town. Many generations of my family had gone through this very high school. Some of them were highly respected athletes, therefore I think this garnered me some type of an early pass. This seemed to help in the first couple weeks of school, but I knew there was sure to be some type of venom headed in my direction.

After the first two-week grace period, the hazing came my way. This big mountain of a guy nicknamed, "House," came towards me and a couple of my burnout friends. House was a notorious bully. Not only was he intimidating in stature, but he was actually a grown man. He had stayed back a couple of times and rumor had it that he didn't mind as he loved torturing the underclassmen. There were rumors that he was in his early twenties. Surely that couldn't be true, I thought. All I know is that I prayed that he didn't get held back a third time.

Watching House walk towards us was like watching a grizzly bear coming for his food. His menacing 6'5", 350-pound frame imposed itself over us. We were at his mercy. House barked, "All right, line up next to each other and start doing jumping jacks. As you do them, yell as loud as you can that House is your master!" I started doing as I was told. I mean, no big deal.

Then suddenly, my older cousin, Angela, who was a junior at the time came over. She looked at House and pointed in his face. She said, "That's my cousin right there, he's not to be touched."

My female cousin coming over to save me had House kind of dumbfounded, but he reluctantly told me to stop. I just kind of squirmed away but I was a little pissed off at my cousin. I didn't want any special treatment. The way I looked at it, everybody should have to go through this. It's like a rite of passage. Plus, I didn't know if there'd be any backlash when she wasn't around. I knew after my cousin had stuck up for me I would be on House's radar. Boy was I right.

Everything seemed fine for the next month or so. Then one day in the gym locker room, three seniors surrounded me. House was there with two other large bullies.

House exclaimed, "Your cousin isn't here to protect you now, is she?"

They started wailing on me, everywhere except my face. When they were finished, I could barely feel my arms. I was black 'n blued all over. I never told my cousin, or anyone else for that matter. I just sucked it up like a man. At that point, I really knew how to take a beating anyhow. I was numb to the pain.

The worst of it came during wrestling season. At this point, I was developing a wise mouth. I would take the senior's abuse, but I would always talk back. They would beat me up worse for my wise-cracking mouth and my continual sarcastic remarks, but I didn't care. The beatings never deterred me as I was steadfast with my rebellion.

During wrestling practice, there were a couple of us who were defiant. My buddy Jack and I would always talk back and even mock the upperclassmen. I didn't care. The way I saw it, I was going to take a beating anyway, so I might as well get some enjoyment out of it as well. We made up nicknames for almost everybody. There was "Mud-Back" who had a giant brown birthmark on his back, there was "Wolf Pack Jack" who was hairier than an actual wolf, and of course there was "Senior JV" who was the senior that couldn't make the varsity team. This was quite an embarrassment for him as all seniors were supposed to automatically make the varsity squad, but he couldn't beat anyone to actually earn his spot. "Senior JV" was understandably enraged with his nickname and he would often partner up with me in order to torture me during practice.

When practice was over and the coach was long gone, that's when we'd endure the most damaging beatings. One day I found myself surrounded by several upperclassmen. That day will forever live in my mind. Two of them tackled me to the ground and one of them began to choke me. My body flailed around like a fish out of water as they continued to choke and suffocate me. My breath was leaving my body and there was no end in sight. My face turned blue, and looked like a pipe ready to burst. The alarming sight finally put an end to the agony as the perpetrator mercifully released me.

Even though that was the worst beating I ever took, I didn't give a shit. I had been beaten so much to this point in my life that I didn't even feel anything. Even as the breath left my body and my mind went to another place, the pain couldn't break me. Pain was now my friend. I was impervious to the pain and my mind would drift elsewhere during these beatings. This time, my mind drifted further than ever before as I was so mentally immune to it at that point. I never even cried like I would have when I was a kid. My crying days were well behind me, as I was eerily conditioned to all this torture.

Another day, we had to go for a two-mile run during practice. My friend, Jack and I were antagonizing one of the seniors who was about ten paces ahead of us. We kept going and going until he snapped. He turned around and tackled both of us at once into a patch of bushes. Another senior came over and held us down. They pounded us into the bushes until they were exhausted. We returned to practice, covered with pine needles hanging off our beaten bodies. Back then, the coaches didn't care. This was all normal behavior. The rest of the team saw our green covered carcasses and they all laughed at us. Jack and I even found it somewhat amusing. Actually, we found it to be very funny. That's how you laugh off a beating!

In wrestling practice, there was one kid in particular that I especially picked on. His name was Colby and I despised him. He was a year older than me but that didn't matter to me. Colby was not easy prey because he was easily one of the best wrestlers on the team, but I sensed a weakness in him. You would think that other upperclassmen would have his back, however, nobody really liked him. He was made to be an outcast because he was intelligent, well-spoken, and eclectic. He was smarter than most of the rest us, making him somewhat of a pariah. He was highly respected as a wrestler, but other kids still viewed him in a different light. Although he was a gifted wrestler and extremely intelligent, he was pegged as a social pariah.

His social standing led me to ridicule him more times than I remember. The weird thing is that Colby was a far superior wrestler than me and I had no place mocking him, but that didn't stop me. I felt like I could actually kick his ass off of the wrestling mat if I had to. That probably wasn't the case as he was actually a tough kid, however in my warped mind, I was tougher than I actually was. My complex made me feel like I could pound Colby in a real fight, and this emboldened me. I don't know if I could or couldn't to be honest, but that confidence was all I needed instilled within me to make him the focus of my verbal and mental bashing.

On a couple of occasions, Colby spit a little when he spoke, so I emblazoned him with the nickname "Slimer" from the movie *Ghostbusters*—a green ghost that would land on people and slime them with this green mucus-like substance. Even though Colby probably only spit as he spoke a couple of times, I deemed it necessary to brand him as Slimer. Therefore, Slimer was born, and everyone in school followed suit. When I brandished people with nicknames, they spread rapidly.

Every day, I would harass Slimer and tell him I was going to kick his ass. I called him every name in the book; "nerd," "dork," "geek," "weirdo," "faggot," whatever filtered through my deranged brain to my filthy little mouth. There was something about Slimer though; he would take this abuse and let it build up. He was like a glutton for punishment, and I couldn't wait to dole it out. Instead of giving it back to me verbally, Colby would punish me whenever we had to pair up in wrestling practice. He would smother me and maul me on the mat. He often made me look like the fool. Colby was above name calling as he was extremely mature for his age as opposed to me who was obviously immature.

One day, I pushed Slimer to his limit. We were running in circles around the mat for wrestling practice. I noticed Slimer was wearing a funny looking hat. I ran right up next to him and I shoved his head knocking his hat off. I ran away from him laughing at him every step of the way. Others near me saw and began to laugh with me. I continued my way back near him, again shoving his head and this time his hat went flying into the nearby exit door. At this point, everyone knew what was going on and began cracking up. The whole team started yelling at Slimer and saying he was a pussy.

He stared at me and said with malice, "Do it again and see what happens!"

Well, I couldn't wait to do it again and see what would happen. I wanted to bash his face in. So, I went back one last time and I went to push his head once more, only this time he grabbed my arm and in one motion, he swung me into the unforgiving exit door. He slammed my head into the door, and I collapsed into an embarrassed puddle. Now everyone attending the practice was laughing at me instead of Slimer.

I wanted to get up and fight him, but coach was fed up and had enough of our out of control horseplay. He blew the whistle and ordered me to go run two miles by myself on the track. My need to bully had cost me once again, but this seemed a small price to pay, as I undeniably enjoyed torturing others to the point of mental anguish. A couple of miles on the track wasn't going to slow down this bully train.

"Slimer" and I had multiple run-ins over the span of high school. I continued to mock him for being offbeat. As I look back at it, I can honestly say that I disliked him because he just wasn't the kind of person that I liked to hang with. That being said, I should not have ridiculed him and made him feel he was different. Colby was actually a good guy and didn't deserve the verbal abuse I dished out to him. It shouldn't matter if he was different; the way I acted was unacceptable. It is better just to keep your mouth shut and stay away from someone who you dislike. Just because you dislike somebody, that does not give you a license to bully them, mock them, ridicule them, or do anything demeaning to them. They should be left alone. All people are different, and some are really different. Let them be different and do not harass them. If they are different and keep to themselves, how is it your business to victimize them?

The fact that we are all different is what is great about the human race. No two people are the same and this should be celebrated, not mocked. Colby should have been praised for being highly intelligent, mature, and an outstanding wrestler. Instead, we mocked him and disrespected him. This should never be the case. Kids need to wake up and realize that people like Colby are the kind of people they should strive to be. I would rather have a generation of highly intelligent and mature kids, than a generation of immature bullies like me!

Victimizing other kids for being different was my specialty back then. Freshman year was when I developed and sharpened my bullying skills. I bullied kids that I knew were weak and had a lower social status. I attacked kids that couldn't stand up for themselves. I was well on my way to becoming a master bully. I needed something to further propel me, and that was coming soon in the form of a newfound friend.

Freshman year continued with more of the same shenanigans. As the year progressed, I became a sharp-tongued wisenheimer. I was a wise ass to the highest degree. I endured a lot of abuse, but I began to dish it back even harder. That summer, I met someone that would match my wisecracking prowess and things would never be the same.

That summer, I met Patrick and we instantly clicked. I was in a transition, as Donny had moved the summer before. My best friend was gone leaving a void in my life. The Don had given me a blueprint to becoming popular. Patrick helped me to take that blueprint and assemble the frame that put it all together. I was desperately craving a transformation and I wanted to catapult into the popular stratosphere of high school. The wrestling team was a good start as I had started to develop more friendships. It also helped get me in shape and I was moving on from being the fat kid. I was tired of being the fat kid. I was tired of being an outcast burnout as well.

I dumped all my burnout friends and my new BFF became Patrick. I was a real jerk about it, too. Instead of severing my friendships like a man and telling my burnout crew that I didn't want to associate with them, I avoided them at all costs. I wouldn't answer their phone calls and I wouldn't go places in which they frequented. If I went somewhere and they were there, I would leave immediately. I shut them out. I still have guilt over my cowardly actions to this day. Most of them were good people and didn't deserve this treatment. I hope they can forgive me. I now realize that at this transitional time, being popular meant everything to me. I would have done anything to gain the popularity that I so rabidly desired. I was sick of being the "Fat Chink" and I saw an opportunity to be cool. I wanted to feel that high of being a bully again, like that day I pounded on the "Jew Boy."

My past time as a victim was exactly that, in my past. I had now developed what I refer to as a Bully Complex. All the victimizations I had suffered made me want to inflict pain upon others.

Patrick and I were inseparable from that point, and we were two terrors that were ready to take our high school by storm. That summer, we made fun of everybody and everything that was in our sights. Many of the kids we mocked were beginning to hate us. We'd make fun of our victims right to their faces and then laugh boisterously, to the point that they whimpered from humility. We made up stories about other kids; that they didn't shower, they had lice, and their moms were whores. We had joined forces to become two unrelenting menaces.

When school started that year, I was ready to cause some mayhem. We used to tell mother jokes back then (yeah, I know, old school). I was going back and forth with this nerdy kid and he was actually pretty good at mother jokes. He must have practiced at home or something. Anyway, he really managed to get under my skin and I wanted to get him back. I made up a story about him when he was in eighth grade, since he had attended school in a neighboring town of Garwood until high school. Kenilworth kids made up the majority of the student body, therefore not many of them knew this Garwood nerd.

Here's the story that forever brands this victim to this day. I told people that there was an eighth-grade field trip to a farm. At the end of the trip, when the students gathered on the bus, the teacher took roll call. There was one student missing. We'll call him "Tim" to protect him from further humiliation. The teacher sent two responsible students back to look for Tim. Well, they opened the barn door, and to everyone's shock and awe, Tim was banging a sheep! The kids were mortified and ran back to the bus. They told everyone what they had seen. The whole bus ride was filled with the sound, "Baaaah! Baaaah!" Of course, I then stigmatized Tim with the cold-blooded nickname "Sheep."

Now, you might ask what about the other students from Garwood who actually went to eighth grade with Tim? Well, first off, the story spread like wildfire and by the end of the day, nearly the whole high school had heard. Secondly, he was not very well liked, as not one kid who went to school with him said it was a lie. From that day on, Tim was known as "Sheep." To this very day, many people will refer to him as Sheep. I am not proud of this as I pretty much ruined a child's high school experience. Tim hated me then and probably still does and I do not blame him one bit.

Sheep was just the beginning of my fabrications. I made up stories about one of my ex-burnout friends as well. First off, I nicknamed him "Big John" because he wore Big John brand named jeans. They were jeans bought from Bradlee's which we referred to as the poor man's store. You could get items at a deep discount and it was not somewhere you would want to buy your wardrobe from. I of course realize now that Big John's family didn't have money to afford name brand jeans, but those are not thoughts that crossed my mind at the time. I let my Bully Complex do most of my thinking for me. Instead of having compassion for somebody who was poverty-stricken, I branded him as Big John and made him a pawn in my sick game of bullying. Even though we had previously been friends, I did this without a second thought. My Bully Complex was amplifying at an exponential rate.

I tortured Big John that whole year. I would put signs on his locker emblazoned with his new nickname. I told everyone in school that his mom didn't wear underwear and that she was a whore. I even made up a poem about his mom called, "A Whore Named Claire." I passed the cold-hearted composition around all my classes giving everyone a chance to read it. I had the whole school calling him Big John and many referred to his mom as a dirty whore. My actions were repulsive and revolting, but I couldn't help myself at the time. I was the epitome of a nasty, unrelenting bully and I relished every moment of it. I am disgusted with the person I once was.

Sophomore year was off with a resounding bang. I began to dish out pain to others that were undeserving of my despicable actions. I wanted others to endure pain like I had. This was becoming a sickness growing inside of my ever-blackening soul. "Sheep Boy" and "Big John" were just the start of my detestable, degrading, and bullying ways. Patrick was always causing chaos by my side.

That year, something remarkable occurred. Somehow, we became two of the most popular kids and simultaneously the most hated kids in school. Every innocent kid we shamed loathed us with justifiable reasons, but the other kids thought my victimizations were rather comedic. I was starting to become popular with the "cool" kids. They actually wanted to be around me just to see what shenanigans I would cook up next.

One time, in art class, I recreated this kid's sneakers. All the cool kids wore Nikes, Reeboks, and Adidas. This one kid owned a pair of sneakers adorned with a brand that was unheard of. They were called "Voits." I thought this was hilarious. So, in art class, I turned my Nikes into Voits. I painted a little piece of canvas and glued it to the side of my sneakers. That day I walked around and tried to follow this kid wherever he went. His nickname naturally became Voit. Before days end, I had half the school yelling "Voit!" at this poor kid.

What's ironic about my calling him a poor kid, is that back then I didn't realize why this kid owned a pair of Voit sneakers. I was young and I didn't care. Since his sneakers were perceived as not being cool, I rode this kid and preyed on him. Now that I am older and I can assess the situation, I realize that this kid was literally poor. His family had no money and therefore could not afford the popular sneakers of the time, much like Big John's family. Instead, they had to buy cheaper shoes that just so happened to have a strange name. Well, a name that was strange to me and many others. I made fun of a kid whose family had no money to afford luxuries like designer sneakers. What a scumbag I was, in retrospect.

Imagine how this child felt when he went home to his family. He was either too ashamed to say anything about what had occurred that day, or he hated his family for being impoverished. Either way, I unquestionably gave this kid some damaging mental issues. He couldn't help his situation. He was only a young kid without any control over his family's financial situation. Leave it to the big bully to only make it worse.

Why don't bullies think about their detrimental actions? I wish I had thought about what I was doing.

Some things never change. Kids still mock others for the sneakers and clothing that others wear. If a kid doesn't have the newest Jordans, then they are open to ridicule. Young boys and girls of today are open to even more scrutiny for their clothing choices. Society needs to examine this, because not everyone can afford designer clothing. We need to teach our children that when they are given designer clothing that this is a privilege and not all families can afford such luxuries. I wish someone would have put me in my place back then. My parents had no idea I was doing these things, or they certainly would have. I'm sure of it.

During that time, I never thought about any of my grotesque actions as there were countless kids I made fun of. There was the one kid I constantly yelled at to "Get into the choppa now! Gooo! Gooo!!!" Those are lines from an old Arnold Schwarzenegger movie. The kid had an accent, prompting me to yell that at him across the high school hallways. He was a foreigner and he was different, so of course I pigeonholed him. It didn't matter to me that he couldn't help his accent. I was unrelenting and I made his accent a school-wide mockery.

There was one kid that I couldn't seem to break no matter how much I harassed him. I used to beat on him with fellow bullies. Yet he always just sat there and took the beatings. His name was Dan Liddell and I made him one of my primary targets. Dan wasn't the best looking guy so I nicknamed him "Handsome Dan." I would often try to use another pawn in my sick game to try and break Dan. I would try to get people to fight him and punch him in his face. There was one kid who would always volunteer named Ricky Polomini. Nearly every day that I could, we would surround "Handsome Dan" and try to get him to fight Ricky. This led to many fights and Dan just took the beatings. It bothered me that he took everything without so much as a whimper. Ricky was always by my side when it came to torturing Dan. Maybe Ricky thought this made him cool or something. Whatever reasons Ricky had, he could have realized what we were doing was wrong. I hope he has changed as I have.

"Handsome Dan" had something else that was unique about him. He was known as the stinky kid. He stunk of something fierce and had major body odor. My fellow bullies and I made it a point to tell him and mock him for it. We presented him with sticks of deodorant in the boy's locker room. We would constantly spray cologne, tell him that he needed to put some on and wave it in his direction. We called him "B.O. Boy" and over the course of the year, it seemed our message was not getting through loud and clear. One day, a group of us bullies gathered around "Handsome Dan" in the boy's locker room. We had wrapped string around bars of soap. We surrounded the helpless boy and started whipping him with the bars of soap. For the first time, he squealed in agony and cried out for help, but his screams went unheard. We were relentless in our mauling. The misfortunate boy just had to sit there and take that soap-tinged beating. I smiled because I felt I had finally broken him.

There was one kid in school with a large amount of acne on his face. His acne covered the entirety of his face and it was excruciating to look at. This boy was named Russ. In grammar school all the kids mocked him and branded him with the moniker, "Puss Faced Russ." Russ seemed to be a pretty tough guy, especially in grammar school, or so it seemed. He would not back down from a fight as he always went after those who mocked him. This made me fear him a little during our freshman year together. However, as high school wore on, the entire narrative changed. My newfound popularity and pack of bullies as backup provided me with false courage. I tormented "Puss Faced Russ" and told him that looking at his acne burned my eyes. I told him he looked like a pepperoni pizza and that he disgusted me. Russ definitely wanted to fight me, but I never made fun of him when I was alone. I always had my bully wolf pack behind me, backing me up.

I was spineless, just a fake tough guy who needed an entourage to feel emboldened. This is not being tough, nor will it ever be. This is cowardly. Just as bullying gives you false confidence, bullying gives you false toughness. I was the furthest thing from being tough. I was a complete coward.

The perceived confidence and toughness that people attain from bullying is all false. This is not true confidence or true toughness by any means. When you get into the real world, you will receive a harsh reality check. You will realize that you manufactured confidence and toughness through bullying and demeaning others. You will realize that you are insecure. Your insecurities will take over as you realize the false bravado is only a mask that you wear. Your true colors of being a coward will eventually shine through.

My own cowardly ways even led me to make fun of certain girls in my school. There was Vicki who I called the "Dragon Lady" because her voice was soft, and she spoke almost in whispers. I mocked her voice and said she sounded like a hissing lizard. There was one girl who had huge eyebrows, so I dubbed her "Caterpillar Eyes." I told her she had hairy ass eyebrows and I would sing a song whenever she was in my vicinity: "Jeepers, Creepers, where'd you get those Peepers?"

There was a pair of twin sisters who were considered to be extremely ugly. Their last name was Givens, and the Givens twins became one of my primary targets. They were outcasts and many other kids already laughed at them, making them easy prey for me. Since they were known widely by most of the school as the ugly twins, I made fun of their looks. I would call them the "Uggo Twins" or if I saw one of them alone just "Captain Uggo." I would run up to them and yell in their horrified faces, "Givenzzz Twinzzz, YOU'RE GORGEOUS!" Of course, I had the whole school yelling this at the vilified twins. This was not meant to be complimentary, rather it was a jab at their rough looks. I would always tell people who were considered to be "Uggos" that they should be in a beauty pageant. Anyone that wasn't considered attractive, I would relentlessly degrade with my malicious sarcasm. I was a sarcastic, mean, and remorseless bully.

Finally, there was one more girl who I badgered constantly and that was "The Girl Who Wrestles Bears." She was much larger than other girls in high school, and she became an easy mark for me. That dejected young girl probably looked in the mirror every night and cried because of me. There also was her "boyfriend" who I nicknamed "Sasquatch." Sasquatch wasn't actually her boyfriend, but I paired the two together, because they were two misfits that I continually persecuted. They were both large for their age, so to me, pitting them together was funny, further humiliating the two of them. Sasquatch was an oversized hairy fellow who was in many of my advanced classes, giving me lots of opportunities to badger him. I knew I used to piss him off and he probably wanted to fight me. Looking back now, he probably could have kicked my ass. Why didn't he, or anybody else, you ask?

A small handful tried, but I did what any bully would do. I only fought those I knew I could beat. If there were kids who fought back and I wasn't sure I could take them, I would have reinforcements ready as there was always a pack of bullies backing me up. Would you expect any less from the big bad bully with no backbone? The challengers almost always backed down, or they would receive a beating from several of us. I mean that is true bully status right there, four kids pounding on one sitting duck.

What a tough guy I was. But as I have said several times, usually the bully is afraid, and that's why they try to overpower somebody with actions and words, not physicality. Most bullies will back down if challenged. That was me, a gutless jerk who just took out his issues on the less fortunate. How dumb could I have been to do that, when I was the one on the receiving end of this torment for many years?

It was as if all those years I had been bullied and been the victim had suddenly vanished. My newfound power erased any past scars, or at least I thought it did. Maybe I thought this was like some kind of twisted karma. I mean, I had gotten mine, now it was someone else's turn.

All of this was all too ironic. I was in all the "smart" classes because I was a fairly intelligent young man. I had all the advanced classes and that made my immediate classmates all the perceived nerds and geeks. All the people that I would torture and relentlessly use as my prey were right there sitting next to me in class. The irony was, *I was one of them*. I had been in the advanced classes since grammar school. I was somewhat of a nerd disguised as a cool kid. Was it all a ruse? Even when I became popular in high school, I still maintained many nerdy qualities. I was a part of the school newspaper and poetry magazine. I even joined the school play during my junior and senior years. It was almost blasphemous that I made fun of these people. It was as if I had turned on my own. I was indeed one of them, but because others enjoyed the way I constantly ridiculed the lower end of the social demographic, I continued doing it. The feeling of being popular was intoxicating. I felt powerful being the hunter and not the pathetic hunted. This is a sad but true revelation. Somehow, I had broken through to the other side and there was no turning back!

For the record, being on the school newspaper, being in school theater, band, color guard, or even an academic club doesn't make you a nerd. And even if it did, being a nerd nowadays is actually cool. There are plenty of people who find this an attractive quality. After all, most of these activities require a higher degree of intelligence. Don't most of us find intelligence to be an attractive quality?

In all seriousness, just because you join any of these clubs or engage in any of these activities DOES NOT mean you are a lesser person. Sadly, my actions towards other kids who joined these clubs were remorseless and rotten. Join all the clubs you want to. Be a part of a group where you feel accepted. Engage in any activities that make you feel happy and alive. Don't let jerks like me discourage you. People like me shouldn't undermine your happiness. I know what I did and how it deterred kids from wanting to be in certain social groups. I tortured kids to unspeakable heights, and it was terribly wrong. Kids should be themselves and join any group they desire, without ridicule. Be yourself and be proud of the groups you associate with. Being part of these groups is healthy, and feeling accepted will make you happier.

High school can be an extremely confusing time in a child's life. There's so much going on, as this is when kids are developing and growing into young adults. Kids are seeking acceptance at this age. Many kids turn to bullying in order to fit in. We need to teach our children to be more accepting and not to bully those who are perceived to be less popular. I wish I had someone in my ear telling me that what I was doing was extremely wrong.

Bullies are often dealing with emotions that they don't know how to deal with. That's why many kids turn to bullying, whether the emotions stem from a broken home or from being victimized in one way or another. Some kids are abused whether it's at home or in school. Some kids are bullied and have pent up anger. This unquestionably described me as I had anger issues I could not escape. I had no idea how to cope with my prior victimizations. I had no idea how to deal with my newly burgeoning popularity. I felt like if I didn't bully and show others that I belonged, then I would lose my social status.

Pushing others down does not make you popular, it just makes you a weaker person. Putting others down should not equate to popularity in any way. It *shouldn't*, but unfortunately, sometimes it does. Sometimes the popular kids are the ones who are the bullies. We need to change this mentality. All kids should be accepted. After never being accepted in my early childhood, I should have known better. I explicitly should have been more accepting. After all, I knew how it felt more than anyone to be excluded and isolated.

I was the farthest from being an accepting person, as I consistently made other kids feel like they were outcasts. I put an unneeded spotlight on my victims, and I made them feel as if they didn't belong. I went beyond the point of human decency. I not only tortured and ridiculed these poor souls, but I quite literally ruined a few of their lives. A few of them probably remain scarred to this day. This fact does not make me proud, nor have I sought all these people out to make amends. I fear the damage I may have caused. I am afraid I may have gone too far with some of them. I have joked over the years that some of my victims might have me targeted, that some of them may even want to kill me. Even though I joke about it, I know this could be a very real possibility. Yes, actual murder. I think joking about it gives some levity to the situation. I don't want to think about someone wanting me dead.

I recognize my wrongs and I realize the mental abuse I doled out, but I don't think I deserve to die over my insensitive actions. If you think this is a preposterous thought, I remind you of the Columbine incident. There have also been other incidents where kids are incessantly bullied and victimized until they reach a breaking point. Although bullying was certainly a major factor, we do have to remember that there are usually other factors at play when talking about school shootings. These victims are usually pushed to the limit and then they sometimes retaliate with murderous intentions. These kids are sometimes bullied so badly, that they felt the only answer was to kill their perpetrators. I do not condone these actions in any way, I am simply illuminating the seriousness of the bullying epidemic. Torturing someone to the point that they could snap and kill, is something we need to take seriously.

I'm just happy that I lived in simpler times when hazing was almost commonplace. Even though hazing and bullying was wrong, it was widely accepted by everyone. Teachers, administrators, and even parents recognized that hazing went on and it was even endorsed and encouraged at times. I remember a few times I had acted up in school and my wrestling coach slammed me into a locker. I told my dad about it later and he said, "Good! Maybe you'll learn your lesson!" I was shocked, but I realized that these were all practices that my dad had grown up with. He had told me stories of when his coaches or teachers would "knock some sense into him" as they used physicality to try and curb his behavior. Nowadays, these actions would never be condoned. Teachers also knew about the bullying and hazing, but they almost always turned a blind eye unless there was something considered to be too serious to ignore. So, at the time I grew up, all the bullying seemed to be the norm. It's almost as if bullying and hazing were accepted during the time I grew up.

Several generations after I passed through school is when things started to turn. Kids started showing up to school with weapons in order to confront their perpetrators. Had I grown up in a different time, I'm sure I would have been gunned down or knifed to death.

There's no overstating the pain I've caused. As I continue to reflect, I too was once bullied. I was a victim at one time, and I didn't seek personal revenge, and I wouldn't even think of retaliation at this point in my life. I realize that it is more than wrong to strike back and to hurt others. Even if they have hurt you, you should be the bigger person. You should only fight back if you are forced to. I never wanted to do any permanent damage to anyone who victimized me, no matter how much anguish I was forced to endure. I pray that anyone I've inflicted damage upon feels the same. After all, we were only kids. I never meant to leave permanent scars. Anyone who gets bullied just wants the pain to go away. Anyone who gets bullied just wants it to stop.

Although, now I recognize my wrongs and the pain I have caused, I never had compassion when I was inflicting the torment. There were two specific kids that I tortured past the point of human decency, and I know that they must have scars. Not only did I taunt them on a regular basis, I made their lives a living hell. I didn't even brand them with nicknames. Their actual names became their mocking call. Steve and Bill became the biggest laughingstocks at our high school. I disliked both of them for different reasons. To be honest, I didn't even dislike Steve that much, as he lived a few houses away from me. I grew up with him and we spent a good amount of time around each other. Despite all that, I still made him a victim of my incessant bullying. I knew that if I said something, it would be perpetuated and would soon catch on like wildfire. I was now popular, so if I said someone was the color blue, they became the color blue. That's how powerful bullying can be. The mob mentality is highly pervasive. Bullies come in packs and often gang up on the weak. What's ironic about Steve is that he was actually not all that fragile. He was a strong fellow who could have positively blasted my teeth out of my mouth. As I've stated, I always had a pack of predators behind me, which made it seem like there would be consequences if he touched me.

Steve lived nearby and he would often come by my house unannounced. The problem wasn't that Steve came over to my house, the problem was that his timing was impeccable. He somehow always made his way over when food was being served. We had a grill in our backyard that was often cooking all sorts of delights.

I used to mockingly say, "What, did you smell the grill, Steve?" So, from that day forward, my friends and I would joke every time the grill was on that Steve would be strolling over at any moment. We would joke that Steve's mom didn't feed him and he needed to come over for some free grub. When he actually would show up while the grill was going, we would all laugh. It became a thing to say when someone would mooch off of you. "Stop being a Steve!" "You're acting like a Steve!" I had turned his name into a noun that our whole school and even some parents started to use. You did not want to be told that you were acting like a "Steve!" Talk about sheer humiliation. His name had become a public disgrace.

Bill on the other hand, I genuinely disliked. He was someone that tried to latch on to our group and tried to bully others. But I would have none of it. I never accepted Bill as an equal. We would let him drive us around and hang out only on my terms. We had a group that always played cards and Bill was always invited to the card games. I loved winning his money, but when he beat me, there was nothing worse. I loathed when he beat me in cards. When he did, I would mock him profusely, as if I needed a reason.

I was relentless concerning his most obvious flaw, his bucked teeth. "Hey Bill, where do you work? The BUCKingham Palace?" We called him "Uncle Buck" after the movie of the same name. Anything that had the word "buck" in it or any way I could fit the word in around Bill, I would. I would often say, "Pass the Buck" or "The Buck Stops Here" in his presence. I verbally harassed him endlessly. I even brought his family into the harassment. His dad was a barber who owned a local barber shop. Bill was learning the trade, which of course prompted me to ask him if he would cut the customers hair with his bucked teeth. I just had pure unbridled disdain for him.

I came up with this demented game of sorts regarding my two favorite targets. Anytime that anyone was caught hanging out with Steve or Bill, you were given "points." It was like being given demerits, and we never actually kept track. It was just fun to say, "Hey you were playing cards with Bill, you got points!" "Oh, don't go to the sub shop now, Steve is there, you'll get points." I had turned nearly an entire school against these terrorized victims. To this day, I know Bill holds a grudge. As far as Steve, I have not seen nor heard from him. He disappeared and has not re-emerged. Maybe I forced him into an obscure life and for that I'm truly sorry. It's possible that Steve is scorned from his tainted high school experience. I am unsure of what the truth is, but I know that I feel awful for whatever I caused him, as he surely did not deserve any of it.

My bullying was not confined to other kids; just as I did in grammar school, I bullied anyone I could, including teachers. There were several of them that felt my wrath in high school. There was "Doof Dannery" who was just a goofy dude who reminded me of most of the kids I harassed, except he was all grown up. I was probably his worst nightmare all over again. Surely "Doof" suffered from the ire of bullies back in his day. Here I was back to remind him of who he was. Yeah, I know I was a little prick. I didn't care about consequences back then; I actually relished the punishments. Suspended? Bring it! Saturday school? That's my specialty!

"Doof" wasn't the only teacher I tortured, as there were plenty of others. I gave plenty of my educators the "Miss Pisto treatment." You remember, the one I gave toilet water to? No, I didn't hand out any more toxic liquids, but I did play a prank or two. I remember a specific caper that I concocted in chemistry lab. I had come up with a devious plan. I can't recall the teacher's real name, but we called her "Mrs. Stinkysworth." Her stench was one of legend. Her distinct smell would waft and emanate from her unclean body and permeate throughout the classroom. The stink was like a day old, dirty diaper combined with musty, moldy Muenster Cheese. It was so remarkably bad that I even penned a song in her honor called "Give Soap a Chance."

One morning, I gathered two other like-minded bullies to sing the song over the loudspeakers for all to hear. There were announcements each morning and I was able to get a short segment over the air, in order to promote our literary magazine. The song was going to be published for all to see, but now I had the school listening to the song in all of its evil glory. I wanted the whole school to revel in the majestic composition that I had written in Mrs. Stinkysworth's honor! My song was the stuff of legend and everyone knew it was penned for Mrs. Stinkysworth. I'm sure the poor science teacher knew that I had written the song for her, and that gave me a sick sense of satisfaction. Somewhere deep down, I was losing who I truly was. My innate goodness had been replaced by evil. I couldn't stop it. I was wrapped up in this newfound confidence and everything that came with it. My intentions were malevolent. I executed a sick and perverse agenda.

My evil-minded agenda led me to another sinister plan that I had in store for Mrs. Stinkysworth's chemistry class. Everything went swimmingly, well almost. We were studying the process for the dissection of frogs that week in class. We had dehydrated frogs that we would perform our dissections on. However, there was one live frog kept in class, which was there for observation purposes. First, I had to find a way to get that frog out of its cage without Mrs. Stinkysworth seeing. So, one day, I had an accomplice who pulled the fire alarm for me. Next thing you know there was a chaotic fire drill situation. We had it all timed out where I would be in the bathroom when the alarm was pulled. I came out of the bathroom when I knew the classroom would be cleared. I made a beeline right for the frog's cage. I quickly snatched up the slimy little animal and made my way towards the stairwell. There was still a line of students and teachers wrapped around the stairwell making their way down to the exit door. So, I headed into the group holding my slimy little friend. A few of the girls saw it and they all start squealing and yelping. It was fantastic. Then a buddy of mine spotted the monkey business and he started cracking up. He came near me and said, "Let me see."

Next thing I know, he smacked the bottom of my cupped hands and suddenly there was a flying frog soaring through the air. The frog went from the second floor of the stairwell and landed at the bottom. Young female voices screeched and shrieked. When I finally reached the bottom, a disappointed Miss Logan was waiting there for me, shaking her head. Someone must have ratted me out.

Now, you must also know that Miss Logan was another one of my targets. I often bullied her and acted up in her class. She was a short, stumpy woman with bucked teeth just like Bill. She had the worst set of bucked teeth I had ever seen. They protruded out of her mouth like mollusks. She glared at me intently and said, "Pick it up."

I looked her dead in the eye and I coldheartedly said, "Why don't you pick it up with your teeth?"

There was one moment of silence, due to the malicious words that spewed out of my mouth. Everyone was shocked as this was extremely harsh, even coming from me. There were several different reactions, as several young ladies gasped with disgust while most of the guys started cackling with laughter.

Miss Logan's jaw dropped. To mock a teacher was one thing, but to deride her personal appearance, especially about something that was an obvious glaring flaw was another. Her face turned as red as a Jersey tomato, first in rage, then embarrassment. She was first enraged. But as the cackling continued, you could see a sadness come over her. Instantly, she transformed from raging bull to silent lamb.

I could see a tear shimmer down her cheek. She began to cry but I couldn't show any sign of weakness at that moment, even though I actually felt bad. Instead I scooped up my slimy little friend and scurried off.

The frog story became a school-wide sensation. For weeks, Miss Logan was haunted by the phrase, "Pick it up with your teeth." She was never the same after that. You could tell that she lost her authority, her dignity, and her pride all in one malevolent statement. I was not only capable of ruining the lives of young men and women, but I even had the power of destroying full grown adults. I seemingly tore down their walls of invincibility that they projected. I made it seem that just because they were our teachers and authority figures, that didn't mean they had power over us. I had reached a new level of bullying.

I had no boundaries when it came to being a bully. Like I've said, nobody was off limits. Well, for the most part. I did not make fun of the handicapped kids, with one minor exception. I know what you're thinking, what kind of a person makes fun of handicapped people? And, to my credit, I was pretty mild when it came to them. There were a couple of bullies who were really bad and mocked every handicapped kid in our school. There was one janitor named Gary that I picked on. He did not seem to have all of his mental capacities and he was unmistakably slow. If you threw any type of coin on the floor, Gary would scurry to pick it up. So, of course, I gathered a pack of bullies and we would proceed to torture Gary the janitor. We would throw pennies, nickels, and dimes on the floor and watch Gary waddle swiftly and scoop them up. Then we would all yell, "Get to work Gary!"

One day after school had ended and the hallways were relatively cleared, I really wanted to mess with Gary worse than usual. I glued some pennies on a string and placed them at the end of the hallway. A few of us were giddy with anticipation. We watched Gary waddle around the corner and then suddenly he started to pick up speed, as he saw the shiny rewards glimmering in front of his awe-struck eyes. He then went diving for the pennies, but this time I pulled the string as he grabbed for them. Gary then began to move faster towards the pennies but to no avail, as I continued to yank them away from his fat fingered paw. He was getting frustrated. Every time he waddled closer, we started yelling, "Get to work Gary!"

Gary then erupted with ferocity and started waddling at full speed, barreling at us like a locomotive going off its tracks. He had a wild look in his eyes, so we all took off running, yelling, "Get to work Gary!" all the way down the halls.

Gary was the only slow adult that I messed with. When it came to the handicapped kids, I left them alone. All except this was one girl named Akeema. I did mess with her, partially because she was *fresh*. Let me explain. She would often give students the middle finger or she would cuss at us. So, I would often give it back to her. So what if she was slow? Akeema was smart enough to give us the finger from the confines of her wheelchair, wasn't she?

Because of her wiseass antics, we often had back-and-forth banter which usually took place in our home economics class. This class was well-known to be a haven for hijinks and shenanigans. I had only taken it because I heard you could goof off. I had played several practical jokes on Akeema to this point. I had put ants in her sugar jar. I often switched ingredients on her, and I always let her know that it was me after the fact.

One day Akeema came into home economics with a brand-new haircut. I was smitten with her new hairdo and of course, I would let her know it. I did what any bully would do, and I instantly started a chant in class. I looked directly into Akeema's eyes and I began chanting, "I like your haircut!" I used to use this inflection in my voice that was certainly a mocking tone. The voice inflection used to piss people off immensely. Actually, it still does piss people off sometimes, as I will use that tone in a sarcastic manner to this day. Some fellow bullying classmates had now joined in, "I like your haircut! I like your haircut!" The chants began to get louder and louder. I could see Akeema's face begin to fill with outrage. She started up her electric wheelchair and started coming towards me.

Then something outrageous occurred. Akeema stood up in front of me, grabbed the cane that she carried, and began beating me with it. The entire class was astonished. She had stood up! She continued the onslaught of the cane whipping and elicited only one reaction from me—laugher! The entire class was besides themselves with laughter at this point. Up until then, nobody knew she could stand.

Akeema was a celebrity after that. I actually left her alone the rest of the year. However, the joke, "I like your haircut," would live on to this very day, as many still sing the infamous jingle.

In our town you could get mocked so badly that your real name could actually become something else entirely different. There was

Bobby who became "Wally"—from the TV show "Leave it to Beaver". There was Greg who became "Myer," which was taken from this goofy comic that some of my fellow bullies used to draw. "Myer" was depicted in these sketches as having overly large teeth. The character was obviously made to be goofy looking and he would display his eccentricities by yelling strange things at people like, "Grr!" There was Tony who became "Bones." I am pretty sure it was because he was a big, chubby guy so it was to make fun of his weight by referring to him as skinny bones. Either way Bones just stuck.

Bones took a lot of abuse from my group of friends. He may have been a little slow and he was an easy target. Bones would get drunk and talk about killing himself. At first, I felt bad for him. I even talked him down a few times. But after high school, he became the boy who cried wolf. He continuously talked about killing himself, would cry and bang his head against walls. But in the end, he never did anything to hurt himself. Since it seemed as if it was for attention, we started making fun of him for saying he wanted to kill himself. I know, shameless. But you must know by now that nothing—and I mean nothing—was off limits for me to make fun of. I'm just glad that Bones never acted on his suicidal vocalizations. I would have been one of the people to blame, and I don't know if I could live with that type of thing hanging over my head.

My group of friends used to rent a shore house every summer down at the beach. We were all underage, so this was a thrill for us to get a house where there were no parents and essentially no rules. We used to drink, party, play loud music, and invite girls over to the house. We needed a good number of guys to rent a house because it was pricey for kids our age. Because of the cost, we had to invite a couple of undesirables. One such invite was extended to Bones. We needed his money, plus we'd have somebody to ride and mock for the week.

The first night of the shore house was always crazy. We were all drunk and the girls hadn't made their way to the house yet, so we had to keep ourselves entertained. Well, for a couple of us bullies, Bones was all the entertainment we needed.

My buddy and I threw him onto a bed and held him down. We laid him on his stomach and tied his arms to his legs. We bound and gagged him to further humiliate him. Several of us were laughing and mocking him. I believe that Bones may have been a little bit slow or something, so we mocked his speech and spoke as if we were mentally challenged. Looking back, this was something we shouldn't have engaged in, as it was terrible. Nobody should mock a slow or mentally challenged person. But for me there were no bounds and I dragged several of my bullying buddies down with me into a heartless abyss.

Bones struggled as he squirmed around. He attempted to cry out, but his cries were muffled by the gag. I pulled the gag down and he screamed, "Let me out! Untie me!" This outburst only made us laugh harder. Instead of relenting, we mocked him even further.

We had him tied up for a while. This wen0t on for a good half hour or so, until Bones got angry. He started yelling louder and louder, "Let me out! I'm going to take a taxi home! I'm going *home*! I'm going to call a taxi!"

So, what did we do? We continued our unsolicited punishment. We started yelling, "I'm calling a RAXI! Ret me go! I'm raking a RAXI *home*!"

We always changed words and placed the letter "R" in words in order to mock Bones and we always called him retarded. He was constantly the butt of our jokes, from as far back as I could remember. One time I instigated a fellow bully named Aldin to whip Bones with a stick. I said that Bones was saying disparaging things about Aldin, even though he wasn't. The likeminded bully began a vicious assault. He started whipping Bones over and over with a long, bendy stick. Bones was screaming out, "Aldin stop! Aldin, stoppp!" Aldin saw me cracking up and this just exacerbated his already barbaric behavior. He relentlessly started spinning the powerless victim in circles and when he finally let go, Bones went barreling into a bevy of bushes.

Even though we tortured Bones, he continued to hang with our group of guys. Our torment of Bones went on for years and years. Bones just took all our abominable abuse and we continually dished it out. My cold and unrelenting heart had taken his spirit on many occasions. I want to personally apologize to Bones for all the years of torture and humiliation that he had to endure.

Now I want to be clear about something. I had a large group of friends and not all of them were bullies. I would say that there were only a few of us. However, none of the others tried to stop us. Sometimes they would half-heartedly tell us to stop, or merely just turn and look the other way. Somebody might actually say they thought he had enough, but there was no real resistance.

The reason no one really spoke out was because of peer pressure. If somebody were to stand up and say that what we were doing was wrong, we may have ousted them from the group or mocked them for sticking up for someone. I know for sure there were members of my group that thought what we were doing was wrong, but they would not outright go against what we were doing.

These are the pressures that students face on a daily basis. They are often pressured to bully in order to fit in and to feel like part of a group. Or they are often made to watch others get bullied and say nothing since they are in fear of losing their friends.

I will tell you this: you should say something. If your friends oust you or end their friendships because of it, then they are not your true friends in the first place. Be strong and stand up for what you believe in. If you see someone getting bullied, try to help that person and attempt to intervene. If you are truly a strong person, you will lift others up and not put them down. Reaching out and attempting to help someone could save them from a tragic ending. If your efforts are rebuffed, then report what you saw to an authority figure immediately.

Nobody reported my bullying back in my high school days. Other kids were afraid to tell someone because they were afraid they would be my next target. Kids today are afraid to report the bullying they see because they rightly fear they will be the next to be victimized. If anyone would have told on me, I certainly would have come after them. I would have tormented them and made their life a living hell.

My friends who didn't speak up probably wish that they had. As I've mentioned, I grew up in a different time. Bullying and hazing were accepted to some degree. That's definitely part of the reason none of them reported what was happening. These practices can no longer be tolerated. Even though times have changed, kids are still fearful to report bullying.

Kids should not have these fears. We need to breed a new culture where kids feel safe if they report something. If kids are told they will be protected from bullies, then maybe we can start a new trend. All kids deserve to be safe and protected but that is definitely not the case. Many schools do not intervene enough when bullying occurs. Teachers and administrators are still often turning a blind eye. If there are no consequences for bullies, then why would they stop?

Bullying is wrong and it needs to be reported. We need to encourage kids to stand up to these bullies. I am here to tell today's youth that you need to tell an adult what is happening. You could save someone's life if you take the appropriate actions.

The bully never thinks of the consequences of their actions. The bully just wants to shame you in front of others to look cool and for their own entertainment purposes. A bully doesn't care nor consider the feelings of their victims. This is what makes them a bully. I had no care or consideration for any of my victims. This is a disgusting revelation, yet it is sad but true.

I encourage you to make your own way. You don't always have to follow the crowd, especially if the crowd is doing something that doesn't seem right. If there is bullying going on in your circle of friends, try speaking up, and see if you can foster a change within your group.

PART 2: A BULLY'S RISE AND POTENTIAL REFORMATION

"Three ill-tempered men wielding knives charged at me all at once."

My junior year of high school was a great time as my star was rising. I was at the height of my popularity and I felt like I was on top of the world. Somehow I had become popular and I didn't even play football. You see, most of the football players were gifted with instant popularity. I envied the football players for a long, long time. I had craved what they had since my freshman year and now I finally had a taste. I had also finally slimmed down as I had grown about five inches since the eighth grade. I had shed the "Fat Chink" moniker that had haunted me all throughout grammar school. I was feeling somewhat better about myself. This empowered me and accelerated my already out of control Bully Complex. All this perceived power was a breeding ground for my reprehensible actions and bullying ways. It was unquestionably a thrilling time for me, and it was certainly a stress-free time to be on the wrestling team. I no longer had to worry about being choked out or abused by the upperclassmen. I was now in the power position and I could bully the underclassmen without recourse. There were no longer beatings to be had from the upperclassmen, as I was now the one with a high ranking. I could make up as many nicknames for the underlings as I wanted and there were no consequences. I was loving life on the wrestling team.

One weekend, we went away for a wrestling trip to the state championship tournament in Atlantic City, New Jersey. This was a huge thrill for a bunch of high school kids. Since we were so young, we didn't have much money, so we had to get a bunch of us together in order to afford the hotel room. I honestly think we crammed about ten of us into a room with two double beds. Needless to say, it was unpleasantly tight. None of us cared at the time, as it was for one night and we wanted to see our peers compete.

That night we jostled for position in the tiny room, and next morning, the room was filled with a stench. I woke up gagging and scanned the

71

room in hopes of an answer. None was to be found. The room was probably filled with such a foul odor from having too many teenage boys confined to a small space. But leave it to me to turn it into a bullying situation. I panned across the room and on the floor near me was a freshman who we called by his last name, Yarm. Yarm was a short, pudgy fellow who was extremely quiet and kept to himself. I saw that his socks were off, and his feet were extremely amusing to me. By now, everyone in the room had noticed the permeating stench. I was about to burst with laughter, but I managed to call out, "It's Yarm's FEET!"

A few others looked at me and said, "What?"

I said, "The stink, it's Yarm's FEET!"

The room erupted with laughter after my comical quip. Yarm sat there dejected as he was just a powerless freshman. He was demure to begin with, but you could see him crumple into a cowering ball.

For the rest of the day, he became known as "Yarm's Feet." As a matter of fact, he is known by this hideous moniker to this very day. Yarm has never escaped that day or that stench in that room. The disheartened kid probably scrubbed his feet for years and years afterwards in an attempt to scrub away the insensitive incident. That incident would not go away though because when I started fires, I fanned the flames so they would continuously rage. The fires I started wreaked havoc and were everlasting as they burned down many reputations.

I remember seeing Yarm months later at a party. He probably hoped that the foot jokes would have subsided, but he didn't know me that well. There were a bunch of people playing cards at a table, including Yarm. I took off one of my shoes and one of my socks, and slyly proceeded to the table so no one would see my bare foot. I then lifted my leg and plopped my bare foot right on the table in front of Yarm. The entire room exploded with laughter. Yarm turned fire engine red with embarrassment.

He looked up at me and said, "Very funny Los!" as he tried to just brush it off.

I was cackling and said, "OK you got it, Yarm's Feet!"

The rest of the night I played songs and made up my own lyrics. Each song was about feet or Yarm's feet. I was relentless. I will tell you what though, I give that kid a ton of credit. He just sat there and took all my nonstop verbal abuse. This was one tough-minded kid. Most others would have cried or begged me to stop or flat out left the party. But not Yarm, he sat there all night and ignored me as best he could. I give him props for being a strong-minded person. As for me, I was obviously weak-minded and had a long way to go before becoming a strong person.

I have stated over and over that I was a chronic bully. My only soft spot was for the handicapped. But that did not include people with deformities or what we now refer to as little people. One kid named Greg Clock had a nub for one of his arms. I used to look at him and point one of my arms to the sky and shorten the other one and yell, "It's 3 o'clock!" For me, it was perfect that his last name was clock because he had one long "hand" and one short "hand," just like a clock. In reality, this is probably one of the most defenseless people that anyone could mock. Had Greg Clock been able to, he probably should have clocked me in my insensitive face!

I also mentioned little people or as we called them back then, "midgets." Yes, we had a couple of little people in our school and I even tortured these undeserving victims as they were the easiest of marks. I would sing the "Oompa Loompa" song from the Willy Wonka movie directly at them. I would squat down, and I would persistently ask them, "How's the weather down there?" I was such an insensitive jerk back then.

Years later, I remember seeing one of the little people I had previously victimized, his nickname was Little Jimmy. He was sitting at a table in the bar I worked at. I don't think Jimmy knew I worked there. I came over to his table. He was sitting with several of what looked to be his co-workers. I could see him squirm in his seat and swallow hard as I approached. I think Jimmy was preparing himself for me to embarrass him in front of his peers. However, this was the new and improved me, the non-bullying me. At the time, I was in my mid-thirties and I wasn't 100% changed, but I was well on my way.

I smiled at him to reassure him that I would not embarrass him amongst his peers. I politely asked if there was anything I could get for them. Jimmy looked at me with shock and awe, as he stammered, "Yes, we'll have a round of drinks." The rest of their stay proceeded without incident. I was hoping he would come back into the bar after that day, but he never did. Jimmy probably thought I was having an off day and that my assault would be unleashed upon him at some point. He certainly didn't know that I was a changed person at this time in my life, or perhaps I had scarred him so deeply that it disturbed him to even glance at my face.

All he knew was the person that I used to be, who would blast him in the high school hallways. All he knew was the person that had no compassion or care in his callous heart. I wanted to show Jimmy that I had changed. All these thoughts and possibilities raced through my head, as I felt something I would have never felt in my repugnant past: extreme remorse. I realized though, there's nothing that can be done to change my unsavory past. Every nasty, vile act I had committed can never be undone. I was a monster in high school, and I have to deal with that now. I can only move forward and be a better person from here on out.

I wish I could have been a better person back then. Saying I was a problem child in high school is an understatement. I was a complete nuisance. I degraded students, teachers, janitors, and anyone I felt superior to. I cheated off other students using forceful measures. I intimidated teachers and threatened to beat them up. I drank beer, partied, and smoked cigarettes. I even started gambling with the other cool kids in school. We would play cards underneath the stairwells hours after school. We would play into the early evening, when all the educators had dissipated and only the janitors were left. We would not abandon the game until a janitor would eventually catch us and threaten to report it to the principal, had we not broken up the game.

My friends and I at the time were obsessed with mafia movies, in particular *Goodfellas*. I loved the movie so much that I wanted to be in the mob. That's part of the reason I started gambling, because gambling was glorified by the mob. I bought a pinky ring and acted as if I were a real-life mafia boss. I would bully kids, as I made them kiss my ring out of respect. I took everything to the extreme as I idolized these mob movies. My friends and I even started our own "mafia" group. We had "colors" which you had to display, and you had to be inducted into the group. Of course, you also had to gamble to be a part of the group.

I began to gamble fanatically, and I was addicted to it at an early age. I was a sixteen-year-old kid putting in sports bets. I ran card games out of my house. One weekend when my parents were away, I held an event called "Los Vegas" at my house. It was a play on words since my last name is "Los-pinoso" and Las Vegas is the holy grail of gambling. I thought the event was so cool. I thought *I* was so cool. The event *was* actually pretty cool, though. I had three different blackjack tables and a roulette wheel. All the boys I deemed worthy enough and a couple other outliers were welcomed over to gamble their allowances. Girls didn't partake in these activities back then and especially at that early of an age. As a matter of fact, girls probably found our behavior repulsive.

I eventually branched off from my casino night and just became a full-fledged bookie in high school. Yes, at sixteen to seventeen-years-old, there I was taking bets from other students. What had started as a tiny hallway card game had now evolved into a full-blown gambling ring. Patrick was my best friend, so naturally he was my partner in crime, literally and figuratively. We had half the school placing bets with us. We took their bets on anything. Football was the obvious big attraction, but we would take any bet. If you wanted to bet on soccer, women's college basketball, NASCAR, or even professional wrestling. You name it and we'd accept your wager. We were pretty idiotic to say the least.

Some of the school administration had caught wind of our gambling ventures and they were determined to put a stop to it. Although they were not completely sure who was behind the monetary mayhem, they had an idea or two. I was summoned into a counselor's office to speak to him about my problems. This was not some ordinary counselor. This was a counselor for troubled children; children with suicide issues, children with extreme behavioral issues, children who were continuously in trouble and couldn't stay out of it.

Even though the school wasn't 100% sure that I was one of the people perpetuating the gambling ring, they had other probable cause to assign me to the extreme counseling. I was a habitual troublemaker and quite frankly, they could have used any number of reasons at that point. I had constant conflicts with teachers, I was generally defiant, and there was of course my consistent torment of my fellow students. I was an all-around menace and that made me a prime candidate for these intensified counseling sessions. I had been in lots of trouble at school before, but this was the first time that I was told I needed to see a counselor. The unfortunate man that would have to deal with me was named Cliff Callahan. I am sure Mr. Callahan was a nice guy and I am sure he meant well. But to me at the time, he was creepy, and I wanted nothing to do with him. I was deemed a trouble child, so now I had to attend an hourly meeting with Cliff once a week. I despised these depressing get-togethers. Cliff poked and prodded at me, but I mostly gave him nothing. Every week it was the same line of questioning from "Cliffy Poo," as I nicknamed him.

Cliff would ask, "So, Anthony, did you go out drinking this weekend? Have you done any drugs? Have you recently engaged in any gambling activities?"

I would always respond, "Of course not, *Clifff!!!*"

"It's Mr. Callahan!"

"Yeah, OK, Clifffff!!!!!"

I had zero respect for him, and I was never going to fold to his rigorous line of questioning. My father taught me when I was growing up to never be a rat and to never squeal for anything. He always said, "Don't give yourself or your friends up to anybody. Don't be a squealer!" The mafia movies I idolized repeated the same rhetoric. This guy had no reasonable chance to capture a confession from me. I was tight lipped, and I am sure it frustrated "Cliffy Poo" to no end.

As each week passed, and Cliff began to annoy me more and more, I began to scorn him and the monotonous meetings I was forced to endure. One weekend, my mounting angst prompted me to acquire Cliff's phone number out of the phone book. My friends and I were drunk. I had slugged down a full bottle of gin all by myself. I drank myself into a stupor and decided it was time to call Cliff. I was the master of prank phone calls back then and I was determined to get good old Cliffy Poo real good. I called and disguised my voice. It was fairly late at night, probably midnight or later and I had woken Cliff up from his slumber.

"Who is this?"

I responded in my disguised voice, "This is Steve!"

"Steve Who?"

"Steve Marcelli," I answered.

Steve Marcelli was one of the two kids that I made a school-wide mockery out of. One of the two kids that others would receive "points" for if they were to be caught hanging with them. Cliff was probably aware that Steve was made to be somewhat of an outcast.

Agitated, Cliff said, "What can I do for you Steve? It's quite late."

"I want to kill myself, Cliff! Can you save me?"

My friends giggled and jeered in the background.

"Well, Steve this is very serious, and I will do what I can to assist you. Can I offer a phone number for a help line?"

"No Cliff, I need *you* to help me! Please Cliff!"

"Well, I honestly think you might need to talk to someone who is professionally trained in this matter. But why are you feeling this way, Steve? What can I do to help you?" Cliff responded with a tinge of sadness.

"All the kids in school make fun of me and I hate them. I hate school and the kids make me want to kill myself! That's what's wrong, OK, *Cliff*?" I answered with resounding emotion.

"OK, well I am always available to speak with stu—"

I cut him off, "Well alrighty, Cliffy *Poo*! CLIFFF! *CLIFFFFF!!! CLIFFFFFF!!!!!!*" I just began bellowing his name at the top of my lungs as all of my aggravation and contempt towards him poured out into the phone. He abruptly hung up the phone.

That week's meeting with Cliff was quite awkward as I had a feeling that he knew the prank phone call had been executed by yours truly. I squirmed in my chair and I could barely look him in the eye.

A lot happened in that strange prank call. I usually never had a script when I made those types of calls; everything I said was improvised. Looking back, I see so much underlying in this phone call besides the obvious.

Why had I chosen to say I was Steve Marcelli? This was someone that I had made a school-wide mockery out of. I think I had guilt over my insufferable actions, and I was projecting how I thought I may have made Steve feel. I am not saying that he felt suicidal because I do not know for sure. But in my mind, maybe I thought I had pushed him to the brink of such feelings.

I also think I had unearthed some pushed down feelings of my own. Maybe there were times when I was younger that I wanted to give up because of the continual torment I received. I had an immense amount of emotion running through me during the phone call as I can recall the details fairly vividly.

I want to make my amends to Cliff and Steve; I apologize to you both. Cliff was merely doing his job and I gave him a ton of grief he didn't deserve. As far as Steve, he was just another unfortunate victim on my relentless bully crusade.

The counseling never curbed my issues. I continued to drink, gamble, and most of all, I continued to bully. In fact, that summer I would have a run-in with the Jewish kid that I had beaten up in grammar school. The first kid I actually beat up. We have always had a contentious relationship since I have known him, to say the least. I despised him, and still do, to this day.

One day that summer, out of boredom, I decided I was going to kick the dirty Jew's ass one more time for old time's sake. One of my friends contacted one of his friends over the phone. At first, there was somewhat of a jovial banter between both our groups. His group of friends were laughing, so were my group of friends. It seemed like a big joke, but I wanted to fight him in all seriousness. It did not take much goading because he still despised me. I went in deep though, and for the first time in my life, I have to admit I went way over the line. I was always near the line, maybe even a little past it. But this time I went too far. The two friends who were negotiating the fight finally handed the phones over to the combatants.

I got myself so worked up that I said something that should never, and I mean NEVER be uttered to a Jewish person, no matter the circumstance. I bellowed with ferocity, "I'm going to throw you in my oven, you dirty Jew!"

There was silence from both sides. As soon as I made the anti-semitic comment, everything escalated, and the situation became stone cold serious.

Needless to say, their group of friends came immediately to confront us. The dirty Jew's friends went from a jovial instigating bunch, to an angry mob. What ensued wasn't pretty, and I am not proud of it. But we all clashed and mauled each other with raging fists. There was a tornado of punches that culminated in a blood-stained hurricane. The only thing that stopped the cascade of blood and tempestuous brawl was the sound of sirens in the distance. It was a good thing too, because this was getting ugly and probably would have led to someone's hospitalization. It may have very well been mine. Who's to say?

My racist tendencies were always displayed on my sleeve. I never held back, and I didn't care if you liked what I was saying or not. I disliked Jewish people, as I habitually made them my targets and I always participated in target practice. I was persistent with Jews, but they weren't my only targets. I also had animosity towards Indian people for some reason. I hated their food, and I couldn't stand the stench. There was a lot wrong with Indian people besides their food in my atrocious opinion. Indians were just stinky people to me, and they had nothing to offer me.

There was an Indian restaurant in the center of Kenilworth called Neelam and I detested the fact that it was in my town. I couldn't understand why this Indian restaurant was in the middle of a predominantly Italian town, and I was determined to make them feel uncomfortable, thus making them my new target.

I started my devious plan to run them out of town. I began with prank phone calls as I was an expert at those. I would call and it would go something like this:

"Hello, Neelam, how can I help you?"

I would always feign an Indian accent when I called, "Hello, yes I would like to order some food. My name is Zagbar!"

"OK Zagbar, what can I get for you?"

"Oh yes, I would like a pizza with— "

"Sir, we do not have pizza."

"Yes, I would like to order pizza with goat balls and curry!"

"Sir, we do not have—"

"Roooo Toooo Ayyya! Roooo Toooo Ayyya!" I would bellow at the top of my lungs.

I couldn't even tell you what these noises meant. To me, they were mocking Indian people and I couldn't get enough of yelling these racially-tinged sounds at these undeserving people. The calls went on for months, but I wanted to up the ante. I had a plan to really rattle their cage.

One day, I had my buddy drive me to Neelam and had him park right next to the restaurant. I went inside and started up with my shtick. The man's skin somehow went from brown to beet red, as he instantly realized that I was the evasive phone bandit who had been terrorizing him for months on end.

He jumped over the counter and came at me. I was shocked but I quickly darted for the door. The man gave chase and I could see my friend cracking up in the car as I ran towards the door. I swiftly jumped in and he took off. We could see the Indian man in the rearview mirror cursing and yelling vehemently.

You would think that this would have curtailed my behavior, but the chase only exacerbated it. I was far from deterred as we would go back every weekend and the employees became aware that I was coming. I would just walk in now and scream, "Roooo Toooo Ayyya! Roooo Toooo Ayyya!" at the top of my lungs, turn and run out the door. Sometimes they would give chase, sometimes they just let it go.

This went on for several weeks until one day, the employees decided to put an end to it. I walked in and things were different this day. They came at me full force and caught me this time. They pinned me up against the wall and they put a meat cleaver up to my throat. They said that if I came back again that they would slice me.

I sat there with a big shit-eating grin on my face. I was a crazy little bastard; I wasn't even the least bit scared. I snidely said, "OK, no problem. I will leave you guys alone."

But instead of ending the harassment, I decided to change things up a little. There was a side door to the restaurant, and I made this my new point of emphasis. I ran up to the door and screamed in my racist tone, "Roooo Toooo Ayyya!" I banged on the door and when they opened it, I would throw water or soda on them. Then I would run to the getaway car.

They soon caught on to my new tactic. I had barely knocked on the door when suddenly it swung open. Three ill-tempered men wielding knives charged at me all at once. I ran as fast as I could, but they were right on my tail.

My friend rolled down the car window and said, "Jump in! Jump in!" as he started to pull away. I ran as fast as I could, catapulted my body through the passenger window and into the passenger seat. I looked out and I had just barely evaded the impassioned mob. I was a jackass at the time, so I continued screaming, "Roo Too Ayya!" out the window all the way down the block as my friend and I cackled the whole way home.

I never drove the restaurant out of town, but I positively pissed them off and made their lives miserable. In my mind, that was a victory, because part of being a bully is basking in the misery of others. Hurting others actually gave me a sick sense of satisfaction. My ghastly gratification accelerated my objectionable behavior.

When you look at it, the truth is, this should not give anyone fulfillment or joy. We should pick others up and not put them down. These people did not bother anyone in my town. They were just trying to run a decent business and make an honest living. I only disliked them because they were Indian and for no other reason. This is the wrong way of thinking and we need to change this pervasive racism that runs rampant in our country. If there's somebody that you dislike, you need to stop and think why you don't like that person. If the answer is because of their skin color, race, or religion, then you need to evaluate those thoughts. These are not valid reasons to dislike someone. Racism should not be tolerated, and I am glad that I have looked inside myself and made changes. We can all make changes for the better.

Kenilworth was a very small town, in fact it was a tiny town: about a mile by a mile and a half. This is why I grew up extremely close-minded; I was not exposed to many cultures, races, and different types of people. My parents certainly weren't racist, so they didn't influence my racist tendencies. My tendencies developed from lack of exposure. The small town is why I didn't know many Jewish people or Indian people. This is why I wasn't open to people of other races and cultures.

I was also close-minded because I did cross paths with a few individuals in my hometown who were explicitly racist. There were a handful of racist people, but for the most part Kenilworth is not like that at all. Again, not everyone in K-Town has a racist mentality, but there is certainly some cultural divide. In fact, I personally know many wonderful people from Kenilworth, who are far from being racist. I've met some of the greatest and most accepting people hailing from my fabulous hometown. But obviously, there's always a few bad seeds in a bunch of good people and there were some who were blatantly racist.

One time, there was a house for sale on the corner of my street. I remember my neighbor, Johnny, calling me over. He told me that an Indian family had looked at the house and that we couldn't allow them to move into that house under any circumstances.

I asked, "Why, Johnny?"

He looked me dead in the eye and said, "They'll stink up the whole block!"

I started cracking up, mostly because I could tell Johnny actually believed it.

My disturbed neighbor then said in a deadpan, "No really Ant, we can't have it! I'm calling my brother and I'm making him buy THAT house!"

I thought Johnny was kidding, but a month later, his brother had bought the house and he moved in. This is how serious some of those bad seeds from Kenilworth are when it comes to our town. I thought this was crazy but then again Johnny was quite insane.

You see, Johnny was somewhat of the town drunk. He was at the bar six to seven days a week. He was a strange bird. And it's not that I didn't like Johnny, but he was a rather delusional person. My friend and I ran into Johnny at the bar about a month after the 9/11 incident. The drunk told us the most outrageous story I had ever heard. He said he was in the World Trade Center during the 9/11 incident, even though everyone knew he never left Kenilworth. I had heard he was on a bender the night before and I even saw his car in the driveway the day of the tragedy.

Johnny told us he was thirty stories up when the tragedy took place. He said he carried two bodies, one over each shoulder all the way down thirty stories. My friend and I started laughing as we thought Johnny was joking, but his face became serious. He turned red with scorn and a near psychotic look came over his glowing red face. He furiously declared, "What are you laughing at? I am an American hero!" We ceased our laughter, fearing he may become unhinged, and we proceeded to commend him on being a"hero." I just smiled at him and sarcastically said,"That's great, Johnny." We left that bar and cracked up for days after.

I don't know if there was a race problem in my town back then. Johnny certainly felt that way, as he was adamant about not letting the Indian people move onto our block. However, he was delusional, and certainly could not represent the entire town. Yet there were not many different races of people in Kenilworth. One group I was also unfamiliar with was African Americans.

For some reason, K-Town only had three blocks of African American people; it was the "black section" of town. It was not three blocks spread throughout the town, but three consecutive blocks. There were a few black people throughout the town, but there were not many.

One of my early best friends named Brian was a big influence on my younger years. We were friends from a young age starting from around the third grade. He could be a good guy if he wanted to, but Brian would rather cause trouble. It didn't take much to twist my arm. Trouble was something I could never avoid growing up.

Across the street from Brian's house was one of the few with black people living in it on our side of town. We used to call them "shads." That was our name for black people at the time. There was a kid our age living there named Kenny, but he was white. We never understood why his family was black. He had obviously been adopted, but no one had illuminated what this concept was to us at the time. Admittedly, we were young ignorant kids but that is no excuse. We were harsh to Kenny as we assumed there was something wrong with him. We would mock him and call him the "Shad in disguise" and "Shad Lover." Kenny hated it when we verbally abused him. But we didn't care, he lived with a bunch of "shads" and they were living in the wrong part of town, in our jaded eyes.

Kids can be racist at a young age. Certainly, some of this is learned behavior. However, there are times that kids just mock what they do not understand. I believe Brian and I were in that category. Our parents were not racist, we just made fun of Kenny because we didn't understand. Young kids need to be taught that making fun of other people because of differences is extremely wrong. When I was young, I was isolated and made fun of for being Asian. I received racist remarks firsthand. As I've stated, in the beginning I didn't even know what a "chink" or a "gook" was. I just knew that I didn't like being called those slurs. Brian and I would isolate Kenny because he lived with black people and we knew little about them. Looking back, I can tell you that we were too young at the time to be intentionally racist, but what we were saying was undeniably racist.

Kids say things often without even knowing what they mean. We need to better educate our children about different races, cultures, and ethnicities at an earlier age. This will help to eliminate racism at earlier stages.

Being young and ignorant, we decided to make fun of what we didn't understand. We always found a new way to mock them. I did some research and found out how to say black person in different languages. I soon spread the racial rhetoric around the whole town. The derogatory words spread like wildfire. All black people were now "shads," "chadnas" and "shizaks!" Of course, with me being Italian, above all they were "moulinyans." I remember the first time I heard the word. I was at the local sub shop with my older cousin. We were in the white, all Italian part of town. There were two black guys walking down the street. My cousin looked at me and asked, "Ant, what are these Yans doing in our part of town?" I looked at him dumfounded and confused. He said, "These MOULINYANS! These spades, eggplants, black people! They don't belong here!"

Later on, I told my dad what had happened, and he said that my older cousin was wrong to say that. My dad was not racist in the least, but my cousin was a different story. My jaw dropped, but I loved what he said at the time. What my cousin had said was like sweet music to my young innocent ears. I was enthralled with the new word I had learned. I guess even at a young age I had an insatiable hunger for racism. I didn't know at the time that what he had said was radically wrong, I just thought it was the funniest thing I had ever heard. Not to mention, I thought, it was true! What *were* these Yans doing on our side of town? Who did they think they were walking in our part of town anyway?

This was not the first time I would hear these racial epithets roll off of my older cousin's tongue. I once attended a boxing match which was shown on a big screen in an Atlantic City show room. There were all types of people in the room but that did not deter my outlandish cousin.

Somebody asked him who he was rooting for and he proudly proclaimed, "The white guy!" My cousin was nearly possessed with madness as he yelled and screamed, rooting for the white guy. He was yelling, "Get that moulinyan!" over and over again. He even dropped the "N" word several times. That racially insensitive bomb caused a disturbance.

Finally, an African American man confronted my cousin, but he was not backing down. My older cousin told him that he would drop him, just as the white boxer was going to drop that "moulinyan" in the ring. They nearly came to blows, but my father thankfully calmed down the situation. My father was equally taken aback by my outlandish cousin's actions. He talked the African American gentleman down, and soon peace was restored. But I was barely a teenager, and this left a lasting impression on me.

The racist mentality was pervasive and impossible to avoid. I had been brainwashed. Luckily, I am not one of those people to get stuck in their ways; with time, I became vastly open-minded. I would eventually be exposed to many, many African American people. I would eventually have African American friends and I even dated a couple of black girls once my racial walls finally came crumbling down. This was all a part of my transformation process, proving that race is no longer an issue, in my now mature mind frame.

Kenilworth was not just devoid of many Jewish people and black people, but it seemed devoid of other races as well. As mentioned previously, this was the effect of generations and generations of people staying in the tiny town and never leaving. The early perceptions I gained from my older cousin and several others caused me to have a racist outlook. The town overall was not racist. I referred to it as sheltered, and I stand by that. But growing up in such a small area can lead to skewed perceptions. As a young impressionable kid, these are the perceptions that I formed. The fact that my hometown was not culturally diverse should bother me. After all, I am half Asian and I should have been offended when other people discriminated against Asians, as my mother always reminded me. But I grew up feeling

Italian, as I was almost exclusively surrounded by that culture. I always associated with being Italian at a young age. There was a point in time that I embraced my Korean heritage, but I despised it for so very long. I was embarrassed to be half Asian, as I was constantly taunted for it and mocked for being "chinky." I was known as the "Fat Chink" nearly my entire grammar school existence. Why would I want anything to do with being Korean? I eventually grew up and I realized that this makes me who I am and now, I am damn proud to be Korean.

I am proud to be Korean now because this makes me distinctive. I am always told that I have a unique look and this gives me character. I wouldn't change who I am now, and I especially wouldn't alter my heritage. I am proud to have grown into the person that I have become. I am proud of all the pieces that have come together to make me whole. Sure, there are things that I would like to work on, but overall, I am content.

Being content with who you are is extremely important. You should embrace who you are as a person. Your heritage and your culture make up who you are. Your likes and dislikes make you an individual. Stand tall for what you believe in. Be proud of where you came from and what you stand for. Don't ever let others put you down for being who you are.

I am extremely happy that I can now be content in my own skin. I am proud of everything that makes me the person I am. I have finally gained a great deal of self-confidence and I even think I am a fairly good-looking guy. I don't think I'm a '10' or anything, but I think I'm slightly above average. I am constantly aware of and take care of my appearance. I have always been well-kept and I am proud to be clean cut. I was always a neatly-kept person growing up. Even when I was friends with the burnouts, I was the clean cut one of the group. My group of friends after that were quite different from the burnouts. These guys have always been a clean cut group of guys. Some of us may even be considered borderline "metro" with the lengths that we would go, in order to look "fresh to death." We wore nice clothes, good smelling cologne and always bathed on a regular basis.

The reason why I tell you these things is because we would make fun of others who weren't "clean." Guys with long hair and scraggly beards were always in our sights as a source of laughter. You know, the types that I used to hang with, burnouts! I especially liked picking on people with mullets. There's something especially hilarious about mullets and the way they look. We made up a term to describe these people, so we could talk about them right in their faces without them knowing. We called these types of people "DUSTY." For example, if there was a dude with long, greasy hair and a scruffy, dirty beard, I would say, "Look at Dusty!" If there was a guy with an outdated mullet who looks like he's stuck in 1985, we'd yell "Hey Dusty, nice MULLET!" My insensitive taunts and bullying weren't just of the racial variety, they were for physical appearances as well.

Now, put a couple of drinks in me and I would pretty much go up to anyone and say anything. My friends would tell you, it's a wonder how I didn't get my ass kicked for my leaky faucet of a mouth. I marched right up to many "Dusty" characters in my past and just flat out said, "You look Dusty!" I would tell them to take a shower and to cut their hair. I'd call them "Scruffy Mofo's" and "Dusty Dirt Bags." The list of people that think I'm an unforgivable jerk just grew exponentially.

All of my racist tendencies and judging ways would lead to a bevy of harassment on my part when I attended high school. My actions were despicable, and nobody should replicate the things I said or did. The barbaric brute inside of me was unleashed in a big way during high school and it would take an awful long time to change the monster I had become.

Being a monster among everyone caused me to bulldoze a path of destruction and nobody was safe. I had an unquenchable thirst to bully everyone. I would even bully people I considered to be friends. I had a large group of friends in high school and beyond. Sometimes these friends would branch off away from each other, but there were subgroups of friends that all associated with each other. In each subgroup, there were new people to meet who became intertwined in your life. Sometimes these groups would intermingle. When this happened, there were bound to be people that not everyone would get along with.

I remember one particular kid that most of my friends found to be a little odd and out of place with us. But he was good friends with one of my best friends. Instead of bridging the gap and saying, "Hey guys, he's a good kid, he's OK, let's give him a chance," I saw an opportunity to mock and make fun of someone. His name was Phil Drogon and whenever I was alone with him or with our mutual friend Pete, I would treat him normally. Pete was and still is one of my best friends. He's the most good-hearted guy you could ever meet. He was friends with Phil without any caveats. But not me; I did not want my other friends to see me acting cool to this "unpopular" kid. Hence, whenever we were around a larger group of our friends, I would openly ridicule him. His last name Drogon rhymed with a popular professional wrestler of the time named Hulk Hogan. That, of course, prompted me to call him Phil Hulk Hogan and yell Hogan's catch phrases at him. I would scream, "Oh *yeeeaaaahhh brotherrrrr*," and laugh in his face. I always did this to impress my other friends. I could tell Phil hated it, but I didn't have any compassion. I just wanted to look cool at any cost. His feelings meant nothing to me, at that time in my life anyway.

After many years of me acting like this, Phil resented me. I remember Pete and I were going out drinking one time and he was on the phone with Phil. This was during a time when I working on becoming a better person, and I wanted to treat Phil better than I had in the past. Pete then asked Phil to join us for drinks, which made me very happy. I could hear Phil speaking through the phone rather clearly and he said he had little money and could not join us. I told Pete to tell him that I would spot him and pay for his drinks. Pete told him what I thought would be uplifting news. But when Pete mentioned my name and that I offered to spot Phil for his drinks, I could hear his voice change. Phil deflated instantly with the utterance of my name. He said, "Oh, you're with him? Nah I'm good," and hung the phone up.

I felt dreadful. I could hear the distress and sadness that I caused him in that moment. His words came through the phone like a lightning bolt and struck my inner core. This was someone that was supposed to be my friend. But I had used him as a public whipping boy for others to laugh at, just so I could maintain my social status or whatever. I was disgusted with myself at that moment. I have never officially apologized to Phil, but we seem to have made amends since that day. Especially since I made a conscious effort not to deride Phil in front of the group any longer. I have treated him with respect since I found out the way he actually felt about me. I no longer wanted to shame him in front of others. I am ashamed that I did that to Phil, as I was in no way a true friend to him. He is truly a great guy and he didn't deserve that disgraceful treatment. I would like to apologize to Phil after all these years. I have harbored some guilt for the way I treated him, and I know I was wrong. What I did was egregious, especially to someone who was supposed to be a friend. If somebody treats you in this manner, if they ridicule you, mock you, demoralize you and are just flat out a bully to you, they are NOT your true friend!

My bullying caused some troubles in maintaining some of my friendships, and it's no wonder I had ample problems when it came to girls. As I've said, I was not too smooth when it came to dating girls in high school. But my junior year, I was able to finally land a girlfriend. Her name was Jaime and she was my sister's best friend. It was a little awkward at first. Jaime and I had developed a strong bond, as she confided some dark secrets to me that shall not be talked about here. Also, I had such low self-esteem at the time that I thought Jaime might be one of the only girls that would actually go for me. Not that she was ugly or anything, I actually thought she was beautiful. We had forged this bond over her pain, and we cared for each other deeply. I thought the emotional bond would endear me to her and I could make her my girlfriend.

I remember the day that I built up the courage to kiss Jaime. It was my very first kiss at what I thought was the old age of sixteen. I don't know if I've ever actually admitted to this before, because I was embarrassed for a long time that I didn't have my first kiss until the age of sixteen. After all, I'd witnessed boys and girls kissing for the first time in the seventh grade! But now in the grand scheme of things, it doesn't matter. I was a late bloomer as they say. I fancied myself ugly and Jaime was this beautiful angel that was actually willing to have me. She became my first everything and we dated pretty much my entire junior and senior years. I thought I was in love with her and maybe for that age I was. I realize now she was only my first love and it was just "puppy love." Nevertheless, at the time, my feelings were intense. The inner heavy metal burnout inside of me was exceptionally proud that I had finally gotten a girl to be with me!

By my senior year, everything was going swimmingly. Jaime and I were full throttle, I was one of the most popular kids in school, and I felt untouchable. At this point, I did relent some of my bullying ways. I calmed down somewhat on the teachers. I had caused so many waves in high school that there was a serious threat to have me thrown out of school. I knew that if that actually happened my mom probably would have killed me. Well, obviously not true murder like many of my victims probably wanted for me, but she may have thrown me out of the house. Therefore, I continued to skate through and mostly only bullied the underclassmen during my senior year.

Even though I was still a bully, I could feel myself changing slowly. I remember one particular wrestling match that tugged at my heart strings. Our team was at a dual meet where we faced two different teams. I came out with a win in my first match, but it was the second match that left a lasting impression on me. My coach pulled me aside and said he needed to speak to me before the match. Coach usually just gave us a pep talk and told us to make him proud. However, this time, Coach was serious. He told me that my opponent had Down syndrome and to go easy on him. He said to take him down softly and pin him as quickly as possible. Also, he told me to smile at the boy and make him feel comfortable.

My mind was racing with a thousand thoughts at once. Part of me wanted to let this kid beat me. I wanted to make him have a special moment. The other part of me knew I couldn't lose to him because my friends on the team wouldn't understand, and they would ridicule and mock me. I thought, *I could at least let him take me down.*

I only had seconds to process all of these thoughts. Suddenly, time was up, and I had to face him. I smiled wide at him and gave him a nice handshake. I said, "Good luck, buddy!"

After the whistle blew, I could hear some of my buddies giggling on the side of the mat. This gave me even more conflicting feelings. I knew the guys were laughing because I was wrestling a kid with Down syndrome. Pretty ironic, the Big Bad Bully is facing the ultimate victim who cannot defend himself. Their giggles made me want to lay down and let him win even more. But I wasn't ready for that just yet.

My Bully Complex took over and I did what I thought I had to do. I locked up with him and brought him to the mat softly. I quickly pinned him and then proceeded to hug him. I told him he was amazing.

He was still upset because he had lost. My heart was broken right there on the spot.

I wish I had done the right thing, even now. What a moment it would have been for him. I probably could have made a special moment that would have lasted a lifetime for him. Instead, more selfishness ensued, as I was only concerned for what others thought about me. I was still mentally weak. I know deep down I had it inside me to let that kid win that match. I just couldn't get past my own complex.

That match left a lasting impression on me, as I toned everything down afterwards. I bullied, but not like I used to. My heart was starting to feel hurt. I eased up on everyone. My only run-ins with teachers at this point were mostly harmless pranks. We had this one teacher that we all loved, Mr. Fernandez, who taught history and English. We nicknamed him "El Sid" after the famous NY Mets pitcher from the eighties. El Sid was the man and put up with a lot our shenanigans. I didn't back talk nor was I generally disrespectful to El Sid. If anything, we always had a playful banter. One day, this would culminate in the ultimate prank.

I had been fresher than usual on this one particular day. My behavior caused El Sid to lock me in his private office. Before he led me to the office, I told one of my friends to have the video camera ready for a prank I was going to pull, since we were in the middle of our final video project and we were allowed to have our video cameras in class. El Sid said I was to stay in his office for the duration of the class and study my history book. I'd had this plan for a while now but hadn't known when I could execute it. This was the perfect time. I waited until I knew I was alone and then picked up his phone and called Domino's Pizza. At first the Domino's employee was very hesitant.

"Wait, you want me to deliver a pizza right to your classroom?"

"Why yes," I said, "No worries, we are having an end of the year pizza party to celebrate."

"Are you sure your teacher is OK with this?"

"Oh yes sir," I said convincingly, "Mr. Fernandez just wanted me to call because I am the head of the class. I assure you, everything is fine."

"OK then, we'll be there in a half hour."

Now I was about thirty feet down the hall locked in what was essentially a small closet. I could not hear the prank going down, but my friend was able to get the whole incident on video tape. The delivery man surprised the entire classroom, and Mr. Fernandez had laughed about the good-natured prank.

My exchanges at this point had become nothing more than buffoonery, funny business and foolish antics, rather than with malice. There was a certain lunch lady that I used to torture in good fun. I remember my amusing banter with her pretty vividly.

"Hey lady, look, dog meat for lunch! Looks pretty tasty!"

"Oh, go in the other line kid, stop bothering me!"

"Mmm high school lunch is great, what a selection! And the service! What service from a cranky old lunch lady!"

"Oh, stop pestering me, kid!"

Lunch became a comedic forum for me. Every day I would come up with something new in order to harass "my favorite" lunch lady. There were cups of apple juice or fruit punch in the buffet-style line and I would often chug every drink on the tray before getting to the register. This would invoke laughter from those who were close enough to witness my lunchroom monkey business. Most times, the laughter would cause me to get caught after my thievery had been committed.

"Hey kid, that stuff's not free ya know! Next time you'll pay!"

I'd always leave the lunchroom with a great big grin. I think the lunch lady was entertained by me as there was never a next time. She would engage in our banter but would never charge me. I'm glad that she didn't take her job that seriously. Maybe she thought that I was just a kid having fun, therefore she let it go. Either way, I was happy to get away with being the little troublemaker I was.

It wasn't before long that all the lunch ladies had learned my name. They knew who the resident clown was. And I was more than happy to entertain all those who were in my vicinity during lunch break.

I continued my lunchroom antics as I upped the ante. I graduated from drinking all the apple juice. Now I was brazen, as there had been no previous consequences. This encouraged me to start unwrapping sandwiches and I would boldly take a bite. If I didn't like it, I'd put it down and leave it.

"Anthony, you can't just bite that and leave it! Now you have to pay for it!"

"I just wanted to sample it. How do I know if I like it or not?"

"Well, this isn't a sampling station or a salad bar!"

"Of course it's not, it's a slaughterhouse and the mystery meat of the day is chopped up monkey! C'mon lady, you know you love me!"

I loved busting that one specific lunch lady and I think she actually enjoyed my busting, because she never charged me. I mean I actually took bites of sandwiches and put them back! Who does that?

My senior year, I toned down my act, even with the lunch lady. But I do remember a certain incident that left an impression on me as the lunch lady showed me that she did indeed enjoy my clownish behavior.

"Hey, miss lunch lady, look at this sandwich, it has mold on it!"

"That's not mold, Anthony."

"Then what is it? Dried snot?"

"No, you wise guy, it's the peanut butter seeping through the bread."

"Yeah, and that meat is from a cow!"

"You know what, Anthony? To show you my appreciation for you all these years, I'm going to give you this 'moldy' peanut butter and jelly sandwich on the house!"

Believe it or not, I was rather speechless. Now I wasn't sure if the sandwich actually had mold or not. Was the lunch lady just giving me this sandwich as a joke and some sort of twisted revenge? Was her intention for me to eat the sandwich which quite possibly had a piece of mold glaring back at me? Either way, that gesture was a show of appreciation that the lunch lady had for me. I recognized her appreciation and took the sandwich which was actually quite tasty by the way. That put a nice little bow on our lunchroom relationship, and I will never forget that lunch lady to this day.

My run-ins with teachers and lunch ladies may have quelled to a minimum but I soon found myself entrenched in other controversies. I was not only social amongst the lunch staff, but I had an active social life in general. Along with popularity comes partying. My drinking had become slightly out of control. I was partying and drinking every weekend.

My drinking ways would even spill into my bullying ways. My friends and I used to play tricks on unsuspecting people at parties just to look cool. We used to do this shot trick with alcohol. I would challenge some kid and we'd bet money. We were supposed to go shot for shot with vodka and the one who dropped out, passed out, or puked would be the loser.

Well, the person running the game was one of my best friends. We would set it up so I would take shots of water while my opponent took shots of the real stuff. Obviously, I always won and destroyed whoever the pawn was in our sick game. We expressed unusual enjoyment from this game. We loved watching some idiot get drunk while I threw back shots of water! Yes, this is another form of bullying.

You should never make people drink alcohol. There were times during my college years while pledging a fraternity that I was forced to drink alcohol. I must tell you how dangerous this is and that you should never subscribe to such practices. My actions were deplorable, and I hope that people reading this will realize that alcohol is not something to fool around with. Drinking haphazardly and not responsibly could cause serious damage to someone. People have died from ingesting large amounts of alcohol. Please be safe when consuming alcohol and only drink if you are of age to do so.

Drinking, doing drugs, and smoking cigarettes are all practices that I am firmly opposed to, regardless of what I did in my past. I do not condone doing any of these activities if you are underage; they can be damaging habits, even if you are of age. I am not proud that I drank alcohol and smoked cigarettes as a young man. These habits can sometimes be glorified, but let me tell you, there is nothing glamorous about them. They are disgusting habits and can be extremely dangerous to your health.

Despite the fact that I know better now, I clearly did not back then. There was one day in particular that my drinking spiraled out of control. My friends and I were drinking heavily at the Don's house, because he had the house to himself that weekend. We filled up a blender with beer. First, we would take a shot of booze and then chug the beer-filled blender. Needless to say, after several rounds of this, we were all blasted.

We decided to roam the streets of Kenilworth. In our inebriated state of mind, we had only one mission: TROUBLE!

We walked down Passaic Avenue, past a line of parked cars. My friend Brian exclaimed, "Watch this!" as he suddenly jumped onto the roof of a parked car. He began gesticulating and bouncing on the now convulsing automobile. Brian bounced to another car, and another, until *SMASH!* His colossal foot slammed right through a windshield.

We all stood in awe, not knowing what to do. Then it suddenly clicked to all of us at once—RUN! So, run we did. Brian and the Don ran through backyards and hopped fences. I was with my cousin, Rose, and neither of us were in any shape to leap fences, so we ran down the dimly lit street. I ran faster than I ever had, speeding toward the glowing Boulevard, the largest main street in K-Town. This was unquestionably a bad idea. Brian and the Don were nowhere to be seen as they surely had gotten away. I wish I could say the same for me and my cousin.

As I raced towards the main drag, I felt a forceful tug on my arm. Next thing I know, I'm jerked completely around, facing down a police officer.

He then grabbed my cousin with a hurtful force. This disconcerted me and sent me into a frenzy. I sensed the officer was a bit shaken himself, so I slapped the officer's hand off of my cousin. He looked at me in amazement, then began backing me into a parked car, pinning my hands into my chest.

With all my mounting rage, I exploded forward with one of my pinned arms and struck the policeman with full force.

I backhanded a person of authority.

My cousin Rose and I were both arrested. She was released shortly after into her father's custody.

My fate was much different. I spent the drunken night in a jail cell. The night was blurry, but I could remember yelling and verbally abusing the arresting officer from my cell. I could see the shaken police officer filling out paperwork nearby. I glared at him with sinister intentions. I berated him and told him I was going to kick his ass when I was let out of there. I continued to bully the officer for the majority of that night.

The next morning, my parents were called to come pick my drunk ass up. I was given a slap on the wrist since my dad knew half of the force. They gave me a stern warning despite the arresting officer's protest.

On top of spending that night in a jail cell, my parents grounded me for two months. Even with all of that, this would not be my last run in with authority figures or law enforcement. There was more to come and my incessant need to feel power over others would land me in more trouble.

After enduring my punishment, senior year was almost over. The end of the year was like what most people experience. It was sad because I would be leaving a lot of friends to go to a new school. It was also exciting as college and new experiences were on the horizon. The end of the year events brought about exhilaration. I was especially looking forward to the Senior Prom. I really thought I would get voted as the Prom King. I thought I was the King of the school anyway. I was definitely the King Bully; therefore, I would need a proper crowning.

However, at prom's end, I was not crowned the king, deflating my ego somewhat. Maybe I wasn't as popular as I had previously thought. This only brought out my insecurities more than ever. I thought to myself, maybe I was still that young loser who was perpetually bullied on the playground years prior. Eventually I would realize that being prom king didn't matter, nor should it. I should have been proud of myself either way. More importantly, I never should have referred to myself as a loser. I was not the loser, the people who had bullied me were the losers. If you are being bullied, you are not a loser. Please always remember that.

There was one more big event left in my senior year and that was the senior class trip. We went to Great Adventure, which is more widely known as a Six Flags theme park. But anyone from New Jersey will tell you, it's definitely *Great Adventure*. Now, on this class trip, I did something special. Something that I would have never done in the past. When the teachers chaperoning asked which of us would take a handicapped student as a partner, I raised my hand.

I have to admit that at first, I raised my hand in order to skip all of the lines. The handicapped kids and their partners were able to wait in the handicapped line, which basically put you at the front of all the long, winding lines. Yes, quite distasteful, but that's the kind of person I was at this point in my life. However, that day changed me and would leave a lasting imprint on me. I ended up being partners with a handicapped girl named Christine.

In high school, I have said that no one was off limits when it came to my victimizations. I however, embellished slightly. Everyone was on my bully radar except handicapped kids. The lone exception was the girl named Akeema. You might say to yourself, "Who in the world would bully handicapped children?" But let me tell you that there is indeed a select breed of bullies, who actually do pick on the handicapped. I have witnessed this type of bully, as they harassed the most helpless of the helpless. The handicapped kids had zero chance to defend themselves. So, yes there were actually a few first-rate bullies that were shockingly worse than even me. The fact that this rare breed of bullies existed should not be that astonishing though, as the ultimate idea of a bully is someone who picks on another person who most likely won't defend themselves. The handicapped are easy prey for the bully to feast on. Now the key here is that they "most likely won't defend themselves." Occasionally, there will be some of the victimized who stand up for themselves. More often than not, this is not the case. But if they needed to, they could defend themselves, nonetheless. That's why picking on the handicapped is reprehensible and beyond unforgivable. The handicapped for the most part cannot defend themselves. They are defenseless and often times mentally incapable of fighting back.

I did have that one instance of mocking the handicapped girl named Akeema. I have no defense for this. My reasons were that Akeema actually was able to speak although often garbled. She did try and throw barbs at people and she had a little bit of a nasty attitude. Again, I'm not making excuses, just explaining my reasoning for my one handicapped exception.

There's a huge reason why I didn't victimize handicapped kids. I grew up with a handicapped uncle who also lived with my family at one point. His nickname was Bish and he had a huge impression on my life. If not for him, I'm sure I would have mocked the handicapped, as I was relentless and ruthless. Looking back now though, I am glad that I had these restrictions as far as making fun of the handicapped. I realize I had a heart somewhere underneath my cold and callous exterior. My heart, although cloudy and murky from all the ruthless aggression I unleashed on everybody else, was there somewhere. Somewhere under the hard, bully, fake tough-guy public presentation, there was indeed a warm, loving heart. One day that heart would endure and eventually win over. I am thankful it did. If I had continued on that bully path, I'm sure I'd be in jail or on a path to somewhere undesirable.

My uncle Bish suffered from cerebral palsy and didn't have the use of one of his arms. He is the reason I have a soft spot for the handicapped. His right arm was sort of tucked in and bent as it cradled his body. The paralyzed arm would not move from its position. His left arm, however, was extremely powerful since he used it for everything. I heard plenty of stories about him growing up. His left arm strength was that of legend. One particular story my dad told me was about how Bish tossed a kid on his bike who was bullying my father. Supposedly, my uncle lifted the bully in the air with his one arm and flung him to the pavement!

When I was about eight, Bish came to live with my immediate family. During that time, I often had to help him with everyday life. Due to his handicap, I had to assist in daily tasks that he had trouble accomplishing, from going to the bathroom to getting dressed. These are daily routines that most of us take for granted and it opened my eyes to see someone struggling to accomplish them. These early encounters left a long-lasting impression on me.

My uncle Bish was a funny and outgoing guy. I admired how he lived his life and went out and met as many people as he did. He never let his handicap hold him back and I had high admiration for that. His handicap could have made him depressed, but it didn't. I would often go on walks around town with him. He would introduce me to what seemed like everyone in our entire town and I loved going on those walks with him. I used to go down to his room to watch the NY Mets with him, and I have remained a loyal fan to this day.

Unfortunately, my uncle passed several years later, but the impact he had on me remains to this day. Although I was an unrelenting jerk to most, I was always sensitive and sympathetic towards the handicapped. I have my uncle Bish to thank for that.

Even though I started with crooked intentions when I raised my hand and volunteered to assist Christine that day at the theme park, I was stoked to hit the rides with her. I asked her which attraction she preferred to ride first, and I was ecstatic that we were in agreement. I quickly pushed her wheelchair towards our first choice and of course we chose a rollercoaster. After all, we were allowed to skip the hour-long line! I rolled Christine up the handicapped ramp, and we quickly found ourselves in the front. The ride attendant looked at me and said, "OK, lift her into the seat."

I thought to myself, *Oh damn, I have to lift her onto the ride.* I had thought there were going to be other people to do that. There apparently weren't, so I lifted her onto the rollercoaster seat, and she was exuberant.

The whole day I pushed her wheelchair to the front of the line and boosted her into every seat. She was extraordinarily happy and appreciative. I had never felt like this before. I was making her entire day amazing and I was in awe. I had to bring her to the bathroom and assist her as she ate. I was suddenly no longer the Super Bully, instead I was a human being. Funny thing is that none of the other bullies judged me because they thought I had taken on Christine only to skip the lines. Even though that was my initial intention, it was no longer the case. I had a feeling of warmth and even love helping this girl that sorely needed it.

For the entire day I pushed my friends and my popularity to the side. For once, being the most popular kid in school, showing off for a crowd or bullying some kid, were not my priorities. I was displaying compassion, sensitivity, and humanity like I hadn't in a long, long time. My heart had been warmed for the first time in forever.

My Bully Complex had actually faded into the background. This was a glimmer of hope that I could change for the better. Somewhere deep down beneath my darkness, there was indeed light.

My friends had asked me to sit with them at lunch, and one of the chaperones offered to sit with Christine. Helping this young girl was giving me a rather euphoric feeling and I didn't want to abandon her for lunch, prompting me to do the unthinkable. I turned down my friends and said I would sit with Christine. As I sat across from her, we had a nice conversation. I actually sat there and listened to her. She told me about her life, and she thanked me for taking her on all the rides. I told her she was welcome and that I would do it any time for her. I actually meant it.

My uncle Bish had opened up my heart, but Christine had further warmed my soul. That life-changing day, Christine and I truly bonded as we shared laughs and meaningful conversation. Years later I saw her at our ten-year reunion where our connection would be reaffirmed. Our bond was still there, and it opened my eyes to the person I could become. I believe that this fateful day with Christine was the first day that facilitated change inside of me. There was plenty of work to be done, but I was changing for the better.

At the very end of my senior year, the changes became apparent as I slowly softened my hard-edged exterior. I spent time repairing some of my relationships with the teachers I had scorned. I actually became close with Miss Logan, which was rather stupefying, considering I had made her cry just a couple of years earlier. Miss Logan was the advisor to the school newspaper and poetry magazine, and I had done both activities since my sophomore year. We had a rather tumultuous relationship to say the least prior to my senior year, when I actually became editor of both publications. I was somewhat of a productive student even with all the clowning around. I had accomplished becoming the editor of these publications and my relationship with Miss Logan had slowly mended. I was actually proud to have made amends with Miss Logan. She even wrote me a letter of recommendation for college and gave me a good luck card!

I felt the utmost remorse that I made her cry in the past and was appalled at how mean I had been. It was sweet redemption that we had mended our relationship. After all the shit I had put Miss Logan through, she was instrumental in helping me get into college. That shows what a truly amazing person she was. If I were her, I would have told me to go shit in a hat.

Miss Logan had taught me something incredible though; that people can change their view and perception of you. I probably didn't deserve her forgiveness, but she gave it to me anyway and acknowledged that I had changed. I was transforming from a foul-mouthed, brash bully to a genuine, nice young man. I still had a long way to go and a lot more to learn, but I was taking steps. Baby steps.

SECTION THREE

COLLEGIATE AWAKENINGS

PART 1: PASSING JUDGEMENT

"For the first time in my life, I could see pain in someone's eyes."

That summer between high school and my first year of college was a bit tumultuous. As I write this, it is quite strange to think about, because I buried this summer into the back of my cavernous mind.

I had decided to go to school at the University of Miami. Jaime and I broke up because we thought it was best. After all, I was moving to Florida and she would be staying behind in good old Kenilworth, New Jersey. It was an excruciating breakup for me. I had truly thought I was going to marry her. I mean, I fell in love and this was it, *right*? But maybe this actually wasn't it. Maybe we weren't going to be together forever or whatever. After all, I was heading to Miami.

I don't even think I ever truly thought my college decision through. I applied to a handful of colleges and when my acceptance letters came back, Miami was one of the schools that had accepted me. When people heard that I was accepted to be a future Miami Hurricane, their heads began to spin. They came up to me in the hallways asking me, "So you're going to the University of Miami?" They told me how awesome the weather was down there and just how spectacular Miami University was going to be. My friends and family talked about it like it was a foregone conclusion, even though I hadn't really decided yet. I almost felt like I *had* to go to Miami, or I would be letting everyone down. Everyone was expecting me to go there. So, off to Miami I went.

That was a tragic mistake. I was completely miserable after my first day. I tried to talk to and like my roommate, but we didn't have much in common. He was from Florida; his life was totally, completely opposite of mine. He wanted to go roller blading and to "catch some waves."

Huh? Oh yeah, and he wanted to listen to the Beach Boys and bad ska music. Don't get me wrong, the Beach Boys are classic, but my young ears did not appreciate them at the time. My ears felt poisoned by such blasphemous musical overtures. I wanted nothing to do with my roommate, and by the second day he knew it. He left me alone to wallow in my own misery.

After my disconnected attempt at trying to chill with my roommate, I was left in a bored, lonely dorm room staring at the pale white walls. As I stared into nothingness, blanking out, I became lost in the doldrums of that room. Something began to take over my mind and would not stop haunting me. I kept thinking of Jaime. I could not get her angelic image out of my mind. I would close my eyes and she was still there staring back at me. I could do nothing as I was frozen in a melancholic, cathartic state. Tears rained from my face and formed puddles of sorrow beneath me.

I cried for nearly two weeks, non-stop. I barely left my room. I think I went to a class or two, but I really couldn't tell you because my time at Miami was a blur. During that miserable two-week time period, my parents often called me as they were worried about my despondent state. I was getting worse by the day. I decided to call Jaime after the two weeks of perpetual misery, thinking it would cheer me up.

We spoke for a few minutes and I could tell something was off. She was acting aloof and did not seem like the same loving, jovial Jaime that I had left behind. I was extremely perturbed. Her standoffish behavior agitated me, and I curtly asked, "Are you seeing somebody else?"

Silence.

My heart dropped and at that moment, I knew that she had found someone else. A new suitor had supplanted me, making me yesterday's news. I felt like a discarded piece of trash. My sorrow relented and immediately turned into rage. I was a bubbling volcano ready to erupt. I could hear the fear in her voice as she finally mumbled that she had met someone new. I slammed the phone down on the lifeless receiver. I melted into a pile of somber mush. Tears streamed down my face.

The next two days I laid in my bed, numb to the world. No classes. No food. No sleep. I felt like I didn't want to live. My parents left several messages. Finally, I summoned the strength to call them. My father could hear my words fading and my tone faltering as my soul was withering through the phone.

He finally said, "Listen, if you want to come home you need to decide now. We can recover most of the money and you can attend community college or something."

This was like the voice of God speaking to me. I let out a glorious, "YES!" It was the first time in weeks that my pathetic, emotionless body felt a charge of positivity. I would be heading back to Kenilworth in just a few days and I couldn't be happier.

My arrival back to Jersey was met with much fanfare. There was a bevy of mixed reactions. Some people were ecstatic while others were confused, and some were angry that the Big Bully from the Block was back. Many were dumbfounded and asked, "Why would you leave Miami?" People would say it with such contempt that I almost felt like I had committed a mortal sin. Honestly, I didn't care because all I cared about was being back with Jaime. That was my primary focus.

Although Jaime was my main focus at that time in my life, I can look back and say that I realized who my true friends were and still are. I have many friends that have come out of Kenilworth, and I am glad to say that we are all great friends to this very day. Kenilworth is a special place where you form special bonds. Many people stick together and are lifelong friends. Not many places in the world are like this special little town that I call home. I am grateful to have these lifelong friends. Never take your friends for granted, because no matter what, your true friends will stick by you.

I was probably a horrible person to be around when I returned, because all of my energy was focused on Jaime. That's all I talked about or wanted my night to revolve around was *Jaime, Jaime, Jaime*. I was madly obsessed with her so much so, that it was completely unhealthy and borderline insane. Jaime, if you're reading this, I just want you to know that you did nothing wrong and I needed all of this to happen to me. All of these deranged and irrational experiences fostered a change within me. They assisted me in my maturity and growth process.

The other sentiment I rode back into town with was fear. Everyone who knew me was fearful that I was about to go on a rampage and go after Jaime's new dancing partner. I asked everyone and their mother what was going on with Jaime. I wanted to know who she was dating. I was furious and I was ready to win the love of my life back. I mean, I was going to marry her, wasn't I? I now know I was immature, unrealistic, and completely unhinged at that time.

After some serious probing, some of my best friends finally broke down and told me that Jaime was now dating some guy named Rich. Rich was the new kid in town and had just moved here from Florida. How ironic was that? I had just gone to Miami and had been there for three weeks. In those three weeks, Jaime had found a new beau who was actually from Florida. My blood was boiling. I was ready to rumble. This guy Rich from Florida had no clue what was coming his way. I was about to unleash the beast inside, and he was going to feel the venomous wrath of my Bully Complex.

I began harassing both Jaime and Rich. Well, I tried to harass Rich, but I didn't know where he lived. I would incessantly call Jaime's household and threaten Rich's life as Jaime implored me to stop. I would scream through the phone with fury knowing that Rich would hear my psychotic rants. My adrenaline pumped even harder knowing that he heard me and was probably cowering in the corner consumed with fear, or at least that's what I thought in my warped mind. My constant phone calls and challenges were going nowhere. I decided I needed to take things to the next level.

One night, my infuriation had finally built into a crescendo. I was ready to pulverize this poor patsy and plaster his face all over the pavement. I gathered a couple of my close friends to join me on my crusade to go snatch this fool up. I only brought along friends for backup in case Rich had friends of his own with him. I was extremely enraged which gave me little doubt that I could smash him to pieces all on my own. I was now a seasoned fighter and an even more seasoned bully. I knew I could shake him with words and beat him down mentally to begin with. My words would soften his mind and then my fists would harden his face. I would crush him!

We arrived at Jaime's house like a mini lynch mob ready to persecute the sinner. I began banging on Jaime's window like a mad man, yelling and screaming for Rich to come and confront me. I had snapped and I was ready to commit some dirty deeds. My yelling and screaming did not seem to summon the Floridian fool who was now dating my darling dame. I was rattled.

I picked up what looked to be a metal pipe from the side of Jaime's house, and I began to pound on the side of the house. The house rattled and began to shiver. I pounded the pipe over and over imagining I was pummeling Rich's powerless skull. The house was reverberating, and it sounded like a gong crashing over and over again. The scene was frightening, and Jaime finally decided to open the back door to yell for me to stop. Her angelic voice was crackling as I could hear the fear dribbling out of her mouth.

This lulled me into a brief calm, if only for a moment. I approached the door as she implored me to stop. Her pleas were soothing, and the beast was about to be tamed. But as I stared through the screen door, I saw Rich about ten feet behind Jaime and he seemed to have a sly grin across his smug face. I stared Rich down through the screen door as I dared him to come out. Jaime began to scream in anguish and threatened to call the police if I made any further advances. My wild eyes scanned up and down the screen door, as I envisioned plowing through it with ease and then tearing the smug look off of Rich's face.

I stood there; my shadow was imposed on the kitchen floor. I certainly thought I was imposing to Rich, but he seemed to be smiling which only infuriated me more. He must have known the police were on their way as the faint sound of sirens neared. But I was dead to the sirens as I was locked onto Rich's smug face leering back at me. I was ready to tear that grin clean off his face.

I was getting ready to blast through that screen door when my friends finally intervened, yelling, "What are you, crazy? The cops are coming!"

That's the only thing that could snap me back to reality for a mere moment, as I hated the police. I relented and then retreated. We ran from the house in fear that the cops were well on their way. We were a few blocks away and I could now hear the faint sound of sirens. We had narrowly escaped, but Rich was still on my raging radar.

I had arrived back in K-Town during early September that year. The University of Miami had started classes two weeks before most schools. The first week had some extra orientations that other schools didn't. This afforded me an opportunity to apply to Monmouth University, which was only a few days into their school year. Luckily, I was accepted and did not have to go to Community College. I am in no way condemning Community College. It can be a great start for some people. However, in K-Town, we used to call it the 13th grade, as if it were just an extension of high school. It was like you didn't even leave high school and you just took one tiny step up. A good portion of my senior class went to Union County College. If I had gone there, I know my life would have been totally different. I probably would not have made it out of there and graduated college. I think I would have been consumed with my friends and drawn into my persistent bullying. I would not have gained the culture that I needed to open my mind either. I needed to branch away and experience life outside of Kenilworth. My mind wouldn't have been right, and my focus definitely would not have been there. For all of these legitimate reasons this would not have been a good choice for me. This is personal to me and if Community College seems to be a good choice for you, then by all means, you should attend. Community College can be an amazing choice for some people.

I was able to attend Monmouth University and it was the best possible situation for me. There was minimal housing available as I had applied late, but that was fine with me. I wanted to be as close to Kenilworth and as close to Jaime as possible anyway. I was more than happy to make the forty-five minute commute, five days a week. My mom was fine with it as long as I was going to college and obtaining my degree.

That first year was a bit of a blur as far as school was concerned. I went to all of my classes and I was focused on my schoolwork. I was detrimentally depressed, to the point that I didn't even want to fool around, therefore I paid attention and actually received stellar grades. I wasn't in my troublemaking mode, like I had been the majority of high school. I even gave bullying a break for the most part.

There was only one person that I wanted to bully, as my mind was consumed with thoughts of loving Jaime and destroying Rich. I could only think of three things, Jaime, Rich, and school. I am happy school was one of my main focuses, otherwise my life may have gone off the rails.

In October of that year, my younger sister was turning sixteen, which meant she was going to have a sweet sixteen party. She was unmistakably nervous though, because she knew her older brother had become an insane, incensed lunatic who was hellbent on pummeling Rich. She planned to invite Jaime as they had remained good friends even after our acrimonious breakup. If Jaime was to be invited, certainly her new boyfriend Rich would be as well. The thought of this must have given my sister nightmares. My sister begged and pleaded with me to leave Rich and Jaime alone. She was continuous in her pleas, so I begrudgingly acquiesced.

When the day of the party arrived, I tried to stay calm, but I was a smoldering inferno. While setting up, I had visions of Jaime and Rich slow dancing and then me coming over to smash Rich's head in with a bat. It was unhealthy and maniacal to say the least. Some of my friends arrived early, surely to try and buffer the situation. As guests began to arrive, my heart began to race like a prized racehorse. I sat there and stewed as I knew the moment was finally about to commence.

In order to calm my nerves a bit, I went over to a widely known troublemaker. He was somewhat of a derelict, but I had a feeling he would do my bidding if I paid him. I offered him $100 to beat Rich up after the party. I told him it had to be afterwards and outside somewhere, where my unsuspecting and innocent sister wouldn't know about it until later. Even though I wanted to see the destruction of my sworn enemy, I also did not want to do it at the expense of my sister's happiness.

Right after the conversation with the town derelict, I made my way back to my seat and an instant later Jaime and Rich walked in. I stared at them and my blood boiled. It took every fiber of my being to remain seated and not lunge at Rich's throat. A few of my wary friends saw my face then immediately came over to me and told me to simmer down. Have you ever tried to lower a boiling pot of water down to a simmer? Well, it's still boiling.

I just stared at the two of them from the moment they walked in. I locked eyes with Rich, and he could see my wild eyes were filled with ire and wrath. I slowly made my way to the punch bowl and filled my plastic cup. I sat down and tried to take my mind off of Rich, for had I not, I would have broken my promise to my sister that I would hold my composure.

My rage at that time was challenging for me to suppress. I had major anger issues. I don't know the exact reasons as I had a fairly good childhood. My parents were not overly abusive. I did endure punishments and a few spankings but nothing abnormal. The years of bullying I endured certainly added to my escalating indignation at the time. All of the years that I was continuously victimized, I harbored all that anger towards my perpetrators. I had all of this overwhelming contempt and I think I just didn't know how to deal with my anger issues. I would let it all build up and I would just let myself explode on others. This is never the answer and I have worked hard on these issues for a long time. I am finally in a place that I don't instantly ignite at the drop of a hat.

Even though I was smoldering beneath the surface, I held it together for as long as I possibly could, for my sister's sake. As time slowly evaporated, I fidgeted in my seat. Then finally, I noticed that my sister was taking pictures with just the girls. I seized the moment to stare down my wary and shaken foe. He was alone and helpless, but I would adhere to my promise. I did not say a word to Rich. I had promised my sister I would not say a word to him, and I did not. Instead, I grabbed my plastic drinking cup and I began to chew on it. I stared intently and locked my fury-filled eyes onto Rich's innocent and fearful eyes. The more I stared at him, the angrier I became. I chewed harder and harder on the plastic cup. I chewed so ferociously to the point that I had actually started chomping off pieces of the cup. The more I chewed, I began to bleed. Blood and plastic frothed and dripped from my mangey mouth. My mouth was now foaming with blood, bubbling saliva, and red plastic solo cup. I was beginning to resemble a dog with rabies and everyone watching was mortified by my crazed antics.

Everyone that watched my deranged actions was wondering what in the world I was doing. Finally, someone alerted my sister to the fact that I had begun to act like an untamed animal. She came over and yelled at me. My friends promptly grabbed me and said it was time to go. My unrelenting rage suddenly simmered, and I was now in a haze of emotionless self-pity. I felt like the life had been sucked out of me. All of my escalating emotions from the past couple of months evaporated from my exhausted embodiment. I was so emotionally exhausted that I actually listened to my exasperated friends and left the party.

I left the party broken and at that moment, I had all but given up on getting Jaime back. I even called off the derelict I had paid to beat Rich up. *What would be the sense in that now?*

To this day, the plastic cup incident is still talked about. My friends and I can laugh about it now, but at the time, it was no laughing matter.

I can gladly say that person does not exist inside of me anymore. I would also like to apologize to my sister, Jaime, and especially Rich who was new to town and did not deserve some enraged lunatic psycho stalking him!

Anyway, after that night, I decided to try and move on from Jaime. I was emotionally and mentally drained. My obsession with her was unhealthy to say the least. I decided that she didn't want to be with me, and it was silly to pursue her any longer. It was time to move on. Besides, I had frightened many people with my outlandish behavior including my friends and family. Needless to say, it was a long, cold, and lonely winter.

That year I focused on my studies and I started working part-time. I was consumed with school and work, only seeing my friends sparingly. For most of that year I was somewhat of a ghost. I was there physically but I was mentally checked out. It took me six months to get over Jaime. Six long, grueling months, but by the spring, I was ready to spring into action.

By this time in my life, I had found a little style and the Eddie Munster phase was well behind me. I was gaining self-esteem and no longer thought I looked hideous. I was ready to break out with women in a big way. I was finally single and ready to mingle. That summer I dated around and had a good time. I had a few flings but nothing too serious. I was more than ready for my second year of college and what was to come.

My second year of college began to open my eyes a little bit. I had never really left the small confines of Kenilworth, besides my three weeks in Miami. Our tiny little one square mile town was all I had ever known. People come to live in my town and most never leave. My mom frequently busts my dad's balls and says he'll never leave Kenilworth. His family was born and bred there for decades. His family along with a bunch of fellow Italian families inhabited this tiny town ages ago. Eventually yes, some other races integrated, but the majority of people in K-Town were and still are Italian-Americans.

I know what you're thinking when it comes to my very own race. I myself am Asian, so how many Asians were in my town? Well, there weren't too many. I'm only *half* Asian. My other half was Italian. Plus, I had the Italian last name, Lospinoso. I don't have some "gooky" last name like Kim or Chang. I grew up around mostly Italian culture, which made me semi-legit in my town. But I was only partially accepted, as I've previously illustrated, I was mocked and ridiculed for being half Asian when I was younger. For a long time, this made me ashamed to be half Korean, but this is no longer the case. Things have changed drastically, as I don't self-loath any longer. Don't get me wrong, people may not think this now, but I am proud of my half Korean side, as it makes me who I am. I say most people that interact with me might not believe it, because I often poke fun at all things Asian. Yes, this is true. I mean, I just said that I didn't have a "gooky" last name. I've learned to make fun of myself before others have the chance. Since I'm half Korean, I often start up with some Asian jokes and that usually takes people by surprise. However, when I first meet someone, sometimes I catch people looking at me with side eyes. Sometimes people don't realize I'm Asian and they may have perceived me as racist. Even though some see that my Asian jokes are all in good fun, some people don't get it. After all, they don't know me, so how would they know I'm purely joking and that I am indeed half Asian? I think I need to tone down this aspect of my personality. But as I've alluded to, I am always working on myself to be a better person. This is something I am undoubtedly going to try and be more cognizant of. Even though I am only being sarcastic, some might not recognize that. There is an old saying that if you can't make fun of yourself, you can't make fun of others, but not everyone knows that I am Asian or that I am kidding.

My mom dislikes when I make Asian jokes, and I get it. She is 100% South Korean, off the boat. If you haven't already noted, I have the utmost respect for my mother, therefore I try not to make these types of jokes in front of her. I am a natural wiseass though, which makes it really tough! This is another reason why I poke fun at the Asian culture, because then I feel justified when I make jokes towards other races. I really need to clarify right now that when I make these jokes, I am in no way being malicious. I am completely different these days and I no longer have hate directed towards other races and religions. I am naturally sarcastic, and it is all in good fun. These racially charged jokes are always between friends. I do not partake in this banter with outsiders unless it is made clear to me that I am dealing with another sarcastic individual. Also, this banter is usually volleyed back and forth between two willing participants. When two friends engage in such sarcastic banter, we call this "busting each other's balls." At no time are we serious and it is always meant to be lighthearted good fun. *Bullying* would be doing this to someone who is not a friend and saying racial or hurtful remarks in a defamatory manner. When it comes to bullying, there is no volleying or back and forth. When it comes to bullying, I am an expert and I know better than anyone that bullying is when one person or group is simply attacking a person who is unlikely to fight back.

I have been called a "chink" or a "gook" by someone that I did not know, and it infuriated me. My friends can make jokes to me, but if I don't know you, then you are being racist. Racist as I once was towards Indian and African American people. My friends would often joke with me, but they wouldn't even use those highly racist terms. We would joke about types of food being Asian. We'd joke that I might eat your dog or something, but never in a derogatory manner. Eating your dog is a clear joke because it is something that I would never do. My friends might ask the waiter for chopsticks for their Asian friend when we were out to dinner at a non-Asian establishment. This was all too ironic because I may be one of the few Asians on earth who actually does not know how to use chopsticks! Now you see how we bust balls where I'm from.

OK, back to my sophomore year at Monmouth. On my first day living on campus at Monmouth U, I was in utter and literal culture shock. I had commuted my whole first year of school and I was so fixated on Jaime, that I became somewhat disconnected. I hadn't really noticed my surroundings, as I had buried myself into my studies. Now my eyes were wide open, and I was taking everything in. I was astounded at the amount of cultural diversity that surrounded me. I had never—and I mean never—seen this many black people in my life. I was in awe. I mean I had seen all the movies, *Boys in the Hood*, *Friday* and *Barber Shop*. I'm not saying my first day living on campus was like these movies, but in my mind, it was at first. I'd have to say that I had never seen this many nationalities gathered in one place in my entire life. I honestly had about five to six black kids in my graduating senior high school class. I'd have to estimate that this campus was about 35-40% black. For the first time in quite a while, I was slightly intimidated. I would soon have to change my game plan, which was to bully people, as I had in high school. But it was obvious that this was not realistic at first, so I decided to pull back and assess the situation.

As I've told you, bullies usually tend to run in packs. I decided to do this college thing on my own and make my own way. Now, I could have done otherwise. Monmouth University is in Long Branch, New Jersey. A mere forty-five-minute drive from good old Kenilworth. Naturally there were several other people from my high school who also chose to attend Monmouth. I was cool with all of them, but none of them were my best friends. If they had been, perhaps things would have been different. Since none of them were in my top group of friends, I decided to find a room on my own, so I entered my name into the housing lottery. Maybe deep down I wanted to break away, just a little bit from my hometown ties. I think perhaps I was almost ready to open my tainted eyes and have a more open mind.

I almost instantly regretted my decision to enter the housing lottery. Initially I was gleeful to be living on campus for the first time, but when I arrived at my suite, I was greeted by a gaggle of what I thought of as geeks and nerds. I mean, this was the goofiest group of outcasts that I have ever witnessed. I'm not kidding either. However, I was outnumbered. There were five or six of them. So, I did what any bully would do in that uncomfortable situation, I feigned politeness. I found my room arrangement and I was extremely displeased. I had two other roommates. There were going to be three of us in a room meant for two. My roommates were nothing but eclectic dorks to me. In fact, one of them was seemingly the leader. Ruler of the dweebs! He had a creepy porn star mustache and ironically, he looked eerily similar to Eddie Munster. Yes, I had likened myself to this very character, but this resemblance was uncanny. He was like the twin brother of Mr. Munster. My other roommate was a nice enough guy. He seemed like someone I could get along with, but he was a sloppy mess. Our room turned into a disaster area within three days of living there and I felt like I was living in a scene out of Hoarders. The second roommate also didn't bathe frequently, and he had quite a repulsive stench to him. His pungent odor emanated throughout the entire room. I was none too pleased. As nice as he was, I could not overcome his negatives.

Needless to say, I was pretty miserable for the first few weeks living at Monmouth U. But I was determined to get out there and meet new people. This would be my first time making new friends as I was relatively antisocial my first year. I was in the process of feeling things out and I wanted to give my situation a chance to improve. I didn't want to get too down on the living situation and give up as I had in Miami. I knew there had to be like-minded people here and I would have to seek them out. I didn't know it, but I was innately searching for other bullies to team up with, so we could torture these dorks. I had landed in the world of freaks and geeks; it was a bully's paradise. I wanted out, but there was no leaving for me this time. I was determined to stay at Monmouth and stick it out, throughout any situation. Therefore, I had only one way to make my time tolerable here. I needed to harass and poke fun at these outcasts or I would go crazy.

What was wrong with me? Why couldn't I just do my own thing and leave them be? My insistent need to bully was a true sickness and my Bully Complex was an absolute reality.

Two weeks in, my prayers were answered, and they were right in front of my face the whole time. There was actually one other cool guy in my suite. I met him briefly when I arrived and we exchanged pleasantries, but I never really had a chance to talk to him. I guess we had just missed each other the first couple weeks of classes, as the beginning of the school year can be extremely hectic. But I was ecstatic to finally have an actual conversation with him. His name was Kyle. We instantly clicked since we were both huge NY Giants fans.

We began talking about the suite that we lived in and what a bad draw we had in the housing lottery. He too, had gone in blindly and left his draw to chance. We were both sick of these geeks and we were about to take over the suite. The dynamic bully duo was born and about to make our presence felt. Another part of having a Bully Complex is that bullies attract one another. Kyle and I were drawn together like two magnets. We sought each other out, in order to unleash our victimizations upon our unsuspecting prey.

Later that night, we made up nicknames for everyone else in the suite. There was one particular pushover that we were focused on. Naturally, he was the easiest target. He was the quietest of the group. He was also the hairiest. He was so hairy that his back hair came out of the collar of his shirt. I had never seen anything like it. We instantly nicknamed him the "Wolf Man."

That night, Kyle and I went through magazines looking for specific pictures. We naturally searched for wolves or any other type of hairy beast we could unearth. We cut out normal pictures of guys in T-shirts and we drew back hair coming out of their shirts. We wrote Wolf Man on all of these different pictures. We then started sliding them under his door. Each time we did, we began to cackle. The destitute dork did not come out of his room. I'm sure he had encountered this treatment before. He probably prayed and hoped that he had moved on from it, especially after whatever horrific high school experiences he had endured. He probably thought he had hit the lottery in this suite full of misfits, but he thought wrong.

The harassing went on for the rest of the first semester. Kyle and I ruled that suite and none of the geeks would talk back to us. I have always been a fairly large guy, but Kyle was quite imposing. He was taller than my 6-foot 3 frame and he was wider than me. He was definitely someone you would not want to mess with. I think this deterred the others from retaliating. However, one day when Kyle wasn't with me, I was approached by "Eddie Munster."

My roommate "Eddie" took this opportunity to address me one on one. He asked what joy we received from harassing the bewildered Wolf Man. We also made fun of Eddie, but he could take it. He would even try to dish it back to me when Kyle wasn't around. But the Wolf Man was helpless, and he never fought back.

For the first time in my life, I could see pain in someone's eyes. I could almost feel the pain that I had caused. It reminded me of my own personal suffering that I had endured earlier in my life. Eddie had sympathy for the Wolf Man. I said to him, "I'll lay off of him, if it means that much to you."

Of course, I laid off only when Kyle wasn't around. But bullies always run side by side and if Kyle was there, I had to uphold my image as being cool. Besides, I knew there wasn't anybody in that suite who would mess with my larger than life sidekick. Indeed, when I was alone, I was somewhat nice most of the time to the others after my talk with Eddie. I honestly did feel some remorse for the way I had been acting. I was not completely heartless at the time. I wasn't quite the cold-hearted monster I was in high school. I was unquestionably still a villainous swine, but I was starting to think about people's feelings for the first time.

One day, the others were going to have a small party in our suite. They even invited me. During that party, my vision of the geeks would be altered slightly. There were actually a couple of nerdy girls there and a couple of them were not that bad looking. One of them seemed to be sweet on me. We flirted back and forth for the majority of the night.

To this point, I had only one girlfriend and that was Jaime during high school. I had a couple of flings after that, but Jaime was really all I knew when it came to dating. I dated her for my last two years of high school and I thought she was the one. It wasn't until college that I realized it was just bullshit puppy love and there were many girls out there ready to be explored. This was college after all, and the girls were on their own for the first time. They were primed and ready to break out of their shells. I was more than ready to explore and break out of my shell as well.

Now, here I was at this geeky get-together and this was a rare instance that I had an actual interaction with a girl in a flirty sexual manner. Go figure! I ended up with the nerdy girl in my bed that night. As a matter of fact, we chilled for several weeks after. She ended up being a little too eccentric for me and things ended. But soon after, I started dating another girl from the nerd group. I was on fire with the geeky groupies.

These geeky groupies were making me more confident with women in general. Bullying doesn't actually make you more confident. Bullying stems from insecurities. You project your inner fears and self-loathing onto others. You want to be part of the "cool" crowd and often times, showing off in front of your friends is a big part of it. Your friends, who act as fellow bullies, often give their approval when you perform these treacherous acts on innocent victims. Bullies often gang up on their victims, as there is a mob mentality to it. See, now that I look back, it's easy to see why I transitioned. I wanted to be the one administering the torture, not the one receiving it. Once I was able to flip, there was no turning back for me. I was never going to be the "Duh duh, duh duh, duh duh Fat Chink," ever again!

I brought my new-found confidence and swagger home with me that summer. I had a fun and eye-opening first couple years of college under my belt. Now I was heading back to K-Town ready to bully some new blood.

After I graduated from high school, the school unfortunately closed down because it was deemed to be too small. The Board of Education decided that there weren't enough students to maintain our beloved high school, David Brearley. Therefore, the remaining three grades under me had a choice to attend two different high schools. The juniors at the time decided to spend their senior year of high school in the town of Clark. The sophomores decided to spend their junior year of high school in Springfield. I had many friends in both classes. Some of my best friends were in both grades. My sister was two grades below me, and we were close. Therefore, a lot of our groups of friends crossed over.

Anyway, this had brought entirely new groups of people into our lives. The Clark people for the most part were not that bad. I was cool with most of them, but I did harass a select few. I targeted one kid especially because of his name. His name was Benjamin Supperstein. I called him Ben "Super-stein" and I said that he possessed Jewish superpowers. I told him that he could inhale pennies from miles away and he could poop bagels from his ass. This was just the tip of the iceberg when it came to Super-stein. I found his phone number and I used my finely honed phone pranking skills to further bully the "Super Jew." I would call his house, as I disguised my voice akin to an old Jewish man's voice. I would ask for Benjamin and here is an example of how one of those prank calls would sound:

"Hello, this is Ben."

Me (in stereotypical Jewish character): "Ben, this is Rabbi Solomon!"

"Who is this, for real?"

"Benjamin Super-stein, this is Rabbi Solomon! You haven't been to temple in weeks!"

"OK, this isn't funny! Who is this?"

"Benjamin, it's Rabbi Solomon! Hoy! It's so humid in here! Are you coming to temple this—"

Click. The phone call abruptly ended.

Ben would always hang up on me, but I would come up with some new way to call him and use my "Jewish" enunciations. I never stopped with the calls or my general harassing of the him. I couldn't help myself when it came to the Jews. My bullying appetite was voracious, and I enjoyed it more than most of my other victims. I think it all stemmed from the first Jewish kid that I had beat up and bullied. The power I felt that day never evaporated, and I wanted to capture that feeling over and over again.

That's why when my sister decided to attend the high school in Springfield, I was filled with joy and jubilation. This would become the ultimate bully haven for me, because I knew Springfield was home to plenty of Jewish people. To me the town was infested with "dirty Jews." I couldn't contain my excitement. Ben Super-Stein only received a small dose of what I was about to dish out! Suddenly, I was like a shark swimming in a sea full of Jewish guppies.

I didn't like Jews and I had always mocked them openly. My mom always yelled at me and said, "You are Korean, you shouldn't be racist!" I would laugh it off and say, "You're right, Mom!" But I didn't mean it. I just said it to appease her.

When my mom wasn't around, my father told me a story about how one of his friends had bullied the Jews back when he was in high school. One particular story resonated with me. Ironically, my dad also attended high school in Springfield, as Kenilworth had not opened its high school yet. From what my dad has told me, he and most of his friends were sometimes slackers. He told me tales of how he and his friends often partied and did not focus on their schoolwork. My dad and his buddy, who went by his last name "Worth," would cheat off of each other for months in one particular class. However, they still couldn't achieve passing grades. The teacher of one class was handing out graded tests and announcing their grades. He looked at my dad and his friend as he bellowed, "Lospinoso 55, Worth 55. If you guys are gonna cheat, maybe you should cheat off of someone smarter!"

On the day of the next major test, my dad and Worth decided to do just what the teacher had suggested. My dad said the Jews were highly intelligent. Therefore, he started peering over at the Jewish boy seated next to him, trying to copy his answers. He said the Jewish boy covered his paper with his arm making it difficult for my dad to see the answers. Worth tried to cheat as well but had similar luck. They were both pissed off that the Jews wouldn't let them cheat. When they later saw one of the Jewish boys in the hallway sipping water at the fountain, Worth went over to confront the boy. The boy was adamant about not giving them answers, which prompted Worth to slam the boy's head into the fountain. The boy cried out, but this was back in a time when no one was going to do anything or help. Worth said, "Next time we look at your paper, you better not hide the answers!" After the water fountain incident, my dad and Worth passed every test in that class from that day on.

My dad was not truly racist, but if his friend was going to bully the Jewish kids attempting to try and pass the class, then so be it. Hearing these stories made me want to bully Jews even further. In my twisted mind, I wanted to top that water fountain story. My father doesn't condone what Worth did but I took the story to heart. It didn't matter to me that my dad accepted everyone. I should have learned from my father's lead and broken away from racism. I don't know why I couldn't. I was a different person and I wasn't as accepting. I hated Jews at the time, and I wanted to be public enemy number one to them.

My dad is truly good natured and sometimes just told a racially charged joke or two, kind of like I do nowadays. At the time, my dad and I would sarcastically joke about Jewish people. If you were cheap, it was, "Stop being a Jew!" If there was food we disliked, it was referred to as being Jewish food. We might make a bagel joke but that's where my dad left it.

Of course, I took everything to the next level. If someone tipped cheaply, I would call them a "penny pinching Jew!" I often referred to people as "bagels" because Jews ate bagels. So, it became, "Stop being a bagel!" "Oh, you cheap bagel!" "Pick up the penny, you bagel!" You get the point. Instantly, all these newfound Jewish people that had suddenly been brought into my life were in a world of trouble. I was about to unleash all of this hate I had built up inside of me. This was their day of reckoning and I was their Grim Reaper.

I developed hate inside my heart against Jewish people and I didn't even know why. I think my hate developed partly due to my extreme personality and my need to take things to the limit. Yes, I hated the one Jewish boy I graduated high school with, but I realized years later that I disliked him as a person. I think I developed hate over a group of people from disliking one of them. I unfairly associated him with an entire group of people. This is explicitly wrong, and I can't even begin to wrap my head around it. Obviously, my Bully Complex also had a lot to do with my hate. I directed my bullying and victimizations at people who I deemed to be different from me and the group I ran with. The Jewish people were obviously different, and they were also outnumbered in my world, making them an easy target.

Jewish people appeared to be vastly different from all of the people I had grown up with. To me, they ate weird food, wore funny looking hats and their religion was eclectic to me and my friends. Once I found out what Shabbat was, I knew what I had to do. From my understanding, Shabbat is a time period on the weekend when hardcore Jewish people were not allowed to use electrical appliances or answer the doorbell. So what did I do? I went around the most hardcore Jewish neighborhoods of Springfield and I terrorized those poor people. I went up and down the blocks with my fellow bullying bandits and I incessantly rang all their doorbells. Most did not answer, but a few did. We would yell racial slurs at them and run away like cowards. I thought I was so brave at the time, but I realize now just how cowardly I was.

The ringing of doorbells during Shabbat was only the beginning. I started attending all the high school parties in Springfield that summer, ready to demoralize and bulldoze all the Jews in my path. I was first invited to the parties because of my sister. But I think she was undeniably getting tired of my harassment of her new classmates. In fact, I know that she didn't condone my bullying of her new classmates, but she couldn't stop me. I had plenty of friends in her class from Kenilworth and I was always on the invite list.

My initial antics began with dressing up in different costumes. I was a heavy drinker, therefore I'd usually be on keg patrol, manning the tap. Plus, this was the best spot to pick off unsuspecting prey. If you are at a party, you have to make your way to the keg, right?

The costumes changed from party to party. I was a farmer, a burnout, and a junkie. Yes, I did it to draw attention. Mission always accomplished. I became notorious in Springfield. With each costume, I had a schtick to go with it. When I was a farmer, I was a Redneck that disliked the Jews. When I was a burnout, I was a Christian Rocker who disliked the Jews. When I was a junkie, I wouldn't share needles with the Jews. See where this is going? Every Jew at that party would get berated by me in some way. I would yell things at them like: "Kafilta fish! Mozel Tov! Shalom! Bagels with Lox! Yamaca!" I even scribbled these words—misspelled—on paper to further torture them. This was a part of my racist tendencies to misspell their coveted language. I had no care for the true spellings. I was unrelenting with my mockery. Now you ask why didn't these kids beat the shit out of me? Well, of course I ran with a crew. That crew was much respected and were thought of as being a tough group. Because of this, most of the Jewish kids were intimidated and afraid of us. I was able to mock, torture and ridicule at my leisure.

One day, I literally took over my Jewish friend's house. Even though I was a bully, I was nice to girls for the most part. She and her friends were a nice-looking group of girls which prompted my friends and I to start hanging with them often. I became particularly close with this one girl. She preferred to be called by her initials J.G. We were definitely pretty good friends. Since we had developed this nice friendship, I decided to take advantage of that. I insisted since her parents were away that she was going to throw a party. She resisted at first, but with a little cajoling and help from her friends, she was convinced. J.G. said that her only fear was the police being called as there would be a backyard full of underage drinkers on her property. I assured her that I had thrown hundreds of parties and that the police would not come. While it was true that I had thrown many parties in my day, the cops did come once or twice. Also, the parties were at my house in Kenilworth where I knew many people, including police officers.

That night, I went out and bought two kegs of beer. The party was on. Everything was going well until a couple of Jews started a little ruckus. My friends and I were charging five dollars a head to get in. After all, we had two kegs of beer that needed to be paid for. Anyway, two Jews started getting loud with me. "We're cheap Jews, right? Why would we pay five dollars to get into your party? Jews don't pay to get in! We're too cheap!"

There were many people in that town who were fed up with the way I had acted towards Jewish people. I had belittled many of them. I made generalizations and I flat out acted in a disgusting manner towards them. That's unquestionably why these two Jewish kids were coming at me.

They were going on and on, but I would not budge. They would not pay, leaving me no choice but to not let them into the party. I yelled at them and told them to leave if they didn't like it. They left in a huge huff causing a scene. They drove by several times screaming and yelling indecipherable things at me. The scalded Jews would have the last laugh because about fifteen minutes later the cops showed up. I don't know for sure, but I think the loud-mouthed Jews called the cops. I have no proof, but it would make sense and that would have been a good measure of revenge for them. After my despicable actions towards Jewish people, I deserved it.

The cops descended upon the party quickly and broke up the underage crowd swiftly. Now, in Kenilworth I would have known I was safe, as I knew most of the officers. But I was in a foreign town with cops that I did not know. I was the one who purchased the kegs making me the one liable. All I could picture was me going out in cuffs. I did not want to spend another night in a jail cell.

In my mind, I did the only thing I thought I could do. I raced downstairs to try and find a hiding spot. My eyes darted from side to side. There was a brown plush couch which would not conceal me. I saw beige curtains that would not hide my large figure. Then suddenly I saw a sliding door to a closet. I quickly slithered into the closet and closed the door in front of me.

By coincidence, this happened to be the perfect spot. The cops brought my friend, J.G. and several of her close friends into that room. I could hear everything. J.G. was crying profusely and saying that it wasn't her party. She said indeed it was her house, but somebody else had taken over and started the party. The police asked who and she gave up my name rather quickly. "Anthony Lospinoso," she muttered. I was more afraid than mad at this point. All it would take was someone to slide open this closet door and I'd be caught. The officers badgered her, "Well, where is he? If he's in charge, where did he go?" J.G. whimpered, "I-I don't know!"

I think the cops felt bad for her, so they did what they usually do. First, they scared the shit out of her by threatening arrest. But her sobs and whimpers grew louder, and they finally relented, telling her that they would let her go with a warning. The officers then cautioned that the next time it would result in jail. With that, the police finally took off.

The girls huddled in a circle and J.G. was still crying when I emerged from the closet. She pounded me in the chest. "You jerk! You were in there the whole time! You told me that the cops wouldn't come! I hate you!"

J.G. was fuming, but I let her berate me for a minute and then I bolted. This fractured our friendship as she finally saw me for what I was. I was just a coward who pretended to act brave, but when the time came, I let her take the fall. I could have stood there like a man and told the police the truth, but I hid like the frightened coward I truly was. She should have never forgiven me, and I wouldn't have blamed her either. This was just another inconsiderate move to add to my ever-growing list. I was a complete jerk at that time in every sense of the word. I had zero consideration for others, as I was consumed with selfishness.

J.G. was a good person and she did eventually forgive me. We even remained friends for some time until later on at some point when she realized I was insensitive to Jewish people. She had no idea at that time how truly insensitive I was. I wish I matured and realized my wrongs sooner as this would be a fallen friendship that I would later regret.

My harassment of Jewish people was not over yet. Later that summer, I would have one final run in with a group of Jewish kids. A close friend of mine had acquired a job at a Jewish YMCA. I was obsessed with making fun of Jews therefore, I had to go check it out. I watched as my friend lead a group of mini curly headed Jewish kids in an apparent ritual. I will never forget this song as it left an indelible impression on me. The whole group sang, "I brought pennies for Sadaka, for Sadaka! I brought pennies for Sadaka today!"

My ears were overloaded with euphoria. I had never heard such a glorious jingle in my entire existence. The pennies for Sadaka song was like cotton candy to my ears. All at once, it was like everything I had been saying about Jews was true. They brought pennies for some deity named Sadaka! They really did love pennies! This may have been the greatest day of my life in my twisted mind. My ecstasy did not last long, however.

I caught a glimpse of one of the many Jewish kids that I had tortured all summer long. He was glaring at me with disgust. I could see the scorn coming out of his pores and the hatred steaming off of his entire aura. A proverbial mist full of malice and malevolence had risen into the air. The Jewish boy ran over to a cluster of his other friends. Now, I was only there with one other buddy and I realized they were starting to gather. There were about eight of them and they all stared at the two of us and they started pounding their fists into their other hand. I was totally caught off guard. Usually I was the one with the numbers advantage. These kids were coming towards us. They were about to administer to me what I had to them for so very long or maybe even worse. My friend was an unfortunate bystander, but that's what you get when you associate with the Public Enemy #1, Mr. Big Bad Bully! The other kids were coming fast and furiously, ready to gang up on the two of us.

Realizing the imminent danger that we were in, my friend and I bolted out of the building as fast as we could. The gang of Jews was hot on our trail. I started the car and I blasted our way out of the parking lot. However, there were two cars in blazing pursuit behind us, full of angry and hostile Jewish boys. One car was a red race car and the other was a black SUV. I was sure we could evade the SUV but was unsure about the speedy red car. What ensued was a crazy car chase. The Jewish YMCA was in Union, only one town over from Kenilworth. I figured if we rolled into K-Town, I could lose them because we knew the streets better.

We raced through Union, speeding and blowing through red lights. I didn't think the kids would follow suit but whatever I did, they were steadfastly behind us. We all came to a main light, one that we could not run without possibly getting hit by a car or having the police pull us over. The red sports car was directly in my rearview mirror and as I peered over to my right, the black SUV rolled up right beside us. They were trying to box us in.

I gunned the car out of the light at the first sight of green. It was an epic chase at this point and had been going on for nearly twenty minutes. In car chase time, that's like forever, I assure you. Finally, I got to the edge of town and jumped on the highway. It was there I was finally able to create separation. But it wasn't easy. It took another twenty minutes to finally shake those crazy bastards! But for the first time in a long while, I had felt something that I hadn't felt. I felt like I was the one being bullied while those kids stalked me. Maybe I needed that because it had been such a very long time since I had felt that way. I had almost forgotten what it felt like. At this point in my life, this incident would really leave an impression on me. I never wanted to feel like this again. Maybe I didn't want to make others feel this way either. Maybe I was finally ready to take inventory of myself and make some changes.

Besides the car chase, something else strange came out of the Springfield situation. Jewish kids weren't the only ones integrating with the kids from K-Town. One of my best friends, Pete, started bringing around this black kid nicknamed "Sprout." At first, I did not want a black kid around, because I had never really hung around black kids. Pete's a great guy and I couldn't tell him how I really felt because I know he wasn't like me. Pete looked at Sprout as a good guy and didn't look at his skin color. Pete was always like that with anybody. He gave everybody a chance. People I would never dare to be associated with, Pete would befriend. Pete always had some friends that were considered to be the outcasts. That takes courage. Courage that I never had back then.

Pete always said that he looked up to me. I think he looked up to me because he overlooked all the bullying and saw my underlying leadership skills. They've always been there, I just haven't always used them properly, especially when I was younger. Even though Pete was younger than me and looked up to me, I kind of looked up to him. Once I was popular, I never had the courage to be friends with those who were considered undesirable or unpopular. Pete helped broaden my horizons as Sprout was the first black person I ever let into my house. Pete gave him the stamp of approval, making me more accepting of him. I started to let him come around and I began to warm up to him. We used to smoke a lot of weed and Sprout always had weed on him. After he smoked me out a few times, I decided he was a cool cat.

Sprout started to come around a lot. Pete and I kind of took him under our wing. We introduced him to heavy metal. He was really into the music and I thought it was great that we evoked such emotion out of him. We made a black kid get into heavy metal and I was loving it! One day we all proceeded to get high in my bedroom. My bedroom was downstairs in my house, away from the rest of the family who were upstairs. My parents had knocked out a wall and half the garage became part of my bedroom. After the wall was knocked out, I had a gigantic bedroom. One side was normal with a bed and a TV. But the other side was like a lounge with couches, a TV, and a stereo. The room was like a mini bachelor pad equipped for partying.

On this particular day, we were introducing Sprout to some heavy metal. We smoked up and the music started to hit us hard. I had all these empty beer boxes in the corner of my room that had piled up. I saw them all and I initiated a mosh pit on top of the boxes. Next thing you know, the three of us were head-banging and moshing on top of a heap of cardboard beer boxes. I remember smiling and having the time of my life. Music always moved me and made me happier than almost anything, except maybe women. But music was and always will be a priority in my life. Seeing Sprout mosh up and down, truly enjoying the music gave me a newfound respect for him. I truly enjoyed having him around and I have to say he was my first true black friend.

After jumping up and down in a mosh frenzy, we were all starving. I mean we had the munchies from smoking weed, after all. My mom was a phenomenal cook, and she was already cooking up a storm on this particular day. Apparently, my racist older cousin was over for a visit. The three of us all went upstairs to join everyone for dinner. Of course, my mother didn't mind, as she loved feeding people. The three of us then sat down to feast on some good eats.

Unfortunately, my outlandish cousin was at the table and he was giving Sprout some sideways glances. His expression and demeanor were totally dismal. My mind was racing as I had remembered past incidents where my cousin displayed his racist tendencies. He had embarrassed my father and I in that Atlantic City showroom during that boxing match. I was beginning to freak out. My thoughts were racing, and I knew it was only a matter of time before my cousin said something racist to Sprout. Fortunately, we had the munchies and we devoured that food like three vacuum cleaners.

Eventually, the awkward dinner ended, and the fun and games had to end. Pete and Sprout left for the night. After they left, there was a knock on my bedroom door. I was a little alarmed. Was it my parents? Did they know we were smoking pot in my bedroom? I wasn't even sure if my dad would care, as he often told us stories of how he and his friends would light up. My mom on the other hand, she would be livid. But I had no clue who was at the door.

I stammered, "Who is it?"

A stern voice answered back, "Your cousin."

I thought, *What could he want?* I reluctantly opened the door and what he said would never leave me to this day. He looked me dead in the eyes and said, "Why do you have this moulinyan over here eating off of our family's plates?" I was dumfounded and didn't know what to say. It was like the "N" word, but in Italian. My cousin had used this term in front of me before but this time he was directing his ire in my direction.

I used to love when my cousin said that derogatory term, but in this case I was frightened. My jaw dropped and I said, "I-I don't know!"

He continued to stare at me and said, "Don't ever let it happen again!"

I stammered, "I'm sorry, I won't."

As if that wasn't enough, he then called me into the next room. He was holding a glass plate and said, "This is the dirty plate that you let a filthy moulinyan eat off of!"

I wasn't exactly sure how my deranged cousin knew this was the plate that Sprout supposedly ate off of, since my mom washes dishes immediately after we eat. But who knew? He's crazy enough to have kept track of it. Either way, he was intimidating at that moment, as he was staring a hole through me. Suddenly, he threw the plate into the garbage can. *Smash!* He finished off his diatribe, "Nobody can eat off of that now!"

I was flabbergasted for more than one reason. I was stunned by my cousin's actions because I had so many conflicting feelings. I originally thought I despised African American people like my older cousin always had, but the truth was, I didn't. Sprout had changed me. He was without a doubt a true friend. I didn't hate African Americans and maybe I never did. Maybe I just didn't give them a chance as I didn't have exposure to them. Maybe my racist cousin had skewed my feelings before I ever even had a chance.

My dad didn't seem to have these issues. We both grew up in the same town, yet he had African American friends the whole time. I had just made my first African American friend and I was barely out of high school.

There is something you have to understand about my dad. His dad, my grandfather, was off the boat Italian. My grandfather was a hardcore racist and just an all-around intimidating man. The whole town of Kenilworth referred to him as "The Chief" because he was *in charge*. He was someone that you did not want to mess with. But being off the boat Italian made my grandfather very stubborn and racist. In fact, he did not even attend my dad's wedding because he married a Korean woman! I told you, he was hardcore. My grandfather hated Jews and even more he hated the blacks. It's amazing that my father was able to make friends of color after all that. Even though my father was brought up in a racist household, that did not deter him in any way. After all, my dad is not a bad person, actually quite the opposite, he is an amazing man. However, he was brought up the wrong way. I am also not here to disparage my grandfather as I barely knew the man. He must have had good qualities though, as he made six amazing kids including my father. My grandfather grew up in a different time as well, so who knows if things would have been different had he grown up in a different time. My father did grow up in a different time, giving him a chance to break that racist cycle and I'm proud to say that he did. As I've alluded to, my dad will tell you that he had black friends growing up. As my dad always jokingly says, he was down with the "brothers" when he grew up.

In fact, I met one of my dad's African American childhood friends recently. This gentleman's name is Eddie Parrot and he instantly recognized me when he saw me out one night. He grabbed me and began to hug me intensely. Eddie started telling me how much he loved my mom and dad. He told me stories about when he and my father were younger. He was extremely ecstatic, and I could tell that he genuinely loved my father. This put some things into perspective as far as my father goes. I mean he really was down with the brothers! Therefore, my dad was certainly not racist. I mean, he might have some tendencies to joke around about race, but so do a lot of people. My dad always was and still is good natured, as he is a jokester.

I on the other hand, had hate and malice in my heart. I truly used to hate people of different races, religions, and colors, but I now realize, it is because I did not understand them. I didn't understand them because I didn't want to. I didn't want to know them on any level, as I did not have an open mind at the time. This way of thinking was beyond archaic. This is also a toxic way of thinking that everyone needs to break away from.

Growing up and becoming more mature fostered many changes within me. I would change with the times and conform to a more open way of thinking. I grew exponentially as a person and I now am accepting of everyone wholeheartedly and without prejudice. But I will touch on that later on. Whoever says that people can't change, they are wrong because my dad and I are a living testament to this. My dad was able to break away at a young age from the racisms that his own father displayed. My dad was able to block that out and have numerous African American friends. Of course, my dad's greatest act was marrying a Korean woman, my wonderful mother.

If my dad had broken away from his own father's prejudices, then certainly I could change, couldn't I? That process began the first year I was living on a college campus with all types of different people. Being around all these different cultures and races of people started to have a profound effect on me. It even started to lighten me up with the bullying. I wasn't completely done being a bully, because it becomes engrained in you. Sometimes, you just react without thinking. Overall, I was opening my mind, as I had also become much more open to other cultures.

Even though I was making minor changes and becoming more open minded, I still had a long way to go. My college experience was really just beginning and there was so much that was ahead of me.

I eventually moved out of the nerd suite and made a good number of friends. I was becoming a pretty popular guy at Monmouth U. I was very well-known around campus.

My newfound popularity led me to join a fraternity. I loved joining this group and I finally found my place at Monmouth. I felt like I belonged, and this was everything I had been looking for to satiate my need for popularity.

I have to give you some background on the time that I joined my fraternity and how I eventually gained power in the group. In the beginning of the process, I had to endure the bullying, before I could reap the benefits of becoming a full-fledged brother. I went through the process known as pledging. During this neophyte period, the pledges adhered to a roughly six-week program in which we learned to become part of the group. Mostly, this was just the time where we got bullied. If we did something wrong, we would receive some form of punishment.

Often times this was doing pushups or reciting the Greek alphabet. We, the neophytes, had to eat strange food items and chug beers. It was all in good fun, and was not meant to be harmful or malicious. Every week we were put in military style line-ups, where we were grilled with questions. Wrong answers would equal consequences.

I was still somewhat of a chubby, non-athletic young adult. So, doing push-ups was not in my wheelhouse. But I did them until my arms were sore and I collapsed. I endured the verbal abuse thereafter. But what the fraternity brothers did not realize is that this was nothing compared to the bullying I had been through. I grew up as the fat kid who was always picked last in gym class. I had been victimized and endured endless verbal abuse, far beyond anything they could dish out. This was a literal cake walk for me. *Bring it on*, I thought.

Eventually, I would earn my way into the group. The first year, we were still treated as newbies and rightfully so. I mean, we were no longer hazed, but we weren't fully integrated into the group yet. But I was simply happy to be a part of this group and that also meant that I was now able to haze new pledges. I looked forward to that immensely. The bully inside of me had an insatiable hunger to menace feeble prey.

This became one of the things I loved the most about being part of a fraternity. I had pledges to boss around and tell what to do. I degraded them verbally as well. One of my biggest ways of showing my prowess over them was calling them "WEAK!" Calling someone WEAK kind of became my *thing*. I was known for it. My pledge paddle is actually emblazoned with the word "WEAK" in bold, capital letters. This is something I still say to this day. Calling people "WEAK" definitely became my thing. I always bust people's balls and call them "WEAK!" It's one of my favorite things to do actually. Over time, I've said it so much that it has now become just a joke.

Back then, I meant it. I thought these pledges were lesser than me and I thought they were all completely *WEAK*.

Two years into being a member of the fraternity, my star rose, and I became a prominent member of the group. I was one of the more popular brothers and I capitalized on that when it came time to nominate and elect leaders of our group. Soon after, I was voted to became what is known as the "Hellmaster." The Hellmaster was the one in ultimate charge of what the pledges would have to endure during the pledging period.

During this time, I displayed my bullying prowess. I was forceful in lineups and I commanded the pledges with madness. I had a fury in my eyes. The more I bullied these rookies, the more I was cheered and revered. Like some sick game of who could be the biggest bully, I was crowned and named the champion. This was the ultimate fuel for a bully's fire. All the brothers giving their approval and support made me want to lash out at these novices even more. This is one of the major factors in developing a Bully Complex. The group mentality towards a few individuals is like pouring gasoline on an already raging fire. Bullies tend to run in packs and a fraternity is the ultimate bully wolf pack.

I was so exceptionally good at what I did that I earned a nickname from my brothers. I would become the "Bull of Madrid." I was branded with this moniker because when I was in front of those pledges with a group of brothers cheering me and goading me on, I became a Bull. I would pound my chest to intimidate the neophytes. There was practically smoke coming out of my ears. I unquestionably expressed myself as the Bull. I don't know where the "of Madrid" part came into play. It was just a funny nickname. We would laugh about it when the pledges were not present. But that nickname perpetuated my incessant need to bully. Every time we had the neophytes in a line up situation, the Bull of Madrid would come out. Each and every week, I would feel the Bull growing more and more inside of me. I believed my eyes were turning red and I believed I had *become* the Bull. The reality was that mentally I had transformed into the Bull.

Ironically, now that I see the name written *Bull*, I realize it is only one letter short of bully. I might as well have been the Bully of Madrid. Either way, I was the Bull and I was again the biggest bully on the planet.

My popularity on campus and in my fraternity propelled me, as I was voted Homecoming King at one point. This achievement was nothing but a glorified popularity contest. In my mind this was redemption for not being voted Prom King at my Senior Prom.

Before all the popularity and the crowning, I had made acquaintances with some of the outcasts of the school. When I was new to campus and didn't know anybody, I just needed to socialize with somebody. Prior to being in the fraternity, I didn't have many friends, prompting me to latch on to some of the undesirables. I wouldn't say I was friends with these people, but I was certainly friendly. Now that I was popular again, I felt like I could no longer act that way towards them. Or at least I felt like I couldn't treat the nerds nicely any longer. Therefore, I reverted back to the ugliness, a bully, a tyrant, an asshole. I started to snub the unpopular once again. I mean, I couldn't let all the cool kids see me talking with these miscreants. Could I?

I probably could have conversed with the less popular because of who I was and the campus clout I had attained. Maybe I could have made a change and brought people together, but I was in no way ready for that. I should have been, because I always had a bridge to the people who were perceived as nerds. I was always on the school newspaper, on the radio, and in school plays. All these activities were not perceived to be the coolest things to do. There was a good mix of people who engaged in these extracurriculars. With that, yes, a good number of nerds, geeks, and dorks. Therefore, I had always interacted with them in some form or another. I was always nice to people in the newspaper meetings. I didn't act like the jackass I portrayed in front of my friends or other like-minded bullies.

This internal struggle was probably always inside of me. I mean, not many people transition the way I did. I went from being the most ridiculed kid to one of the most popular kids. Most cannot fathom this transformation. But I lived it. It's like I was the chosen one.

With all this power and with all the groups I was in, I probably could have done something about bullying. I could have risen above and stuck up for some of these dejected victims. Instead, I was blindly enamored with my newfound popularity, that I just continued to pile on. I buried the already beaten down. I suffocated them and gave them no

138

chance to fight for themselves. I wasn't a leader and by no means was I a king, as I had been crowned. I was simply a coward, going along with the crowd.

It looked as if things were starting to turn for me in college. It had seemed I was actually beginning to change, but just when it looked like I would be over my bullying ways, I wasn't. I found myself in a similar position as high school, and my mindset was exactly the same. I was once again extremely popular, a cool kid, and I couldn't be seen commiserating with the underbelly of the school. I could not communicate with the perceived lower end of the social demographic, as that would have been social suicide for me. I was constantly consumed and enamored with being popular and I would never give that up for anything. I had so many friends and I always had somewhere to go or something to do. I really felt like a king on top of the social pyramid.

As I've said, in the newspaper or radio meetings I was nice to the perceived outcasts. Very few called me on my bullshit. If they did, I reminded them of who I was. *I mean, who the fuck was I? Who did I think I was?* Or in some cases, I did what I used to do, and I emotionally or physically smothered them to the point that they wanted nothing to do with me. I would bully them into a corner and embarrass them in front of others. However, I maintained somewhat of a relationship with them, after all, I had to work with them on newspaper and radio projects. I was somewhat amicable, albeit an asshole.

When I joined the fraternity, I acquired a whole new group of friends. All of those newfound friends made me start to think that I was exceptionally cool, and I was better than others. This was by no fault of their own. This was all a product of my own inflating ego. The truth is I was no better than anyone and I should have maintained my previous friendships with the unpopular kids. I never had the backbone to do so. I wouldn't have been able to stand it if somebody from my fraternity would have actually seen me talking to these misfits in a social context. The fact remained though, that I still had to associate with newspaper nerds and the radio station geeks. There were some cool people in those groups, but there were also a bunch of outcasts as well. Bullying outcasts and people that are different is a bully's specialty. That meant that most of the friendly relationships that I had cultivated were about to be decimated by my raging Bully Complex.

Over the next couple of years, I was only friendly to my former newspaper and radio station associates when I had to be. For the most part, I was withdrawn in meetings and did not engage with them. When the meetings were over and the advisors were gone, that's when I would strike. I bullied several of them and they were the typical type that I would pick on. They were mostly helpless and never fought back. I would make them extraordinarily uncomfortable in my presence, as I often name-called them in front of others. I would mock them to the point that they became withdrawn. I didn't care anymore how they felt about me. That is, until one day when I needed their help.

As an upperclassman my popularity grew on campus. It all culminated when I was nominated as a prospective candidate to become Homecoming King. It was then that I turned my charm on to my old nerdy associates. I needed their votes now, therefore I feigned niceness to try and persuade them. I was able to manipulate most of them and get them to vote for me. But there were a scorned few who snubbed me, which I totally deserved. I remember one girl's exact quote, "Oh Mr. Popular needs votes now, so he wants to talk to me all of a sudden?"

Another girl said, "Anthony Lospinoso always following the beautiful people!" Wow, that line hit me hard believe it or not. Only because I wasn't sure of its meaning. What did she mean?

I honestly thought about that statement for a while. She was kind of right. I had ditched being friends with people that were considered to be off-putting or different looking, because they had glasses or were perceived to be not pretty enough or because they were too smart. I couldn't be friends with nerds, freaks or geeks any longer. I joined a fraternity with a bunch of pretty boys, and I went to parties to try and hook up with pretty sorority chicks. What she had said was completely true as I wanted to be associated with the beautiful people. Now, I am not saying any of those "beautiful people" were bad people. In fact, I met some of the best people you could ever meet in my fraternity. We honestly had a great group of guys. I am just analyzing the girl's statement and being honest about myself. I was the one who had perception and bully issues, not the guys in my fraternity. For the most part anyway, as a few of them did join in with my bullying ways. I would always rally others to join me. I was the main person with a bullying problem though. I was the one with a Bully Complex. Who had I become? In truth, I knew who I had become. I had managed to go from the bottom of the barrel as the "fat chink" to the top of the brass ring, now as the king of the campus.

Once that crown hit the top of my head and I was named Homecoming King, my ego went spiraling out of control. My ego received validation it didn't need. This would only make me even more insufferable to those I belittled. Everybody that I victimized was somehow going to get even worse abuse. I had become an egomaniacal monster. I would judge people now more than I ever had before, and that's really saying something!

Some good did come out of being in my fraternity. During that time, I made my first Jewish friend. Even though my bullying ways were taking over, I would start to change slowly.

Before I met my fraternity brother, Ryan Ogelstein, I had only disdain for Jewish people. I berated and belittled them mercilessly. I hated the one Jewish kid in my graduating high school class. He was the first kid I ever beat up on the playground. He would account for the only interactions I had with Jewish people up to that point during high school. When I met Ryan, my instinct was, *this guy's a Jew, I can't hang with him*. But Ryan was such a nice guy. You could do nothing but like him. That's when I finally made amends with the Jewish hating part of my Bully Complex. I genuinely have no hate for Jewish people now.

Ryan Ogelstein would be the first to open my discriminating eyes. It was a revelation. I now judge people solely on their personality, their character and how they act towards others. It doesn't matter if the person is Jewish, black or whatever, because good people come in all forms, religions and all races. I didn't know that before meeting Ryan. My initial instinct to dislike him and try to bully him faded away, because Ryan was just a good person. I was proud to call Ryan a friend.

Something needs to be made very clear. Racism is not acceptable in any way, shape, or form. Racism is completely objectionable, offensive, and unwelcomed. My actions will never be justified, as racism can never be tolerated. Anyone who is perpetuating racism is completely wrong and out of bounds. We all need to recognize that there are still racial issues running rampant throughout our country. We all need to do something and speak out against those who are still racist. Racist propaganda is still being spread throughout our society. We need to put an end to all the hate and racism that still persists.

Hate can be a powerful emotion. I used to have hate inside of me and I'm not even sure how or why I harnessed all of that hate. Some of my hate I think stemmed from my friendship with my high school friend Patrick. We were both devout Christians. Even though I loathed Sunday School, I still believed in my religion. Patrick and I both believed in God and Jesus. He used to tell me that the Jews killed Jesus and we should hate them for it. I believed his foolish rhetoric. I was a follower at the time, and I followed his outlandish lead. I listened to Patrick and we would bully Jewish people together.

Some of my hate probably also derived from my racist older cousin and the stories he told. But even my cousin's wrath was mostly focused on African Americans. My hatred definitely wasn't from my father as he didn't hate Jewish people. Sure, he joked a lot, but he was never malicious. My dad was not a hateful person. I was different on the other hand. I used to have hate and disdain in my heart. I truly had hatred for Jewish people and it just wasn't right. It is never right to hate people because of their race, religion, social class, how they look, or whatever makes them different. Hate is never the answer and I truly regret having felt hate the way that I did. I'm extremely glad that the hate no longer resides in my now genuine heart. Hate is NEVER the answer!

Despite all the hate, I did find some lovin' during my college days. I finally came out of my sexual shell. A lot of it was due to the fact that I had finally gained some confidence with the ladies. Throughout college, I purposely did not want to have any serious girlfriends after Jaime, and I decided I just wanted to fool around and have fun. I did not want to endure the heartache and grief that I had felt after my first failed relationship. However, I did end up dating one girl.

I met her at a bar, and we seemed to have an instant connection. She was beautiful and I was enamored with her. It wasn't really serious in the beginning as I knew little about her. But a couple weeks in, we started dating officially. Her name was Lisa and after some time, I started bringing her around my hometown friends. I wanted everyone to meet her, get to know her, and hopefully love her as much as I did.

I remember when we first started getting serious and she met my Kenilworth friends for the first time. I realized that we only had a fling to this point as I didn't even know her last name yet! Somebody innocuously asked her what her last name was.

She squeamishly said, "Steinberg."

The room went quiet. This was the first time I had learned that she was Jewish. A wave of emotions hit me all at once. Even though I had finally made friends with a Jewish guy, this was totally different. Dating a Jewish girl seemed almost taboo to me at the time.

Oh my God, I am dating a Jewish broad! What is everyone going to think? Do I still like her? How many Jewish jokes have we told in front of her? Was she offended by the Jewish jokes? Does this make me Jewish? Does this mean that I loved Jews? Did she hide this from me on purpose?

I know she had to have heard some of our racially charged jokes and jabs. I was certain she had been trying to hide the fact that she was Jewish for as long as she could. She had told me that she loved Christmas and that explicitly threw me off the scent. She never seemed to be offended by anything my friends had to say that was perceived to be racist. She certainly wasn't offended by the racial epithets that always seemed to come out of my mouth. I was more than perplexed by my current situation with Lisa.

The next day, I had a lot of thinking to do. I really liked Lisa, but she was Jewish. I knew I had a hailstorm of verbal jabs that would be coming my way from my friends. Indeed, the very next night, I was mocked and ridiculed. My friends asked me what it was like to kiss a Jew. They asked if I had eaten Matzo Ball soup and washed it down with a glass of Manishevitz. One friend mockingly said, "Don't make fun of him, he's just planting the flag!"

I asked, "What does 'planting the flag' mean?" He replied that I was the first one in our group to date a Jewish broad, so I was planting that first flag. Another friend joked and equated it to landing on the moon. I was the first one to ever enter this territory. The question beckoned though, was I a hero for planting the flag? Or, more likely, had I become the fool of my group? The jokes continued for the duration of that night. I just laughed them off, but the truth was, I really liked Lisa. I wouldn't stop seeing her just because she was Jewish. I continued seeing her despite all the ridicule. That was the first Jewish girl that I dated and there would be one other later on in my life. I dated the other Jewish girl for a brief time when I was a much more mature human being, as were my friends.

Dating these Jewish girls made me realize that you can't help who you like. Religion and race should not matter. If you like somebody and genuinely connect, nothing else matters. Don't let others bring you down and change the way you feel about somebody you deem to be special.

I would never have racial boundaries when it came to dating ever again. My racial boundaries in general were coming down at the time and I am glad that I no longer have a racist mindset.

Even though I was mending my ways with Jewish people, I did continue to bully here and there.

Bottom line is that you should not judge people by how they look, how they talk, how they dress or what their IQ is. Many people do this, and it just isn't right. It took me a long, long time but I've learned to give people a chance and get to know them for who they really are. You never know what lies behind those "nerdy" glasses.

There is another old saying that beauty is in the eye of the beholder. Just because I didn't find any of the outcasts as "beautiful" or "desirable," doesn't mean that they weren't. Everyone has beauty inside of them. I was a superficial jerk and many of these people were beautiful. I was just too judgmental to see it. During my time in college, I always judged people because I thought I was better than them. Being part of a fraternity gave me more perceived power. This would become a playground for my bullying nature.

Being in a fraternity taught me a lot. Even though I was subsequently still a bully, I was still a young man learning how to act. I learned to deal with a large group of individuals. When you're in a group with fifty other guys, you're not going to like every single one of them. I remember having a strong dislike for a couple. We are always going to encounter people that we don't like, don't get along with, and basically just don't click with. These are just facts of life. At the end of our meetings, there was a bunch of stuff we always said, most of which was hyperbole. However, one specific thing I have always remembered because it rings true.

One brother would always say, "There are fifty guys in this room, you don't have to like all of them, but you should respect all of them."

This statement rings true because not everybody is going to get along on this planet. I mean, if we all did, there would be world peace and harmony. Unfortunately, we all don't respect each other either. That's why there's still racism, homophobia, stereotypes, war zones and weapons of mass destruction. If we could all try and have respect for one another, we really could make significant changes in this world for the better.

PART 2: THE POINT OF NO RETURN

"Suddenly, I realized that he couldn't breathe . . ."

There are many things I would like to see changed in this world. I obviously want to change the bullying culture and the racism that runs rampant. Hopefully, I am helping by putting my story out there.

Change for the most part can be good, but of course there are things I wouldn't change. One thing I wouldn't change in this world is music as an expression, especially the music I love as it has changed my life. Heavy metal was my first love when it comes to music. It is somewhat ironic that I gravitated towards heavy metal at a young age. This form of music used to be widely known as the soundtrack for outcasts and misfits. To this day, there are stigmas attached to this type of music. Before my turnaround and unlikely transformation, I was exactly that. I was the hunted and I was the prey for many voracious bullies. The heavy music with loud guitars and pulverizing drumbeats helped me through many tough times and aided in releasing my anger. Metal music can indeed be some of the most cathartic music.

I want to make something clear about this music that I so deeply revere. Even though heavy metal music evokes certain emotions within me and sometimes does get my adrenaline pumping, the music was in no way responsible for my volatile nature, my victimizations, or any violent act I have ever engaged in. Yes, the music does get my blood pumping and yes, sometimes I release my aggression through the music. What I am trying to say, is that in no way is the music responsible for my actions, or anybody's actions for that matter. This type of music I listen to has been blamed for tragedies and fits of rage, for as far back as I can remember. Heavy metal music has been the center of controversy and consistently linked with many incidents, including riots, suicides, and school shootings.

The media, the government, and parents have aimed their ire at this often misunderstood form of music. They have tried to place the blame on the music for these horrific tragedies, when in fact, the music is not the catalyst for these unfortunate incidents. Yes, music makes us feel certain emotions and yes, music moves us in certain ways, but there is no way the music is responsible for people's actions in the end. I have committed countless disgusting exploits. The music may have triggered and aided my anger, but in no way did I do anything because the music made me. That's absolutely ludicrous. Every action or dastardly deed I committed was due my own flaws and the fact that I had become mentally unhinged. My bullying was a product of the complex I had developed. The music never caused that.

Heavy metal never made me do bad things, but it did change my life. There were several bands that changed me and affected me greatly. There was one band in particular that made a huge mark in my life. The band, Korn, released their debut album on October 11, 1994, during my second year of college and it blew me away. I was nineteen-years-old and still finding my way in life. My Bully Complex was running at full throttle. As I delved deep into Korn's debut album, I felt the anger and anguish of singer, Jonathan Davis. If you listen to the album, to this day you can feel his emotions pour out of the speakers.

I was obsessed with the emotion he unleashed; therefore, I began to research what drove him to pour all of his pain and suffering into his art. It turns out that on top of being molested, Jonathan Davis was bullied in school. He spoke out against bullies and stood up for all the outcasts and misfits. Talk about striking a chord with me, because deep down, I still felt like the outcast kid in grammar school who took a beating like nobody's business. Even though I was currently a bully, I could never escape the emotions and consequent suffering that resonated from being bullied years earlier.

Davis spoke about how the song "Faget" in particular was a big "Fuck You" to all the jocks that used to beat him in the locker room and made his life miserable. The jocks and cool kids would pound on him and call him "faget." The following lyrics have been interpreted in different ways. Sometimes Davis is hard to understand because he is yelling and singing with such angst. You can feel the power from his emotional outpouring.

Here I am different in this normal world

Why did you tease me? Made me feel upset

Walking Stereotypes feeding their heads

I am ugly, Please just go away

Why do you treat me this way, made the hate stay

As I walk, I can never seem to escape all the laughing, all the pain

I'm sick and tired of people treating me this way everyday

To all the people that think I'm strange

Davis goes on to ask, "All my life who am I?" Then he screams the word "Faget" over and over again. That's the word that was yelled at him while he was being bullied. The song is extraordinarily dynamic and powerful. Davis was bullied excessively and called a "faget" to the point that it seems he questions himself. It's as if the bullies pounded the word into his head and he almost believed it. This is the true power of bullying. The incessant and unrelenting nature starts to make you doubt yourself. *Am I all these things people are saying?*

I believed that I was the "Fat Chink" because, well, I was, according to so many bullies. I mean, I was certainly fat, and I was Asian making me a "Fat Chink," right? When the bullies called me a cry baby and that I needed my Mommy and Daddy to bail me out of school, they had a point, didn't they? I kicked, screamed, and cried until my parents would come pull me out of school, literally. After all, I just wanted to find safety away from my perpetrators and when my parents took me back home, I finally felt safe again. Home was a safe haven away from the bullying. That's why many kids try to skip out of school and stay home. Staying home allows the victims to avoid the bullying, even if only for a day. These kids are crying out for help, just as I was. I was crying out against all the bullying taking place, but I was so young that I didn't know how to articulate it to anybody. I just acted out in school instead.

If parents see these patterns of behavior, you need to be alert to your child's situation. If your child is constantly trying to avoid school or is crying at school in an attempt to come back home, there is something wrong. Most children will not hate school for no apparent reason. This means there is something significant going on. It doesn't necessarily mean your child is being bullied, but it's certainly possible. There could be some other abuse going on. I don't want to stray too far off topic, but you now know these are warning signs. This signals that it is time for you to take action and find out the root of the problem.

Back to my point about victims who start to believe the words that comes out of their tormentor's mouth. Do you become what these bullies call you and believe you to be? Sure, bullies can make you believe that you are these nasty, vile things that they spew from their venomous mouths, but they are not true! You have to have the intestinal fortitude and guts to believe in yourself. You are not these heinous insults being hurled at you! Everyone has good inside of themselves. You need to find that goodness and harness it. Don't let the bullies get the best of you. Don't let them change who you are. Don't let the bullies make you doubt yourself and get down on yourself. You have exceptional self-worth. You can rise above these victimizations.

We all have flaws and bullies will pick on those flaws. Look at me, I picked on things that people could do nothing about like having foreign accents and the fact that their families were impoverished and couldn't afford brand name sneakers. Be proud of who you are, no matter what or where you come from. Recognize and realize, we are all different. You may be poverty-stricken, or you may be foreign, but it makes you who you are. Going through tough times will aid you in defining your character. This will make you a stronger person and will ultimately help you overcome bullies. Believing in yourself is powerful and is the power you need to combat the bullies. Know who you are and what you stand for.

Heavy metal music will always be a huge part of who I am. I became a passionate fan of the band Korn from the moment I heard their debut album. The Korn debut album also unleashed some of the perpetual anger built up inside of me. One particular victim would feel the wrath of my ferocious temper. My anger issues were undeniable and inescapable at the time. However, I would not totally snap unless I felt provoked. If you pushed certain buttons, I would snap and become a seething lunatic. I know what you're thinking, what about how I had acted towards Jaime's new boyfriend Rich? Rich seemingly didn't provoke the way I acted in any way. Well, in my mind, Rich had stolen the only person I had loved so deeply. I had tortured and harassed him to maniacal heights. But to me, in my demented frame of mind, Rich had crossed me. Even though he didn't know me, that was my immature and highly irrational thought process at the time.

Part of the reason I always listened to heavy metal was due to my aggression and my anger issues. The music was always cathartic for me. Whatever rage, depression, or negative feelings I had I could just funnel them away into the music. The music would blast from my headphones, into my eardrums and pound right into my nervous system. This is how I would release most of my pent-up anger.

My anger would be a lingering problem for years to come. I should have made better choices especially when it came to where I would live and who I would live with. My anger would manifest in horrific fashion. I should have learned to live with people that I was familiar with and not gone into another housing situation blindly.

After the previous debacle of the housing lottery where I ended up in a suite full of freaks and geeks, I modified my living choices somewhat. After all, I had my own group of friends now. I was in a fraternity and I was pretty popular. I next lived with a friend named Carmine, and he was a chill dude. He wasn't a part of my fraternity, but he was an awesome guy to party with. I used to bring him around the fraternity, making him well known to all of my brothers. We would all party and get wasted together. We had a true bond even beyond the partying. I felt like he was one of my best friends.

After that first year of living with Carmine, we decided to live together the next year as well. Most of my fraternity brothers were scooping up rental houses together or decided to trek it on campus for another year. There was an opportunity to live in a brand new apartment complex right across from the beach. The only catch was that these apartments were being rented and regulated through the University itself. They were two-bedroom apartments with two beds in each room, accommodating four renters. After scouring my fraternity and several other sources, Carmine and I somehow couldn't find two other people looking for a place to live. Everyone had their living arrangements set. Well, I had my heart set on living in those apartments, so Carmine and I decided to put our names in another housing lottery, and would randomly get two other students to live with us.

You would have thought that I had learned from my first experience in the housing lottery. But I was bird brained and did not. I didn't think I was making an oblivious decision at the time, because to me, it didn't matter who we were going to be living with. As far as I was concerned, that place belonged to Carmine and me. We would run that apartment. Whoever moved in, they were going to play by our rules, like it or not!

We were allowed to go check out the apartment before moving in, to scope out the size and see how much stuff we could bring. I decided I needed a partner in crime, so I picked up my hometown friend, Larry, for the ride. I told him we were going to "christen" the apartment. We drove down and entered the empty apartment. I showed him around and then we went into the bedroom I had chosen. I opened a drawer where I had already strategically placed some marijuana. Out of the closet, I grabbed a mini bong. I packed the bong and said, "OK, time to christen this bitch!" We both puffed away until our eyes were floating into the back of our heads. We were floating into another dimension, as I never did anything in moderation. I always smoked until I was incapacitated. We were high and feeling good. Now Larry and I, we used to get the giggles when we were high. We started giggling up a storm, when suddenly we both heard keys jingling at the front door.

We both hushed and became stoically quiet. You could have heard a pin drop. I pressed my ear against the bedroom door. I heard a few people bustling about. Unsure what to think at first, my instincts suddenly kicked in, as I scrambled to put the bong and weed away. I scurried back to the door to listen intently. Then I heard in a squeaky tone, "Nice living room. Oh, the couches are comfy. What do you think, Mum?"

In my inebriated state, I was able to ascertain that this must be one of my mystery roommates showing his parents his new living arrangements. I was somewhat relieved. At least it wasn't the police or a Dean from the school arriving to tell me that my time living here had already expired, due to my never-ending need to puff on the pipe.

I went over and whispered to Larry the situation we were in. He was always generally nervous when smoking weed to begin with, and this only exacerbated our conundrum. His eyes bugged out and said, "Kid, what are we going to do?"

I told him to relax, that I would handle this. Then suddenly we heard, "Knock, knock, knock." The squeaky voice came through the door, "Is anybody in there?"

"Yes," I answered in a frantic tone, "I'll be right there!"

I opened the bedroom door and there stood a short, nerdy-looking fellow. He was about half my size and he was slightly pudgy. He was the stereotypical dorky type that I loved to victimize. His squeaky voice had reminded me of a frog. The weed had my eyesight a tad foggy and I was so high that when I looked at him, I actually thought he was this short boy with a toad head. I had to hold myself from giggling in his toad face.

The boy looked surprised. He seemed just as shocked to see us as we were to see him.

I said, "Hello, I'm Anthony. You must be one of our roommates?"

He awkwardly answered, "Yes, I'm Teddy. Nice to meet you."

Then he walked over his parents who were obviously foreign. "Hallo, I am Teddy's Dad." "Hallo, I am Teddy's Mum."

"Oh, nice to meet you, I am Anthony."

I peeked back at Larry and he looked mortified. "Oh, this is my best friend, Larry. We're checking out the room space."

For the next five minutes, we made uncomfortable conversation. I remember thinking about the extreme high I was experiencing and wondering if the awkward foreigners had any clue. What's funny is, I didn't care if they knew. I maintained the attitude that I was in charge of this place and Teddy the "Toad Boy" better get used to it. I was going to smoke weed, drink alcohol, and party whenever I wanted. And that was going to be a lot. A LOT! There was nothing he or his foreign sounding parents could do about it. I was the king of this castle. I was his king and he would bow down to me. I ruled this roost. He would soon learn his role.

Two weeks later, we all moved in. Carmine and I were in our own room. The other room would be occupied by Teddy and someone I was very familiar with. Our fourth roommate was Jerry Dickletz. I knew him from being on the school newspaper together. I nicknamed the two of them the "nerd turds." I had filled Carmine's ear about Teddy and Jerry, telling him what they were like. I told Carmine that this place was ours and the other two would have to comply to our out of control living habits.

Jerry Dickletz was indeed a nerdy type, but he was mostly quiet and kept to himself. He was a nice guy, the type that wouldn't hurt a fly. I had frequent interactions with Jerry because we were both editors on the school newspaper and I had already branded him with the nickname "DICKLIPS." Jerry often corrected me and would say, "My name is pronounced *Dick-LETZ*, Anthony." But I was persistent with my pestering pronunciation and he always submitted to my perpetual persecution. When he corrected me this only accelerated my repugnant behavior. His constant correction added fuel to my engine, and I was always firing on all of my bully cylinders. Jerry would always fall back, and this is how I knew that he would acquiesce to my command. He was a nice guy but had no spine. He was afraid to challenge me, and I knew it. There were a few times during our time on the school newspaper together that he tried telling me how to do something. I was stubborn and always resisted. He always relented, even though he was right most of the time. Backing off was just in his nature, that's how I knew he didn't want to challenge me. The truth of it was, Jerry was a good guy. He didn't deserve the way I treated him, but this was obviously a continuing theme for me.

That first night, Carmine and I decided it was time to christen our apartment and show the new roommates what life was going to be like. We invited over about ten friends and the party was on. We had a bunch of beer and booze, which was being consumed at a breakneck pace. Everybody was having a smashing good time as we all proceeded to get smashed. Well, everyone except for DICKLIPS and Teddy the Toad Boy of course. The "nerd turds" were hiding in their room and we did not see them for the remainder of the intoxicated evening.

For the next couple weeks, this trend would continue. At this point, word was getting out about our raucous and boisterous parties. The get togethers were expanding at this point. With each gathering, the noise level rose as did our neighborly complaints. We had already been warned by the Dean in charge of housing several times. We had even received a letter stating that we would be thrown out of the campus hosted apartment if we kept it up. I took them as empty threats and laughed at the letter. DICKLIPS and the Toad Boy were seriously concerned, of course.

Their concerns may have been slightly warranted. The Dean of housing, Dean Franks, had paid our apartment a special visit. He had received numerous complaints from our neighbors about our excessive partying. Of course, I lied to him, as I said that we had a few people over and that the neighbors were exaggerating. He said that it was fine for now, but if the complaints continued then there would be consequences. I was rather conniving, and I convinced him that all was well and not to worry.

154

The "nerd turds" wanted to have a sit down with Carmine and I after Dean Franks made his visit. I begrudgingly obliged. We were to have our meeting on Monday afternoon. Of course, I had gotten blasted drunk on Sunday and I was not in the mood. Carmine convinced me that we should attend, but there was only one way I was attending this shit show—I took a blast out of my bong and I proceeded to the sham of a meeting at the kitchen table.

Teddy was the first to speak in his froggy tone that grated my nerves. "OK guys, we are in a serious situation here. This letter from Dean Franks is serious business. You two have had enough fun. The fun has to stop. Jerry and I cannot afford to be kicked out of this apartment."

I glared over at DICKLIPS but he stared down at the ground, never looking up. He never said a word the whole meeting. He just stared at the floor as if his life depended on it. As if he would melt into a pile of salt if he took his eyes off the floor. He might as well have been a pile of shit, as far as I was concerned. He sat there spineless as he let Teddy the Toad Boy speak for the both of them.

Teddy looked me dead in the eyes and said, "So is this all going to stop?"

I was slightly taken aback, thinking *this little twit had some balls.* Was he actually not afraid of me? I was ready to bash his froggy little face in. But instead I laughed. I cracked up right in his grill. With that I relieved myself from the "meeting." I heard Teddy saying to Carmine desperately, "Please talk to him! We can't get kicked out!"

Carmine came into the bedroom and asked what I was going to do. I said with a grin, "We'll see." But he knew what that meant. I wasn't about to stop. Not for the neighbors, not for the Dean and certainly not for some froggy little shit!

That weekend came and I decided I was throwing the biggest party yet. I even contemplated buying a keg which was absurd for our tiny apartment. Instead I decided to go with about fifteen cases of cheap beer. I invited over about twelve fraternity brothers, a couple of friends from home and of course a bevy of beautiful ladies. The ladies were what made the party after all.

This particular party started out like any other; reckless, loud, and obnoxious. But the vibe changed slowly as the night went on. "DICKLIPS" was in his usual spot, hiding in his bedroom presumably under the covers. But Teddy the Toad Boy was out in the crowd and mingling! *What the hell was this?* Had he come around? Did he finally come to his froggy senses? What in the blue hell was going on? I was agitated and completely confused.

I began to watch his rather curious behavior. He was hitting on girls and his advances were emphatically rebuffed and unwanted. He continued around the room, trying to hit on every girl, until I was fed up. I went up to him and said, "Hey, lay off bro. None of these girls want to get with you!"

He snickered and said, "How do you know? You don't know until you try!"

"Look, Toad Boy, back the fuck off!" I bellowed.

The Toad Boy's actions were pissing me off. This prompted me to start throwing empty beer cans outside of our front door and into the foyer of the stairwell. The cans began to quickly pile up and the foyer had become my very own recyclable receptacle. I had no care at all for anything at this point. I didn't care about the neighbors. I didn't care about Dean Franks and I certainly didn't care about Teddy the Toad Boy.

As the party wound down, I continued throwing cans out into the hallway and they formed an aluminum mountain. I nixed the dance music as all of the girls had left for the evening. I decided to put on some heavy metal. I put on Korn's debut disc. This album really gets me going and I release major aggression while listening to it. I really needed to let out my anger at that point as the Toad Boy had pushed my buttons. This had become a highly volatile situation as I had reached my breaking point.

Teddy was now visibly intoxicated, and he started to garble in his frog-like tone, "OK, the party is over!"

I said, "OK, Toad Boy, go to bed then, you little shit!"

He wobbled over by the stereo and lowered the music and said once again, "The party's over!"

I immediately jumped off the couch and raised the music, "Don't touch my stereo you froggy little fuck!"

I sat down and once again, Teddy stumbled over to the stereo, lowered it one more time as he garbled, "The party's over! No more music!"

Now I was becoming enraged. My blood was so hot that I actually felt like it was burning my skin. I felt myself turning orange. I once again bounced up and leapt like a cat toward my stereo. I fervently raised the volume this time a little louder. I looked Teddy dead in his eye and said, "Do not touch my stereo EVER AGAIN or I WILL DESTROY YOU!"

I sat down for what I thought would be the final time, because he assuredly would not touch my stereo again. I could not believe the balls on this kid as I watched him flounder over to the stereo one last time. This time he unplugged it completely.

That's when I completely snapped.

I told you earlier, there are certain triggers that will cause me to snap. Touching and messing with my music and its corresponding equipment is a recipe to get your ass beat. I had had it with this toad-faced freak!

I ferociously leapt on the unsuspecting frog boy. I punched him right in his inebriated head, stunning him. He then did the unthinkable; he actually tried to fight back. He was half my size and was no match for my overpowering prowess. Teddy crouched down into a fighting stance and then attempted to swing at me, but I swatted him away like a fly. After swatting him, I tossed him into the wall. I punched him several more times. His blood splattered against the wall and that made me smile.

Then I opened the apartment door and I threw him out into the stairwell. He went flying and smashed into the wall. More of his blood began to dot the stairwell walls. The pile of cans I had compiled clattered around and fell down the steps. *Clang! Clang! Clang!* Cans flew everywhere.

I darted at Teddy and snatched him by the throat. I had him in a firm chokehold, and I said furiously, "I will throw you down these stairs just like the cans and I will finish you off!"

I could see the fear in his panic-stricken eyes. He was squirming and he began turning bright red. His face turned from a crimson red to a ghastly almost purplish color. Teddy was starting to resemble a bruised and battered eggplant. Suddenly, I realized that he couldn't breathe, prompting me to finally release my vice-grip around his neck and let him go.

He wobbled back into the apartment, dripping blood all along the carpet and proceeded to sprawl out on the couch. He was making odd noises and crying out in agony. This is unquestionably when I should have stopped. If we had been alone, I think I might have.

However, my two friends from Kenilworth were still there, and I wanted to impress them. I always had a never ending need to show off. So, I proceeded to play the Korn album again as I undid my belt. Teddy cried out, absolutely helpless, but it didn't matter to me. I began to whip him with my belt like he was my servant and I, his master. He cried out with wicked wretchedness each time I whipped him. His screeches became eerie, but I was someplace else. My mind was no longer there. I had transformed into some kind of monster. All I could see was red. The music also fueled me. I could hear the song "Ball Tongue" playing in the background.

Towards the very end of this hard-hitting song, there is the sound of this cow bell. When I thought of the sound that was coming, it made me want to finish off the Toad Boy in grand fashion. I went to the kitchen and I grabbed a small aluminum pot and a cupcake. First, I unwrapped the cupcake and smashed it all over Teddy's humiliated head. This was just the appetizer to the malicious main course. When the cow bell hit in the song, it made the sound of a banging pot. So, I synchronized with the song, and as the cow bell struck, I came down with full force banging the pot on Teddy's already battered head. He screamed out in agony. Yet the next time, the cow bell struck, I smashed the pot over his crushed cranium once more, this time the handle broke off. My friends were cracking up and this was the first time that everything came into focus.

Teddy had begun to convulse. His body was shaking, and he said in his froggy tone, "I have seizures. I might have a seizure. Please *help me!*"

His speech was now fading. That's when I suddenly snapped back to reality. *What had I done? How would I fix this?*

Teddy squeamishly blurted out, "I need ice for my head! Ice for my head!"

In my first and only act of a little compassion, I ran and grabbed him a bag of ice. This was a tiny gesture compared to the vile, inhumane act I had just committed. I watched as he squirmed on the couch and squealed, "I'm gonna die! I'm gonna die! I will have a seizure and I will die!"

For a slight second, I sat frozen and bewildered. Was he really going to die? What had I done? Would I spend the rest of my days in jail? Was my stereo worth this abominable beating I had administered?

My Bully Complex had taken me way too far. This was far worse than anything I had ever done.

Suddenly, my friends realized the severity of the situation. The three of us huddled in the corner. We talked about our options. For a fleeting moment, I had actually contemplated killing the Toad Boy and ending this reprehensible situation in a morbid manner. For a brief moment a depraved thought surfaced in the back of my inebriated mind: were there any swamps in the area, where we could dump his body? Or was there was a field where we could bury him? I was thinking of obscure places and even more ominous thoughts. My mind was clearly twisted and had me thinking I was some kind of a mob boss. These thoughts raced across my demented, inebriated mind, but I quickly snapped back to reality, as I realized how ridiculous they were.

I am not a killer and I would never kill anyone.

My friends had worrisome looks on their faces, but not quite what had come over my now ghostly white visage. After all, I was terrified, as I was the one who had administered this nefarious beating. I would be the one to take the fall and suffer the consequences. I would be the one that would be locked up in jail. My friends surely couldn't be as worried as I was. They didn't realize the substantial severity of the perilous situation we had found ourselves in. They could have been accessories to a crime, but they were just naive to it at the time. I also think they were a bit scared of what might happen, and they just wanted to get away from there as fast as possible. Suddenly, they both snapped back to reality as they smiled in unison and said, "He'll live."

Their brief reassurance made me feel somewhat like everything would be OK. I smiled and began laughing. "Yeah, he'll be fine! Hey, let's go to Denny's!"

I gathered up the evidence, the pot and its broken handle. I hid the damning evidence in my closet.

The whole time, Teddy squealed for help stating that he needed to go to the hospital. He looked like he was in excruciating pain as blood was dripping off of his battered and beaten head. I just wanted to get out of there as fast as possible. The three of us hastily hurried out the door, scampered down the steps and actually darted to Denny's.

I know, it's beyond deplorable. I should have stayed, called 9-1-1 or taken Teddy directly to the hospital myself, but I didn't. I was cold-blooded and completely heartless as I left him there writhing in agony.

The three of us sat at Denny's and ate Grand Slams as if nothing had happened. We all laughed about it. My friends giggled every time the pot was brought up.

My mind was still somewhat of a blur. I could picture my arm swinging down with full force and smashing the pot over Teddy's battered head. I could hear the pot crack across his cranium and the handle snap off. On the outside I was laughing with my friends, but inside I was a ball of nerves. I was nervous that he might actually be severely injured, and I'd be headed to jail. I was also shell-shocked that I had taken my bullying to a point where I could have killed a person. I certainly wasn't trying to, nor would I ever intentionally. The bullying had gone too far, and I wasn't man enough to say that to my friends. I should have manned up and admitted that what I did was completely wrong. Instead, I sat there spineless and laughed along with them. I was a despicable human being at that time in my life. I was a cold, hard, callous coward.

When I returned from the heartless trip to Denny's, I expected to see Teddy sprawled out on the couch in the same position I had left him. However, there was no sign of him. There were signs of a struggle as the living room looked as if a hurricane had swept through. The living room floor was sprinkled with empty beer cans and CD's. I inspected the couch where Teddy had been recuperating from the vicious beating that I had administered and there were traces of his blood. In fact, there were traces of blood on the carpet and on the walls. I ferociously began scrubbing all of the evidence away. Teddy's blood was literally on my hands and I needed to wash all of this away.

My friends had left to go back home already, leaving me as the only one to clean this wretched crime scene. I was now the only witness to the gruesome aftermath. I was overwhelmed with guilt and I genuinely felt bad for what I had done, but there was no taking it back.

I had to deal with my actions, and I am still dealing with them to this very day.

Looking back, this was the hardest story for me to write. The memories this story dredged up make me feel physically ill. I have shed tears over my gruesome actions. Going back to that place was sickening. It's literally nauseating every time I read this over. I can't believe that person was me. It's as if I was imagining a made-up person and story, only none of this is made up. It was real, IT WAS ALL VERY REAL. That reality would all soon come crashing into my existence as I would be almost thrown out of school for my actions.

The next few days around the apartment were eerily quiet. Carmine had not been awake for the chaos that had ensued. He had passed out from being too drunk. I showed him the pot and told him the story. His eyes lit up and he began laughing. This actually put me at ease for the first time since I had administered the beating of Teddy.

You see, Teddy was alive, and I thought I was in the clear. He did have battle wounds all over his body. He had a nasty black eye and red welts on his arms from the belt whipping I had administered. Carmine's laughter had emboldened me once again and made me feel superior. I again felt that Teddy the Toad Boy had it coming to him. After all, he DID harass girls at the party! Then he had the audacity to touch my stereo! He unplugged it for God's sake. It was a mortal sin in my eyes, and he needed to pay for it. He certainly did pay for it – dearly.

For the next few days, I would come home and grab the broken pot out of my closet. Now I was proud of it. As disgusting as it was, I would take the pot out and I would gawk at it, as if it was a first place trophy in a bullying competition. The broken pot was now my most prized possession. The pot was now a symbol of my power, superiority, and full-fledged Bully Complex. in my mind, that pot had established my dominance in this apartment, and over the whole entire university. I was the alpha male of this domain and of this entire school! I was indeed a king. Nobody could fuck with me now. I was the almighty and all-powerful Super Bully and I reigned supreme!

Everything seemed like it was going to be fine. I thought the days would pass and we would all forget about the hateful incident. Except one day I came home from class and the pot was gone.

I was mortified. How did my trophy disappear? At first I was frazzled, and frantically looked for it everywhere. There was nobody home, so I tried to go into Teddy and DICKLIPS' room, but their door was locked. I knew Teddy must have gotten his grubby little paws on that pot. He must have been planning my demise. A wave of fear and realization suddenly came over me. I would have to go into defense mode. Deny! Deny! Deny!

Later on, when Carmine came home, I asked if he had seen my prized possession, the evidence of the detestable beating, but he said he had not. He was surprised to hear it was missing.

He said, "Uh oh, I hope you-know-who doesn't have it!"

I knew at that very moment that Teddy undoubtedly had the pot, and I was going to have to fight against his accusations. I could not and would not be thrown out of school. Despite the fact that I knew I was wrong, I knew I couldn't give an admission of guilt. I would most certainly be thrown out of school, my parent's house, and possibly face jail time. This could ruin my entire future. I would not let it.

I gained Carmine's reassurance that he would not rat me out. He vowed to say he was asleep and had heard nothing. DICKLIPS was a wild card. I knew he would not take my side, but he might also be too scared to take Teddy's side. I could only hope that he would also say he was asleep and hadn't hear anything. After all, DICKLIPS had not come out of his room that night. In fact, I had joked to my friends that he was probably hiding under the blankets in fear as I beat the shit out of his roommate. Truth be told, he probably did hide in fear. I was scary and uncontrollable at the moment I snapped. I most likely would have given him a beating too, had he tried to intervene. There was no stopping me when I was in that rage-filled element. I used to go to a dark place, one where you wouldn't recognize me. I would snap, black out and see red as I effectively became a deranged madman.

Sure enough, the next day I received a phone call from Dean Franks. I was already on his radar due to the noise complaints from our neighbors. He said that I had to come see him that afternoon or I would be asked to move out of the apartment immediately. I chuckled at him and brashly said, "OK, boss you got it!"

I wasn't taking this seriously at all. What proof did they have? A broken pot? Teddy's account of what happened? I knew what I was going to say, and I was prepared for Dean Franks and his line of questioning.

I went to the office that afternoon brimming with confidence. I thought there was no way he could pin this on me with the insufficient evidence he had. I entered the office and sat down. Dean Franks was a rotund African American man with a beard. He was very tall, probably a tad taller than my own 6'3" frame. Some people were intimidated by him, but I wasn't. I walked in and sized him up. In my mind, I could kick his ass which emboldened me even more.

"What's up Dean?" I said confidently.

"Is there anything you'd like to tell me, Anthony?" Dean Franks asked.

"Not sure what you're referring to, boss. Could you just tell me why I'm here?" I asked.

"Well, your roommate, Teddy, came by to see me. He told me what happened," deadpanned the no-nonsense Dean.

"OK, not sure what you're referring to," I said snidely.

"Well, it seems there was some type of altercation between the two of you," he said sternly as he glared at me. His steely eyes pierced me as if he was going to read my soul.

"Yeah, there was," I responded.

"So, you're admitting to it?"

"Admitting to what exactly?" I retorted.

"That you brutalized and beat your roommate to the point that he nearly needed to be hospitalized!"

I smirked and said, "No, that's not what happened."

"Well, tell me what happened then?"

"We did get into an altercation, but I was defending myself. Teddy swung at me first," I reasoned.

"OK, even if Teddy had swung at you first, the beating you administered was excessive in nature. You whipped him with a belt and smacked a pot over his head!" The Dean was visibly agitated now.

It took everything inside me not to laugh. I composed myself and I deadpanned, looking him directly in the eye and stated, "No, that's not what happened. Teddy swung at me, and yes, I struck him back. But once he went down, I stopped."

The Dean was clearly disconcerted with my flippant answer, and he came at me with a relentless barrage of questioning, "So how did Teddy get that black eye? Where did the welts on his arms come from? Why does it look like he just came out of a twelve round boxing match? Why do you have no bruises or evidence of his alleged attack? Why is he afraid to be in the apartment in your presence?"

I calmly replied, "Look Dean, I don't know what you're going on about. That is not the truth. I told you the truth and that's that!"

"OK Anthony, you can go for now, but you had your chance to come clean. Just be fair warned that this University with my backing is coming after you for what you've done. I believe that you DID administer this heinous beating and you will pay for this. This is not over by a long shot. We will be in touch very soon!"

I left that office not the slightest bit rattled. From everything I had learned from my youth, there was no definitive evidence against me. It was one man's word against another. Carmine had been passed out, which meant there were only two witnesses present—my lifelong friends from Kenilworth, and they would never give me up. Dickletz was in his bedroom for the entirety of the night, therefore he remained a wild card. He could have only heard the reprehensible beating and not seen my grotesque actions that night. I was unsure whether Dickletz would give his account of what he heard or not. Even if he had, I was confident that not seeing the actual events would be in my favor. I was convinced that I would fight this, and I would win. My actions may have been wrong, but I didn't feel like I should lose my entire life because of what I had done.

The weekend was fast approaching, and the big question was: To party or not to party? After this whole debacle, was I actually ready to throw another rager? Would it be wise to do so? Before I even had a chance to fully contemplate my weekend plans, the doorbell rang, and it was Dean Franks. It was rather early for his surprise visit, so I assumed it was something serious. He said that I had to let him up as he had something to serve me. He wobbled his way up the stairs and came into our living room.

He had a domineering look in his eye as he glared at me. He sat only an arm's length away from me and for the first time, the Dean's imposing figure had me slightly intimidated. He said, "Anthony, this paper is being given to you to officially inform you that you are hereby ordered to vacate this apartment, effective immediately, due to your possible actions."

Possible? POSSIBLE? What the hell? I glanced at him with a snicker, "Yeah, OK."

"Anthony this is no joke. You must pack up and be out of this apartment by this evening or you could face expulsion."

This news, as serious as it was, ignited something inside of me. I quickly went from being intimidated to feeling emboldened and furious. I was seeing red again and now the Dean had become the object of my burning inner fire. I looked him dead in the eye and said, "Who's gonna make me?"

"Now Anthony, there's no reason for it to go this way," reasoned the Dean.

"How about you make me leave, big man? How about I toss you down those stairs, too!" I threatened.

"*Too?* So, you're admitting that you assaulted Teddy? I will take that as an admission of guilt," he barked at me.

What had I just said aloud? Why did I say "too"? I quickly retracted my statement, "I did not throw him down the stairs, but make no mistake, I will definitely toss your big ass down them!"

Dean Franks looked like he wanted to choke me, as he roared, "You don't want any of this. I will break y—" he stopped himself. He took a deep breath and continued calmly, "That is it! I am leaving, and so are you. If you are not out of this apartment by the time stated in this letter, you will be removed by the proper authorities. Think about your future, if you even have one to think of." With that, the Dean stormed down the stairs and seemed to pound every step as if he were stomping my face in.

After he left, I sat on my bed and stared at the letter for an hour. Carmine came in and asked, "What's wrong?"

I told him about the letter and the confrontation with Dean Franks.

Carmine looked concerned and said, "Look man, you're my friend and I don't want to see you get kicked out of school. Maybe it's best if you listened to the letter and took off."

Carmine had given me a moment of clarity. If I stayed, I would probably be dragged out by the police and immediately thrown out of school. I had no choice. In my dismay, I solemnly packed up my things and left the tainted apartment. I was reassigned to a dorm room on campus, so I headed there feeling lost, angry, and downtrodden.

I had been living the good life in a fun apartment across the street from the beach, but now I was a recluse in a smelly, small dorm room without any personality. Being an upperclassman, this was a complete and utter embarrassment to be sequestered back in a dormitory. Not many, if any, upperclassmen lived on campus and I was livid with the situation. Although I was reluctant to live there, I had no choice in the matter.

The next week I received another letter informing me that I would have to go to university trial for what I had done to Teddy.

I was ready to fight this and put it behind me. *Let's get it on!* I thought.

The trial came quickly as the school wanted to resolve this issue and the black eye it would leave on its reputation if the truth came out. However, I never intended on telling the real truth. I was ready to carry my lie all the way to the grave. (We know that's not the case, because I am coming clean now. Hopefully, I can find forgiveness for my heinous actions.) No way was I going to let Teddy the Toad Boy and Dean Franks the Dough Boy kick me out of school.

I prepared myself for the trial. I frantically wrote down a bunch of questions. The first set of questions was for Teddy. I wanted to show that he was drunk and being a nuisance at the party. The second set of questions were for my friends from home as they were requested to attend the trial. My friends were the only true witnesses to the "fight" between Teddy and me. I needed all of us to be on the same page. They came down to my disgusting, dirty dorm room where I proceeded to grill them with questions. I channeled all my mind power as I pretended to be a leering lawyer with incendiary intentions. I barraged my friends with an inquisition, and we went over our story hundreds of times. We had to be a united front. I knew we could stand tall together and beat this.

The day of the trial, I was excessively confident. My friends and I had practiced until our stories matched exactly. I wasn't the least bit nervous, but my friend Larry was visibly shaken. Every time I questioned him, his answers changed, and he was making me slightly nervous. I asked him how many people were at the party and he exclaimed, "Fifty!" I would yell "No! I keep telling you to say fifteen! There were only fifteen people at the party!" Even though he had me freaking out a little, I had to try and calm him down. So, I told him not to worry that I would be right next to him during the trial.

The three of us entered, ready to give our accounts and get this over with. However, we were blindsided. One of the school officials said that we were to be separated and questioned one at a time. I was outraged and steadfastly stated that this was unfair, but to no avail. I could see Larry's face as he was visibly apprehensive. Now I was a nervous wreck. This was not good. My friends were summoned in first, one by one.

What was probably half an hour seemed an eternity to me. As each minute passed, my heart sank further into my stomach. I felt like I was in quicksand and I was sinking. A fitting metaphor as my life seemed to be sinking at that moment. I was overcome with an overwhelming feeling that this was going to go terribly wrong.

Finally, the time came, and I was called in. This was not an ordinary trial as this was after all, a school trial. Trying the case were three school administrators, including Dean Franks. Two other high-ranking officers joined him. There were also two honor students with perfect records who were there toobserve and give their opinions to the school officials.

Before the questioning began, I announced that I had something to say. The head of the trial said to proceed. I said, "I feel it is appropriate to remove Dean Franks as one of the presiding judges of this case. Dean Franks has been trying to intimidate me and has been harassing me since I have been accused of these actions. He has come to my home and made me feel threatened. Therefore, I demand that he be removed immediately."

The head Dean stared at me stone-faced and replied, "Yes, we understand that you have had some run-ins with Dean Franks. However, it is the ruling of this court that we take the word of our Dean, who has been part of this University for over twenty years, than that of a student. We acknowledge there has been some friction between yourself and Dean Franks. We also feel that the behavior you have displayed with the Dean is extremely inappropriate and will not be tolerated. Furthermore, your actions with the Dean have displayed your propensity for violence and demonstrated that you are capable of the actions in question."

I was astounded and began to rebut, "But the Dean—"

"There is nothing left to be said on this matter. Dean Franks will preside over this trial with or without your unneeded approval!"

With that, the trial continued with Dean Franks the Dough Boy staring a hole through my stained soul the entire way. I was grilled for about fifteen minutes and asked my side of what had occurred. I repeated what I had told Dean Franks weeks prior, that I had been defending myself. That Teddy had swung at me and I struck him several times until he fell, at which point I relented.

Then they dropped a bomb. They said they were bringing out a key piece of evidence. Suddenly in the middle of the table, appeared the broken pot. The weapon I had wielded and used to wail on Teddy's skull. I had not seen my prized pot since it had mysteriously vanished from my closet. Suddenly, there it was, in all of its glory staring back at me, and engulfing me with all those feelings I had when I had committed the vile act. Surely, they brought the pot out to evoke an emotional response out of me. I was taken aback at first and I'm sure they noticed, but I quickly collected myself and I became stoic. I stared straight ahead and I blocked out the pot as best as I could.

"Mr. Lospinoso, do you know what this is? Have you ever seen this before? Have you ever used this as a weapon? Did you strike Teddy with this object on the night in question?" The inquisition came at me fast and furiously.

I put on my best poker face and stared coldheartedly like I was made of stone, "I have no idea what that is."

Then the trial took another unexpected turn. Teddy was brought out and this was the first time I had seen him since the incident. I could see the fear and shame in his eyes. His black eye had faded but he still looked beaten and run down. They asked if he knew what this object was. I thought to myself, *of course he knows that's the pot I bashed against his skull.* I still somehow had sick thoughts running through my mind. I thought, *if he tells everyone here, I'll beat him with it once more!* This was an immeasurably insensitive and insane thought. How could I possibly think about beating this already broken-down victim once more? My callous, cold-hearted nature had reached a new low. I truly had no boundaries at that despicable point in my life.

Teddy appeared jittery as he responded, "Yes I know exactly what that is." He started out looking shaky, but firmed up for a moment, as he glared at the pot and then over at me. Teddy was convincing when he spoke about the pot. Then he was asked to recount the tale of that cruel and savage night. He spoke slowly and tears began to stream down his face as he told the story. Again, this was done purposely to see my reaction. I could not look at him for too long, as I was finally starting to feel remorse. The more I leered at his demoralized existence, the worse I felt. I had emasculated him and made him feel immensely inferior. As his words came out, part of me wanted to admit my guilt, but I knew I could not. When he was finally finished, I was relieved.

The questioning continued and the examination was fierce, especially after Teddy spoke, but I never folded. I denied everything except fighting in self-defense. I left the trial feeling fairly confident. There were wild cards involved as neither Carmine nor Dickletz were summoned to the trial. Since they were not brought out as witnesses, I thought I was in the clear as far as they were concerned. I'm sure they had been questioned, but I will never really know.

Carmine and I went our separate ways in the aftermath of my reprehensible actions. He was still living with Teddy and Dickletz after I got thrown out of the apartment. I went on with my outlandish partying ways and stayed close with my fraternity brothers. I am unsure exactly why Carmine and I drifted apart. Maybe he didn't agree with what I had done after all or maybe he felt sadness for what I had done to Teddy. In any event, we didn't speak until years later. When we reconnected later in life, I never brought up the Teddy situation, and neither did he.

In my mind, I was getting off because I was innocent until proven guilty. To me, there was not nearly enough information to prove that I was guilty. *That pot didn't prove anything,* I thought. They didn't have enough evidence to ruin me. Even though I thought all of this in my disturbed mind, my heart knew I was wrong and that I was undoubtedly guilty.

My friends and I met privately after the trial. We all said the same disturbing thing, that it was hard to hold back the laughter when the pot was introduced as evidence. They had done the same to my friends as they had to me. Presented the pot and hoped for a reaction. But I will never know what my friends' reactions were, nor did it matter at that point. The trial was over, and my fate was in the hands of three Deans, one whom I had threatened and who probably hated my guts.

It took a while before I heard anything. I had become somewhat despondent at this point. My dorm room was a train wreck of a mess. I hadn't bothered to clean it at all. You could barely walk in it. I went out every night and smoked weed, drank, and partied myself into an oblivious blob. It was as if I had no feelings. I didn't care about anything. This went on for about a month or so, until I received a letter from the University at my dorm.

I frantically ripped it open. This is what I had been waiting for, the verdict of my trial. This is the first thing I nervously read: "This court's findings were such that we believe the incidents in question more likely happened than not, therefore the following sanctions must be abided by. Any infractions against these sanctions will result in the immediate expulsion from school."

My initial thought was, *WHAT BULLSHIT!* But there was nothing to do to change the verdict. I could tell this was set in stone and I had to abide by the sanctions. They included a ban from campus along with all campus related activities for a full semester. This meant no more school newspaper or school radio. I wasn't even allowed on campus at all, except to attend classes and to go to the library. Needless to say, I was banned from any interaction with Teddy. These weren't the worst punishments; at least I had avoided being kicked out of school. For that I was relieved. Sure, the sanctions sucked, but I would deal with them for a semester.

I remember after receiving the sanctions that I was irate with Teddy for ratting me out. I wanted to demolish him once more. I know I should have felt remorse and that I should have been thankful that these were the only punishments that I had received, but I was far from a rational person at this time in my life. I searched for Teddy on campus for months as I looked for another opportunity to pummel him. As idiotic as my intentions were, I was planning on beating him again if I saw him. I didn't think of the recourse this would have and how it could have affected my life. I searched everywhere for him, but he was like a ghost.

Then one day, after months of fervently searching, I finally saw Teddy theToad Boy, or what appeared to be him as he was far in the distance. I couldn't believe my eyes, as I slammed my car door and thought this had to be a mirage. I walked a little brisker in case my eyes or the distance had deceived me. As I gained ground, it became clear that it was indeed him. He began moving swiftly as he now knew I was in blazing pursuit. My brisk walk turned into a rage-filled sprint. I ran full force at the pawn that I had once used as my personal punching bag. He saw me sprinting and he began fleeing as fast as he possibly could. He ran into the Student Center and I gave chase. I was well behind him as he was much more fleet a foot than I. When I barreled into the Student Center, I searched everywhere but he was nowhere to be found.

I was better off for it. Had I caught Teddy that day, there is no telling how much more damage I may have inflicted upon him. There also would have been the permanent damage I would have done to myself and my future. I surely would have been thrown out of school. To say this was all for the better is an understatement.

Don't ask me what I was thinking, as I was clearly not thinking at all. Thinking back, this was probably one of the dumber things I have done in my life and I've done some pretty dumb things. Who knows what would have happened had I caught him that day? I am extremely happy that I didn't. I deserved every punishment and sanction levied against me and probably more. I can't tell you how sorry I am for this conspicuous chapter in my life.

I am sorry to Jerry Dickletz. Jerry was truly a great guy and didn't deserve the way I treated him. He certainly didn't deserve to hear the heinous beating I gave Teddy. I am sorry to Dean Franks. Dean Franks was a good man. He was just trying to do his job, and some snot-nosed kid gave him a hard time. He was only trying to do the right thing and put an end to my vicious bullying. I was out of line and the Dean definitely didn't deserve anything that I did to him. I am sorry to Monmouth University. I hope the University does not disown me, as I am finally apologizing for the egregious mistakes I made while attending this wonderful school. I am owning up to my actions and attempting to make amends. I hope the University sees that and sees the good in what I have written. I probably didn't deserve to graduate from Monmouth U, as my actions were not befitting of a college graduate.

Most of all, I am sorry to Teddy, who I had terrorized past the point of human decency. What I did was absolutely barbaric and undeserved. I can only seek forgiveness for my ill-advised and disgraceful acts. This is what happens when bullying gets out of control. I almost took a human life and I will forever regret it.

Don't let yourself ever be in my position. Recognize the situation you're in and if the bullying is going too far. If someone's life is in imminent danger, then things have unquestionably gone too far. The bullying in my case had gone way, way too far. Teddy did the completely correct thing by alerting an authority figure. If you are being bullied, especially in an extreme situation where the bullying is going too far, you also need to alert an authority figure. Who knows how far I would have gone had an authority figure not intervened?

After I received my punishment for Teddy, I began to lighten up a little on my antics. I mean, I had to. I was one step from getting kicked out of school and my parents disowning me. I had to lay low for a while and stay under the radar.

I had also seemingly taken all my rage out on Teddy. All in one night, I had exorcised my own demons. I pulverized this poor boy and I was initially proud of my repulsive actions. After weeks and months of introspect, I realized that I had demoralized Teddy, just as I had been demoralized and beaten as a young kid. Only this was infinitely worse. I was a young kid when I used to get beaten, probably between the ages of eight and ten-years-old. Teddy was almost a grown man. Probably twenty-one years of age when I humiliated him. I stripped away his pride and I took his manhood.

The bullying that had taken place between Teddy and I is absolutely unforgivable. However, it was the life lesson that I sorely needed at that point in my life. The bullying went way too far as I had committed a vile act. This was the turning point in my life I sorely needed. The realizations that came to me after the incident with Teddy finally pushed me onto the path of redemption.

There have been times when the bullying goes too far and does actually result in someone's death. Many incidents have been documented where hazing and bullying have caused an innocent victim's death. Other incidents have involved terrorized victims coming back for revenge and killing their perpetrators. Suicides have also been reported due to bullying that went too far. All of these tragedies are beyond tragic and unnecessary. I know my own abhorrent actions were certainly beyond the realm of human decency.

This is how serious the bullying epidemic has become. We need to realize that bullying can actually result in death. We must take this seriously and begin to change the bullying culture that has been cultivated over the years. Without change and education, these tragedies will continue to occur. We will continue to lose innocent lives that don't deserve the demise of their fatal fate.

All of the thinking I did for the months after I had beaten Teddy and the punishments I had received for my actions, changed me for the better. I realized that I had gone too far and that my actions were detestable. I had let my Bully Complex take over my existence. I let all the popularity go to my head. That Homecoming King coronation was the worst thing to ever happen to me. My ego exploded after that. Look where it landed me. I had almost beaten someone to death. That crown definitely shattered at that moment as I didn't deserve any accolades. My actions were definitely unfit for a king.

The Teddy situation started to clarify my thoughts. I finally started to see that being a bully may not be the best way to live my life. I wanted to make some serious changes in my ways, but that was going to take time and some more learning. I was subsequently starting to see that I needed to relinquish this bastardly Bully Complex.

College turned out to be one giant learning lesson. Besides the bullying lessons, I was exposed to different cultures and different kinds of people. I was becoming exponentially more open-minded. I was remarkably closed-minded and ignorant before. I was now judging less and accepting of more people. I still had a large amount of work to do on myself to get to where I am now. But at least I was making progress. I was finally moving forward and moving on from the rotten person I was. Change was on the horizon and that was certainly necessary for me.

SECTION FOUR

EARLY MANHOOD:

REALIZATION AND CHANGE

PART 1: SEEKING FORGIVENESS

*"I felt like a superhero when I bullied others,
when in reality, I was the ultimate villain."*

The Teddy incident haunts me to this very day. I honestly had buried the incident into the deep recesses of my mind. For so long, I pretended as if it had never occurred. I pretended that I never contemplated killing another person. Even though it was a fast and fleeting thought, the loathsome thought was still in my mind. For a brief moment, I had thought about taking another person's life. For that moment, I was the most grotesque piece of garbage that one could imagine. I was the scum that you can't quite scrub clean from the bathtub. I was the ugly, smelly, brown stain on the bottom of your toilet boil. Yes, I know, all quite revolting, but indeed true.

Burying this deep into my cavernous mind was the only way that I could possibly deal with what I had done. Even though I buried and suppressed the memory, the truth is, I have had a lesion on my soul ever since. A black, scathing mark on my contaminated soul. There isn't anybody or anything that could wipe away this putrid stench from my wretched soul. This is something that I can never escape, and I know it. As much as I ran from it. As much as I tried to bury it. What I did to Teddy is real and I must face it like a man.

When I think of what I did on that dreadfully fateful night, it haunts me now. I am physically repulsed by myself. I am constantly tormented by my never-ending guilt. How could I have left him lying there in a pool of his own blood? He was crying and screaming out for help, but I laughed it off with my friends. What kind of person was I? Could I ever be forgiven for my deplorable actions?

I still picture Teddy on the couch, clutching the bag of ice that I had given him, squeezing it tightly to his bruised and battered skull. A bag of ice? That's the only sign of compassion that I could possibly muster up? Did my Bully Complex really have that much control over me? I had to look "cool" and show no signs of remorse. Why did I think the cool thing was leaving him there to suffer and scream out in pain? Why did I have this never-ending need to be cool and why couldn't I have changed at that very moment? Would my friends have laughed at me? Maybe, but probably not. If they had laughed, were they true friends? I was the leader and they most likely would have followed my lead.

I did have influence over others, but it was in no way a positive influence. I thought that bullying made me powerful, but that couldn't be farther from the truth. The influence I had on people emanated from being a natural born leader. I did have many leadership skills, but I just used them in the wrong ways. Instead of leading others to do good, I always had malicious intentions on my devious mind. These leadership skills gave me power and influence. I had the capability to influence others and to foster a change. I had the power to help others. I had the power to stop bullying. But I didn't. I was a complete coward.

If I could go back, I would tell my friends that what I did was wrong. I would have told them that we needed to help Teddy and I would have rushed him to the hospital. Immediately afterwards, I would have begged for his forgiveness, which I certainly did not deserve. I would have ceased my bullying at that very moment. I would have gone back and apologized to every single person that I had ever victimized. I don't think there are any words which can truly encapsulate all of my feelings, but here is what I would have said. Here is what I have to say now. Here is a letter to anyone I have hurt, tortured, tormented, degraded, or plainly just bullied:

To everyone I have ever victimized:

You know who you are. Some of you may not want to admit that I bullied you because maybe you are embarrassed. Some of you may have done what I have and buried what I did to you into the dark recesses of your minds. But we both know all the cruel acts I engaged in all those years ago.

You remember, don't you? I singled you out and I turned the school against you. I made you feel inferior. I beat you, I name-called you, and I shamed you relentlessly. I never gave you a chance. I just made you feel as if you were an outcast and didn't belong. All you wanted was to be accepted and I would never allow it.

Remember now? Are those feelings bubbling to the surface? I bet all of your hateful feelings towards me are rushing back and that's OK. I want you to remember. Remember me as a monster and picture me torturing you. Do you have the picture in your mind now?

OK, perfect. Now picture me shaking your hand as my scowl turns into a smile. Picture me smiling, as I suddenly become warm and inviting, as I never was before. Picture me, with a look of acceptance, that you may have once desired. Now finally, picture me looking you dead in your eyes and saying, "I am so sorry." No, sorry is not enough. Sorry will never be enough.

If I could take away the pain I have caused you, I would. If I could go back and change what I did, I would. If I could cleanse your soul of all my viciousness, I would. I would erase your memories. I would change your life for the better, if I altered it in any negative way whatsoever. I would give you back that innocence that I stole from you.

All I can say is that I'm truly sorry from the bottom of my heart and soul. Although I don't deserve your forgiveness, it's all that I can ask for.

Let's meet up. Have coffee. Have lunch. Have a beer. All the things I would have detested doing with you back then, because I was just too "cool." Even though you have all moved on, made lives for yourselves and probably left me far behind in your rearview mirror; I know there has to be a part of you that still needs to heal. Surely, everything I put you through has left some type of negative impression on your life. I know I still have scars from when I was bullied. Certainly, you must too. Let me try and do what I can to heal those wounds. Let me show you that you are accepted, and you always should have been. Let me show you that I value who you are now, even though I never did back then. Let me show you that people can truly change. Let me show you what a different person I am today. Let me show you how I've grown and matured. Let me show you that I truly care about your well-being now, even though it's so hard to believe, because I never cared in our hurtful past. Please let me show you. Give me a chance, the chance that I never gave you.

Sincerely,

The Reformed Bully

Anthony Lospinoso

Maybe, just maybe, if only a few of you can forgive me, then I can start to move on from all the damage I have dished out. Maybe I can move forward and finally feel free of all that has scarred my now blackened soul. I have been tormented with guilt for so long and all I want is your forgiveness. Forgiveness for all the casualties I left in the wake of my destructive Bully Complex.

That letter, although heartfelt and a tremendous show of my change, will never be enough for Teddy. Teddy deserves his own letter. Hell, he deserves more than a letter. Teddy deserves a plea directly from my repairing heart.

Teddy if I saw you now and we spoke—that's if you would allow me to speak to you—here's what I would say:

"I don't deserve your forgiveness. What I did to you is beyond distasteful, disgusting, and deplorable. Nobody should ever have to endure what I did to you. You did absolutely nothing wrong. I was an awful person at the time and that's an understatement. Who nearly beats someone to death for touching their stereo? Who leaves them screaming and writhing in agony? I left you there and went to Denny's for God's sake. That has to be the most detestable part of what I did to you. I left you there without so much as a second thought. I was stuffing my loathsome face with a grand slam breakfast while you were laying there covered in blood. I never thought that I should go back immediately and do something to rectify my repugnant and vile actions. In fact, my only thought was to possibly kill you and bury you somewhere. How can I even ask for you to forgive this?

All I can say to you Teddy, is that I am no longer even close to this monster that I once was. I have taken personal inventory in the aftermath of my nefarious actions and I have made positive changes within, especially when concerning my Bully Complex. I am a changed man now, as I would never even think of hurting someone this badly. I can't even fathom that I used to be this monstrosity. Sure, I was a bully, but our encounter was beyond anything I had ever done.

Teddy, I want you to know that after what I did to you, it changed me. I know I went too far. I also know I can never change what happened. I just hope you were able to move on. I hope you stopped living in fear. I hope you are successful now. I hope I did nothing to derail your promising life after my actions. I remember you were an extremely intelligent young man and if I had to guess, I'd say you are wildly successful now. I can only hope that's the case. Then maybe I can live with myself a little easier. Maybe, just maybe I could move on somewhat. I mean, I'll never totally move on. Like I said, what happened can never be changed or taken back. The events of that dreadful night will never be undone. There is no forgiving what I inflicted upon you. I can only hope that we can somehow move on together. I can only hope you will allow me to seek forgiveness and move forward with you. If only you'll give me that chance. Teddy, would you possibly give me that chance? This, Teddy, is my plea to you."

Sometimes forgiveness is all we can ask for. The wounds we inflict may never truly heal. The wounds and scars I have left in my wake will never truly be healed. They certainly will never be erased. My own wounds and scars will continue to haunt me. I have to admit that the pain of what I did to others far outweighs what was once inflicted upon me. I am well over how I was bullied, beaten, and harassed. I was a young boy and those scars have faded over time. I think, however, that everything that happened during high school will never fade. Memories we accrue from high school usually stay with us more prominently than those from grammar school. All the bullying I inflicted, that's never going away. They say that we make memories to last a lifetime during high school, well I surely made many negative memories for countless amounts of kids. I gave them enough detrimental memories to last ten lifetimes. That time in high school is when kids are really developing into young adults. I stunted that development and I destroyed many experiences. I rewrote that chapter for countless victims, and it can never be re-written. High school is a time when kids start to develop into the people that we are to become. I may have altered that. I may have changed people and I may have changed them in negative ways. I could have affected their growth as a person, and I could have altered their future. They may not be the person they were intended to be. I will never truly know how I affected my victims. I can only seek forgiveness now.

Thinking about this agonizes me. I could have and most likely altered the lives of my countless victims. I may have stunted their development. I shaped their world in a way that was unintended for them. Would they be able to recover? Are they OK now, or did I do permanent damage? I don't know, but I can only hope that everyone turned out fine. But in my mind, I know that cannot be totally true. Surely, I affected one or two people in such a negative way, that their life changed in some way. I pushed them into an unintended direction. Maybe they are shy now, perhaps introverted. Maybe they lost their voice somewhere along the path of my torment. I may have shattered their confidence to where they have trouble functioning normally in everyday society. This is hard to live with. It's as if an anchor is weighing me down to the bottom of the ocean. There I am gasping for air, as I think about the people that I may have permanently scarred. I stare straight into a never-ending abyss and my soul is swallowed whole. I am drowning in my emotions. I gasp for air as I cannot even bear to think that I may have altered the trajectory of their lives in a negative fashion.

I want to reach out to these victims. I want to make things right or as right as I can make them. I want to change their lives for the better. Surely, I cannot make up for the last twenty-something years, but I certainly can assist in making the next twenty years better. I mean, it's the least I could do.

If only I had thought about my actions back then. I mean *really* thought about what I was doing. Most of you who are bullying don't even realize exactly what you are doing and the consequences it can have. You are hurting people so badly that it may even change their lives. I mean, I certainly didn't think about it. I never thought about how I might be affecting the people that I was victimizing, that what I was doing could possibly damage them in a way that they could never come back from. I am thankful that none of the people I inflicted damage upon committed a fatal act. Whether it was coming at me and trying to kill me or even worse, killing themselves. Many victims who are bullied are prone to suicide. Next time you go to bully someone, think about that. Is tormenting someone really worth them losing their life over?

If only I had thought about what I was doing. Then I certainly would have stopped, or at least I hope that's the case. What's sad is, there are many adults that used to bully, and they STILL don't think that they did anything wrong. They are probably still bullies. At least I realize the error of my ways. At least I understand the scope and the magnitude of the damage that I have caused. At least I realize that I was flagrantly wrong, and I know that I need to make amends. If you were a bully in your past and don't realize you were wrong, then I ask, what is wrong with you? Bullying is never right in any situation. Please try to realize the wrongs you have incurred! Join me and try to make amends to our victims.

I had no cares for the countless victims that I was bullying. I was the epitome of selfish. If you were a bully in your past or currently still are, then you too are selfish. If I can get you to start thinking about your actions, maybe we can start to combat this nasty epidemic of bullying. I know it's hard, because I was there. If you're still in high school, you're still a kid. Yes, a blossoming young adult, but still a kid. I know it's easy to follow the group. That's how my bullying began. I started following the group. I wanted to be a part of it and not the brunt of it. Therefore, I followed others when they mocked and victimized other poor souls. I wanted to be a part of the popular group so badly, that I sold my own soul to do so. I had no care or consideration for anybody else's feelings but my own.

Eventually, I became the conductor of a Bully Train. The train was on a never-ending track and there were no stops. I would lead a pack of predators who were hungry to torment and cause havoc on others. I wanted to be the King and have a flock of followers. I wanted to reign over all those who I perceived to be weaker than me. I wanted to be the leader, but not the type that people admired or looked up to. I wanted to be feared and that's where my mindset went off the rails. I did have leadership skills, but I used them in all the wrong ways. I was in no way a king. A true king would never act like I did. My delusional crown was shattered over and over, as I failed as a person. My faults were glaring and everything I did to hurt others was royally wrong.

As I've alluded to, I could have used my leadership in other ways. But I was a coward and I did not. It's easy to follow the leader and pick on the minority. It's easier to follow than it is to lead. Being a leader who speaks out can be difficult. I know it's hard to do the reverse and stick up for the ones being bullied. I know it's hard to go against the group. But we all have to be brave. We can all make a difference. *You can be the difference.* Buck the trend and be a leader who actually matters. Be a leader and stand up to those who practice bullying. Be a leader and help those who need your help the most. Don't be a coward like I was and join the majority. This world needs leaders who can help to make a change. Cowards will never make this world a better place.

That's why I'm here, to give you strength. To show you there is indeed another way. I am here to fight for those who cannot fight for themselves. You can join me and fight for them as well. Nobody deserves to be bullied. You can change their lives by helping them. You can make this world a better place. Stick up for the victims; you won't be sorry! I guarantee you that at some point, that person will pay you back tenfold. You could save somebody's life. Stand up and do the right thing. Be the difference!

We should all be on a quest to make a difference. When everybody works together to make a difference, things begin to change. We can change the bullying epidemic together and reverse its course. Making a difference, making a change, and making things right; this is what I want you to gain from reading this.

I know I have gained so much emotionally and mentally from writing this. I don't even think I could begin to explain how all of this has changed me even more so than I already had. I've gained even more perspective on life. Over the last several years I have realized the error of my ways and I have been engrossed in my thoughts. Constant consternation has brought everything into focus. Writing all of it down brings everything into focus even further. I never thought about the actual damage I may have caused people. Yes, I have remorse for what I have done. I am extremely remorseful for all the bullying executed by my vicious hands. But to sit here and really think that I may have done permanent damage, that puts me in a melancholic state. I am numb and almost lifeless. Paralyzed by my own recollections, I cannot escape my boundless Bully Complex.

I picture myself extending my hand out to all of my victims and shaking all your hands. I even reach for an embrace. Surely, my attempt to reconcile will be refuted by some of you. Surely, I can never fully make amends for my actions. I am now an open book, literally. If any of you want to reach out to me, please do. If any of you want my direct apology, I will gladly give it to you. You deserve that and much, much more!

For those of you who are being victimized, you can reach out to me as well. I will try to help as many of you as possible. I believe this has now become my purpose. It's crazy to think that the Super Bully is now the one who believes he can be a savior. Well, I am not a savior, I am just a man. But now I am a man with a purpose.

For so long, I drifted through life without a purpose. I will tell you that we all have a purpose. If you are a bully, then you are losing your focus and you may lose your way in life. Your purpose will be harder to attain. I know from personal experience. Your mind will be clouded as you are focused on the wrong things. You bully people for being different and you judge others. All this does is hold you back. Your Bully Complex will not get you far in life.

If you are being bullied, I will tell you that you will also lose focus. Don't let what is happening to you bring you down. Don't let the bullying affect you and change your course in life. I know that's easier said than done. Do something about what is happening to you. Do not allow this to derail your life. You must speak out and try to seek help. I promise you that at some point, you will find your purpose. Don't think that being bullied is your purpose. This is nobody's purpose. Think about your talents and your skills. Don't let negative thoughts creep in. You are a much better person than the one bullying you. You will be successful. Stay focused on your goals. If you stay grounded and focused, your purpose will find you.

My Bully Complex has always gotten in the way of achieving my goals. I lost focus and I'm glad to have found my way. I was so focused on hurting others which led me down a bad path. I stopped focusing on the good in life and I gravitated towards being evil. I simply became a bad person. Finding my way was tough, as there are countless components that made up my Bully Complex. This complex not only affected my focus in life but has also affected my relationships. I have met so many contrasting people and my Bully Complex made me react differently to different types of people. Let me explain.

Over the years, I've noticed that when meeting someone new who had a strong personality like myself, I tended to dislike them at first. In fact, I usually hated them. Anyone that seemed to stand on their own and would not be subservient to my bullying ways, I would despise. It was as if I had no use for them if I couldn't make them my victim. This is how atrocious my bullying nature was. This was part of my Bully

Complex. If you weren't going to allow yourself to be bullied by me, then I explicitly had no use for you.

What's crazy is that some of these people later became really good friends of mine. I couldn't even understand why I never liked them in the first place and often times even hated them. I couldn't make sense of it. I didn't realize it at the time, that it was my Bully Complex that prevented me from liking such people at first. Mostly, I think it was because we were like-minded. I couldn't see past their perceived confidence to see that we were exactly like. We were bullies fueled with false confidence. As soon as I recognized this, I would eventually team up with them and indeed, we went on to bully other people together. We were like two bully magnets coming together as we engaged in two on one bullying. As someone who routinely received the outnumbering treatment when he was younger, I surely didn't care if the numbers were in my favor. Heck, I enjoyed the two on one torture that we could execute on others. It was intoxicating because twice the power was so much better. Who was going to fight back against two people? The hallmark of a bully is someone who wants to suppress others and keep them down. Hold them down, rendering them helpless where they won't be able to fight back. Because the truth is, most bullies are scared, and if you fight back, they most likely will back down. I was this type of bully. I only bullied people because I found out that I could and because I was tired of being the victim. I found the kids who wouldn't fight back, and I victimized them. I made them pawns in my sick game and I was never satisfied. My bullying was over the top. My actions were malicious, brutal, and mean. My bullying was incessant, and I never knew when to stop. My hunger for tormenting others was insatiable, prompting me to become the ultimate bully.

This was another part of my Bully Complex. Many bullies have been victimized themselves, which sometimes turns them towards abusing others. I was bullied during virtually my entire grammar school existence as you have read. The first chance I had to break away and bully others, I grabbed it. Many bullies are cultivated the same way that I was. They start as the victims, but they in turn begin to bully others. We, the victims, often justify our actions by saying we have endured abuse. The fact that we were bullied makes us feel that we can victimize others. Let me tell you that bullying is never justifiable. In any situation bullying is never right.

My Bully Complex dictated how I acted, and my actions were mostly vile. My Bully Complex not only propelled me to hurt others, but it drove me to exhibit rebellious behavior. I was an exhaustive nuisance to adults, especially my teachers. I also had issues with people of authority like police officers and Deans. I do not condone any of my outlandish and uncalled for actions that I have executed. The way I treated teachers and authority figures is highly disrespectful and should not be replicated. I am ashamed and remorseful for the way I had acted out. I needed a way to vent and let out my pent-up aggression. My Bully Complex led me to believe that I should torture and harass teachers, when this was totally the wrong solution. My wrongful actions even led me to berate a police officer. There was a time when I had no respect for police officers, however, now I have nothing but the utmost respect for them. Kids nowadays need to be taught to respect police officers as most of them are fighting for good. My issues with authority also led me to physically threaten a Dean. Dean Franks was doing the right thing and I was completely out of line. I wish I had handled myself better and I apologize to all the adults I victimized as well. Kids should never act out against their educators or authority figures like I had. I have displayed that bullying is not only applicable to kids, but to adults as well.

My bullying was never confined or contained. I always acted with malicious intent and the fact that nobody stopped me only stimulated my Bully Complex. The fact that nobody intervened made me feel that I could continue what I was doing and there would not be consequences. This became a vicious cycle for me. Nobody was aware of what I was doing, but we can all start to become aware of our kids now. It is imperative that we start to pay attention to how our kids are being treated and more importantly, how they treat others. If we can recognize the problem early, we can stop the vicious cycle of bullying. Awareness and education about bullying can teach us all that these practices are extremely wrong. Bullying somebody else is never the answer, no matter what you have endured or gone through in life. There are countless ways to find help out there. I am trying to show there are other answers out there. Bullying is NEVER the answer!

All those years I was the one being bullied seemed to disappear because my Bully Complex morphed me into the Super Bully. I felt like a superhero when I bullied others, when in reality, I was the ultimate villain. Bullies can never be heroes. There is some perception out there that bullies are winners. This couldn't be farther from the truth. A bully always thinks they are better than you. This couldn't be farther from the truth. Some think being a bully will get you farther than someone else in life because they are stronger. This couldn't be farther from the truth. Even if a bully found financial success, that's all they will ever have. Unless they seek forgiveness, they will never be spiritually successful. Money does not make you a good person. Financial success will not set you free from what you have done. Your bullying ways will always follow you. Your soul will forever be tarnished unless you seek absolution.

Bullies can never be the winners. The truth is bullies never win! The ones being victimized will eventually emerge as the winners. They will be the ones who go on to do great things. I know in my heart that many who have been victimized will be the ones who are running this country and making changes for the better. They will be successful and will ultimately be the winners. Don't be a bully, be a winner instead! If you are feeling down on yourself, I want to tell you that you are a winner and a champion in my eyes!

You should all strive to be winners. You need to realize who you are and what you're capable of. You need to choose your own destiny and make success a reality. You need to find your own success because success may not find you. Break free from the bullying and pave your own path. You were not meant to be held down and have your inner spirit suppressed. You are stronger than the ones inflicting pain upon you. Rise above the bullying and display your inner strength.

The truth is that bullies are in fact weaker. They are weak-minded and that's what drives them to bully. Deep down inside, they want to keep others down to try and make themselves look good. People who constantly put others down are just afraid of your success. They are not happy with themselves and therefore, want you to be a failure. People who are not happy for you and put you down, instead of lifting you up, need to be removed from your life. They are driven by their insecurities. My own bullying ways stemmed from immense insecurities. I was one of the most insecure kids you could have ever met. Some of my insecurities stemmed from my past where I was beaten and victimized by bullies. But most of my insecurities stemmed from the newfound popularity I found in high school, which I never wanted to relinquish under any circumstances. I was insecure because I never wanted to go back to being the victim ever again.

Bullies want to show off in front of the "cool" kids, in order to feel accepted by them. This is a vicious cycle that we need to break. This mentality is not healthy. If kids would be more accepting in general, we wouldn't have these problems. I understand there are going to be cliques and different groups, but no one should be made to feel like an outcast. Every kid deserves to have friends. Every kid has their own talents and capabilities. If you let yourself shine and let your talents speak for themselves, the bullies will get the picture. The perpetrators will realize that you have worth and will hopefully leave you alone. Your self-confidence is empowering. I urge you to get out there and display whatever skills you have. Whether it's singing, dancing, sports, music, or writing like me. Whatever it is, we all have talents. We all need to shine sometime and be a star. You are all shining stars and you need to harness that from within yourselves.

I know firsthand that bullies are in fact weak-minded. I only bullied people to fit in and to be popular. I only bullied to make others laugh and to seem "cool." The truth is that bullies are the farthest from being "cool." In fact, "cool" is what you make of it. We live in new times. If you are considered a nerd, I say embrace it. There are many people in this world that find nerds sexy. If being in the school band, color guard, or math club is your thing, who's to say that's not "cool?" Whatever your hobbies are, they are "cool" to you and that's what counts. I don't care what people say about you and how they may perceive your hobbies.

To me, you are a star. In my eyes, you are a Rock Star. Be the Rock Star that I know you are and stand by who you are!

I thought that bullying made me "cool" when in fact, this couldn't be farther from the truth. I'm "cool" now without having to mistreat people. I am a much more awesome person now than when I was a bully—actually, than I ever was. Bullying will never be perceived as "cool." I thought I was so cool, but I wasn't. Embracing who you are and showing your true inner self, now that's awe-inspiring. Showing off for your friends is the farthest thing from cool. If your friends think that it's cool when you bully others, then they are not good friends. That's not what friendship should be based on.

Wherever I go now, I feel like the coolest guy in the room and that comes from self-confidence. It doesn't stem from my Bully Complex any longer. I am just a confident person now. When I was a bully, I was immensely insecure and lacked self-esteem. Insecurities and self-esteem are what fuels bullies and their shameful actions. All of these insecurities and esteem issues made me feel like I didn't have any sense of true confidence. That's why I bullied, because of my own insecurities, not because I was confident. Nothing is cooler than someone who carries themselves with real confidence. Bullying gives you manufactured confidence and it's just false assurance. My newfound inner tenacity has carried me and now I am finally finding success. Thankfully, I did not let my insecurities continue to run my life, or I would not be where I am today.

We all have weaknesses and it took some eye-opening experiences to show me just how many I had. But those weaknesses made me stronger. Our weaknesses eventually become our greatest strengths. We can all reflect back to our mistakes and try not to make them again. That's what's great about being human, we can all try and better ourselves. Recognize your weaknesses and try to turn them into positives. Once I realized that I had a complex, I started working on shedding that complex.

My Bully Complex had become my entire existence. I let it consume me and let it dictate who I was. The complex made me attempt to establish myself as an alpha male. I tried to push others down and display that I was the stronger person. I always had to establish dominance over my victims. I thought this truly made me a strong person, but it is so far from the truth. The truth is that I was in fact a weaker person for pushing others down. Now that I have shed my Bully Complex, I can tell you firsthand that you don't need to push others down to establish dominance. I am an alpha male now which comes from the true confidence I have developed and knowing who I am as a person. Bullying does not make me an alpha male. You don't need to suppress others in order to be strong. Being strong and being confident comes from within yourself. Your inner-strength and intestinal fortitude is where you will find your true tenacity. Being a real alpha is finally getting me places in life and I am finally winning.

We should all be lifting each other up and not putting others down. I now surround myself with people that want me to do better. I support others now in a way that I never would have in my past. I don't have any room in my life for so called "Haters." Keep your hate to yourself! Pushing each other to be better and staying positive will push you farther in life. Hate will only drag you down.

From personal experience, I also know that bullies don't get farther in life and they don't always win. My life was a train wreck until I let go of all my hatred towards others. My Bully Complex only served to hold me down in life. Now, of course there were other factors, but I honestly didn't have a clear mind until I changed. I couldn't see the world for what it was through my prejudiced eyes. My bullying ways altered my mind and not in a good way. I put others down and I thought it elevated me to a certain level, when in fact, it did not. In truth, bullying just made me lower than anyone that I ever victimized. I thought I was better than them and that couldn't be farther from the truth. These were all good people and they did not deserve what I had forced upon them. Now that I am living a bully free life, I am finally becoming a winner.

PART 2: REPAIRING RELATIONSHIPS

*"I had a sudden epiphany because all in one moment,
I thought of all the countless people I had hurt in my life."*

Despite the fact that I have shed my Bully Complex, I still make some questionable decisions. I know I need to think about the things I say aloud or post on social media a little bit more, because of the reputation of my unsavory past. The way I used to act makes people that haven't seen me or talked to me in years, look at me in a dubious manner. In the past, I put many people down for many different reasons, but I often focused on race and religion. Because I came into contact with very few Jewish people, they were often the focus of my belittlements. Because of my past reputation of being a Jew hater, I really need to watch what I say more than the average person. You see, I know I have changed, but not everybody knows that. I have hundreds of friends and acquaintances in life and especially on social media that I haven't seen in many years. How would they know all the changes that I have made? How would they know that I am a different person from the one that they knew? How would they know I had finally shed my hateful and repulsive Bully Complex? They would not know that I joke around now and that I'm highly sarcastic, especially about race and religion. I still do make jokes about race and religion sometimes, even though I probably shouldn't. I make more Asian jokes than anybody you know. It's what I call the "Howard Stern rule." Howard Stern would justify racial remarks because he said that he was Jewish, and he made fun of Jews first and foremost. Therefore, by that concept if I make fun of Asians especially Koreans, I can mock other races. I can make fun of myself first, therefore I can mock others.

My point is that I still occasionally will drop a Jew joke or two. On Facebook one year, I posted "Happy Jew Year" on January first. I'll often say,"Shabaat Shalom Hey!" in a joking manner when clinking a drink with friends. As I've alluded to, there are people that don't know that I've changed tremendously. Due to my "Anti-Semitic" and insensitive posts, I had one of my friends unfriend me on Facebook. She was an old friend of mine from back in college. Ironically, she was the same girl who I coerced into having a party. You remember, the one where I had taken over her house, back when I was in college and she was a senior in high school. Her name was J.G. and she was extremely upset with my insensitive post. She told one of my best friends that was the reason she unfriended me. My friend relayed the message to me. J.G. said that I was insensitive to Jewish people and she wanted nothing to do with me. I told our mutual friend, good, because I am only joking and if she can't handle that, then I don't want to be Facebook friends with her.

I hadn't thought out the failed friendship at the time. J.G. and I hadn't spoken since college and how was she to know that I had changed? She saw my Jewish posts and was offended immediately. I didn't realize it then, but now I understand. I now know that I need to be more cognizant of what comes out of my mouth and especially what I post on social media. I have recently apologized to her and I hope we can repair our friendship going forward.

J.G. only knew me as a bully and she never saw my life changes. She only knew me as someone who hated Jewish people. She never witnessed the bonds and friendships that I eventually forged with countless Jewish people. I also made my first black friend and eventually many more. Later on in life, I even made a gay friend. But I have never broadcasted any of this, as I never felt there was a reason to let people know. Why would I just start telling people that I had forged these new friendships? It would seem disingenuous, and all of these were authentic alliances. I am proud to say that all of these friendships and encounters have changed me for the better. I am extremely happy to have a forum to express that now.

I was honestly slightly racist, but I feel like I was also shaped by my circumstances. I lived in a sheltered town and I was never exposed to different types of people and cultures. I also had some racist people in my life making impressions on me when I a young boy, like my older cousin. That certainly didn't help matters as I grew up thinking this was normal. My other issue was, I didn't understand other cultures as I was not exposed to them. I think there is a simple solution to helping kids who grow up in small towns and have a closed-minded mentality like I had. We need to educate our kids about other cultures, religions, and races of people. We need to teach them that everyone is equal and should be treated fairly. I believe that is happening more and more nowadays. I know kids are exposed to many different groups of people, but I certainly was not. I grew up in a different time and people weren't as accepting. I grew up in a mostly Italian-American culture and I did not learn about other races. I was only exposed to the Catholic Church and I had little knowledge of other religions. Had I understood what Jewish people were at a younger age, perhaps I would not have alienated them to the degree in which I did.

Judging people applies to almost any situation in life. I continued to judge people into my twenties and even early thirties. It just changed from a school or campus environment to my workplace and life situations. I have been a bartender for the better part of twenty years. Now, in that time, you accrue knowledge of many different races and types of people. Anyway, after a while you begin to generalize. Every time you see a black person, you expect a bad tip. Every time young twenty-one-year-old customers come in, you expect to be annoyed. Every time parents come in with children, you expect them to try and get money off of their bill.

This is all what I like to refer to as pre-judging. I judged people before I ever even knew them. I assumed what they would do, how they would act, without giving them a chance to prove me otherwise. I was always quick to judge. Judging in any form just isn't right, especially pre-judging which is something that is a persistent problem. Nobody has the right to judge others. So, if you find yourself judging others, it is time to stop and think about what you are doing, because judging of any kind is flat out wrong.

My lack of education made me pre-judge people and then I based my opinion on them according to what color, race, or religion they were associated with. It required actual life experiences to open my eyes and realize that people are just people. Yes, our ethnicity and religious beliefs make us who we are to an extent. But ethnicity, race, or religion doesn't make up your personality. Just because you're Jewish, doesn't mean you're automatically cheap. As a matter of fact, I have met some Jewish people who are extremely generous, and they are the farthest from being cheap that you could ever imagine. The giving nature these people displayed helped me to smash all the stereotypes that I used to adhere to in high school. I now see people for what they are, just people. I have stopped judging people because of their race, religion, or skin color. The fact that I am even friends with Jewish people says a lot about the changes I have made. This really illustrates how far I have come.

Two specific people come to mind when I think of these changes I have made. I started bartending in my early twenties and having continued doing so to this very day. During that time, I've met so many different people from various walks of life. I had a specific Jewish couple that had become my best customers. Their names are Steve and Roberta and they would come in on a regular basis and only during my shifts. They were loyal regulars and became more than that. We grew a special bond over time, and we became true friends. They were also extremely generous people. Besides the charitable tip they would always leave, the couple always went above and beyond to make me feel special. They always gave me a holiday card with extra money, and they invited me into their home. The couple always fed me and whatever friends I would bring as well. They invited me to football and baseball games. I was blown away by their giving nature. This was a far cry from what I had previously thought about Jewish people. All of the stereotypes I had formulated in my mind had become exceptionally untrue. My perceptions were being smashed. This put an end to any lingering doubts or feelings I may have had. I loved these two and it helped me to shed all of my hatred towards Jewish people. Steve had also opened my mind because of something he always said, "It has never been about the color of a man's skin, it is about the content of a man's soul." This particular profound statement borrowed from Martin Luther King Jr. is a mantra that I believe we should all adhere to. People shouldn't be judged by the color of their skin, as what matters is what's on the inside. This may sound cheesy but it's explicitly true. What makes us good people comes from within and nothing on our outside should matter.

Meeting this couple obviously had a profound effect on me and went a long way in changing my hideous and heinous ways. I had made Jewish friends prior, but they made me see a bigger picture. I will never automatically look at a Jewish person and say that person is cheap because that's beyond ridiculous. All of my stereotypes and judgments are just that, totally ridiculous. We have to make stereotypes a thing of the past. This is a new age and it's time to throw out ridiculous past times. Stereotypes are the oldest, most tired thoughts of them all.

Becoming friends with Jewish people, changing my attitude, and altering my prejudices required having actual life experiences. There are some actual facts about my own family, to go along with these experiences, that also helped open my eyes. Sometime after college, my younger brother was doing research on our family. My brother was in high school at the time. He came to discover that our grandfather had a cousin named Guido Lospinoso, who had helped thousands of Jewish people. Guido Lospinoso started as a police officer, then became deputy commissioner, and finally assumed the position of Chief Inspector, in charge of racial relations. He was one of the people in charge of the Jewish affairs in Italy during World War II. Lospinoso was then commissioned to go to Nice, France, where he was supposed to facilitate the roundup of Jews and deliver them to the Germans. However, Lospinoso along with a few others, helped put the Jews into safe houses and hid them in the Maritime Alps. The brave man hid from the Germans and couldn't be found. According to a book written about the time period called, "Hitler's Bureaucrats," Lospinoso used delaying tactics. The book explains, "During this entire period Lospinoso was in Nice, and labored in broad daylight to transfer Jews from the coastal region to abandoned hotels and confiscated private houses in the inland districts. He later claimed ingenuously that he had no idea that the Germans were looking for him, but that can hardly be taken seriously. For Lospinoso, ingenuousness was a sophisticated method for avoiding head-on collisions with those whose intentions were the opposite of his."

My distant relative apparently avoided the German government on purpose, in order to save an estimated 25,000 to 30,000 Jewish people during this time. This is obviously extremely heroic and finding this out hit me like a wrecking ball. I was floored and in disbelief. I almost didn't believe my brother, as I thought this was some contrived way for him to try and make me change. I thought he wanted me to see that my hatred was unfounded and unnecessary. You see, my brother is one of the most politically correct and equality driven people that I have ever met. He often shook his head in displeasure whenever my mouth spewed Jewish hatred, or any other discrimination for that matter. I was already in the midst of my transformation and therefore, I believed him. I took him at his word, and I was proud of this information he profoundly spread into my consciousness. I recently did the research myself, in order to acquire the accurate information, and I have to say that I am even more overwhelmed with pride.

The irony didn't stop there; leave it to my brother to spread even more racial justice my way. Just recently in 2018, my brother took an Ancestry DNA test. The results were shocking. Low and behold my father came out to be 12% Jewish! That means that I am indeed part Jewish as well. Although it is minuscule, I am proud to find out this fact. I am even more proud to say that I don't hate myself. I probably would have self-loathed if I found this out twenty years ago.

The hate that I amassed due to my Bully Complex and sheltered adolescence, finally faded. I am especially proud and happy that I embraced all people and all cultures. I realize that I was completely wrong for how I acted towards Jewish people and I am immensely elated that I am now accepting of them. The most gratifying part of my transformation is that I am now accepting of all people.

Even though I am now accepting of all people, that obviously wasn't always the case. Although I am now accepting, that doesn't mean everybody accepts me. There have been times when I am judged by others and not accepted. I have never hidden from who I am and there are certain aspects of my life that others may perceive to be juvenile. They may look at some of the things I like and scoff at me for liking them. One of those things I love is professional wrestling. I know it is somewhat juvenile, but I just love it for its entertainment value. The only time I may try to hide the fact that I watch wrestling is possibly in the presence of a gorgeous woman. I mean, I don't think professional wrestling is exactly a turn on. But here it is for all of the world to see. Anyway, many people judge others for watching this form of entertainment. They laugh and mock us. They say that it's fake and it's garbage television. That's fine with me, as you can call it fake! Any true wrestling fan will tell you that "it's not fake, it's scripted!" I love it and I am not shy to say so. Yes, in any situation, from now on!

My love for WWE runs deep and I am constantly reading about the wrestlers. I want to know about them personally, because I am intrigued. One wrestler in particular, I came to find, had encountered bullying during her youth. She was made to feel like an outcast due to the fact that she liked wrestling. That Superstar is known as Ember Moon. Moon is living out a lifelong dream but making that dream come true was far from easy for her. During an interview with the New York Post, Moon has said, "When I was younger and I was a kid, I was bullied maliciously for being different, for liking video games, for liking wrestling." Moon continued, "Just no one wanted to be around that. And so, I became like the reclusive person that kind of hung in the shadows and that became me, like I was kind of, for years, afraid to be me and ashamed of being me because so many people disliked me."

There are many kids that are in the same boat as Moon. Countless kids feel like they can't be themselves, because they are fearful that others will mock them. Kids hide their passions because they are targeted for the things they like. If kids like math or science, they are often labeled a nerd. If a young boy likes the color pink, he would surely be called names. The same can be reversed for a young girl who likes playing football. We could carry on and on with examples. The point is, nobody should be made to feel ashamed for what they like. We live in new times, where almost anything should be accepted. I say almost, because we wouldn't accept anything that is illegal, immoral, or where someone could be potentially hurt.

Moon is an amazing example because she overcame what others said and realized her dream. She continued to tell the Post, "And just coming full circle, it's like now everything that people doubted me on or like bullied me for — and that's the word for it — I just kind of proved to be stronger than that. I proved to be better than that. I kept standing up and kept proving that I am not going to follow the group. I am going to follow my own path and it's OK to do that."

Ember Moon is a shining example of what I want to see out of more bullied kids. You need to stand on your own. You don't need to follow the crowd. You CAN carve your own path in life. You shouldn't hide your passions and likes. Be who you are, always be proud of yourself, and everything will fall into place.

Moon was bullied for liking wrestling. Even though I was never bullied for liking wrestling, I was certainly judged. I have been judged in other ways as well. I have continually discussed my love of heavy metal and hard rock. I have never had the typical "metal look" or what people usually associate with the metal scene. I never had long hair, a beard, any piercings, or tattoos. I've never had any characteristics that are often associated with being a metal head. In fact, I was almost always clean cut my whole life. I usually had short, neat hair and for the most part I was clean shaven. When people don't know me, they are usually surprised by my musical tastes. I am more often than not the clean cut metal head and I stand out in the metal community. My musical tastes often get questioned and my "mettle" is tested, when I am often the most metal guy in the room.

Just as I am judged and questioned for liking metal, I used to do the same to the "Dusty" people. I judged the way they looked as they are often not well kept. Many metal heads have long hair and some form of facial hair. I used to mock them and tell my friends that "Dusty needs a shower!" I have realized that I was once again attacking my own. These were all people that have many musical parallels to me. In fact, I would even have offended one of my musical idols. I have mentioned that my all-time favorite band is Metallica. The guitarist of Metallica, Kirk Hammett, was once bullied himself. He has said that he and his friends were picked on for looking different from others. This is a famous musician of one of the biggest bands in the world. Hammett is a guitar and heavy metal legend. To think that he was bullied at one time really puts things into perspective, that truly anyone can be bullied. I am not certain why Hammett was being targeted, but presumably it was for having long hair and wearing leather jackets. I'm sure he was called a burnout just as I was. I don't know why I poked fun of anybody in the metal community as we should all stick together. As a matter of fact, many of the artists say that we are a family. In a way, this is true. When I was younger, metal wasn't accepted like it is now, as we were all viewed as outcasts. My friends and I were often mocked and made to feel like outsiders for listening to the type of music we listened to. Hence, when we all came together in a heavy metal environment, it was an uplifting experience. Concerts had an irrefutable feeling that permeated amongst the crowd. It was as if we were all part of a family; one giant, demented metal family. Therefore, the fact that I would deride these people is absolutely ludicrous. Many of them were just like me. They also judged me, as they questioned if this pretty boy could possibly be a real metal head. I am not saying that when they judged me back it was the right thing to do. I am saying that nobody should judge anybody else. Nobody has the right to judge.

Judging is a huge part of bullying and can be in itself considered as bullying. I don't like country music, but I don't judge people that listen to it. Everyone is their own person and we should all have different opinions. That's what gives us individuality. When you judge people, that brings down our society as a whole. Try and have an open mind. Just because somebody likes something, don't pigeon-hole them. For instance, just because somebody has long hair and a beard, don't assume they like heavy metal music. The same goes for people like me, who are clean cut and like metal, don't question me and call me out because I don't look like a metal head. I am not doing it to be "cool!" This is really what I like. Don't ever judge me!

Judging was a huge part of my youth. All I did was judge people for how they dressed, how they talked, how they looked, their religion, their race, and it just goes on and on. I never realized how immature, ignorant, distasteful, and just flat out wrong I was for judging.

I let my judging ways dictate my life. Now that I have let go of those petty judgments, I am much better off for it. I used to dislike Indian people for no reason at all and I loathed the fact that there was an Indian restaurant in my hometown. Being racist and closed-minded made me miss out on some life experiences for a long time. I have to tell you that I recently tried Indian food and I find it to be delicious. Seriously, that food is bangin'! I have been missing out all these years, because I couldn't get past my racial ignorance. I let my prejudices blind me so much, that I couldn't see clearly. I can now tell you that I find Indian women to be extremely beautiful as well.

I am extremely happy to be in a different place and I am now open minded. I will never judge somebody without giving them a chance to show me who they truly are. I will also never judge different types of cultures in general, as I am now ready to embrace them and learn what I can about them. I am especially ready to try their food.

When I was younger, I judged other kids for things they couldn't help. I didn't realize it at the time, but that's certainly no excuse. That just makes my bullying worse that I taunted them for things that couldn't be changed. I picked on kids for having non-brand name clothing, when they were poverty-stricken and couldn't help it. I picked on kids for having foreign accents who were from another country, when all they wanted was to make a peaceful life for themselves in this country. I picked on kids for facial features like having bucked teeth or extreme acne, when these kids were certainly already insecure about these issues. I was extremely obnoxious, to the point that I even mocked little people and kids with deformities. I made life a living hell for these kids and I regret it all. I want to tell all of you that I am immensely sorry. I am so sorry for making you feel like you don't belong. We all have a place in this world. The fact that I took that away from you is horrendous.

Nobody is to blame for the vile ways I had acted. However, my high school best friend, Patrick, certainly had a lot to do with it. I followed his lead. I watched as he mocked other kids and I watched as those kids wilted. He victimized other kids and I enjoyed watching it. I was tired of being bullied myself, but this was no excuse. I followed his dreadful lead when I had a choice to do otherwise.

I am not the only one who followed when I was younger. Many kids followed me once I began terrorizing others. I had a group of fellow like-minded bullies who followed my every move. They bullied anyone I chose to bully. They followed me into the darkness, and nobody ever looked back.

The Super Bully always led others into group bullying behaviors. If only I would have led my followers to do something good. If only I could have been a stronger leader, a leader who would entice others to do good instead of evil. If only I would have led my followers to believe that bullying wasn't the way. To be truthful, I don't think they would have followed that lead, because I wasn't the only bully. I wasn't on an island when it came to bullying. There were many, many other bullies abound. Maybe they weren't as big of a bully as I was, as not many were, but they were bullies, nonetheless. Surely, those who followed me may have found a new tyrant to follow. I'll never know because I never tried. I wish I would have tried.

What I am trying to tell you is that you can try. If you have a powerful voice. If you have a big personality and you are a leader in your school, then use your influence and try to facilitate change. Don't use your power to bully! Harness your power for good and try to help those in need. I know sometimes it seems easier just to join the crowd and become the bully. But you need to realize that you can make a change if you try! Let the bullies know that someone like you is watching. Make it known that you will do something to try and stop their degrading and abusive actions!

My leadership skills were rarely used in a positive manner when I was in high school. Yes, at one point, I was the editor of the high school newspaper and the literary magazine. Besides my few shining moments, I used my leadership skills against those I perceived to be weaker or not on my level of the social pyramid, even though that couldn't have been farther from the truth. The ones I hurt, were better than me. I was the weak one. Everybody should be treated as equals and should respect each other as such.

My major problem was that I cared too much about what others thought about me. I wanted to look "cool" by bullying and oppressing others. I wanted to make people laugh. I was consumed with being popular. All I ever wanted was to be popular and to feel accepted. Once I was in that position, I never wanted to relinquish it. Popularity was a drug to me, and I was insanely addicted. Most kids just want to feel accepted and fit in with the group. I had an insatiable need to be a part of the popular group.

Nowadays, I don't care what anybody thinks about me. Honestly for the most part, I am carefree, and I rarely get embarrassed. I am silly and often times outright goofy, without thinking or caring who sees me acting as such. I'll dance around like a fool, make funny faces, or talk in silly voices without a care. It doesn't matter if I'm in public or who's watching, as I have no shame in my game. Surely, in situations where I need to be professional, I act as such. But in my everyday life, I am just me without a filter. I am always the realest guy in the room. If you don't like me, then so be it. I am who I am. I don't put on a facade or wear a mask in order to show you something I am not. I will never compromise who I am ever again. If you liked me as a bully, you may not like me now and I am fine with that.

Believe it or not, there are some who definitely did like me as a bully. They loved watching me belittle others. They were entertained by my dastardly deeds. These people were not good people and I aligned myself with far too many of them. I am now living in a bully free world. I have broken away from my pack of bullies and I have never felt freer.

Speaking of past bullies, I bet you're wondering what happened to my best friend Patrick. After high school, we drifted apart. I was changing slowly, and he was still the same old person. After high school, the way we had acted was no longer cool. Sure, I still bullied to a degree, but not at the consistent level that I had in high school and college. College was a mixed bag as far as my Bully Complex was concerned. I had started out somewhat shy and kept to myself. I was too intimidated to bully others in the beginning. However, once I gained popularity at my University, I went right back to what I knew best. After the Teddy incident, I did end up changing. Part of those changes would be to cut Patrick out of my life, if I was to move forward.

My insecurities fueled my bullying, especially in high school. I had been so beaten down and left with little to no self-esteem prior, that I wanted to inflict that feeling onto others. Somehow, I thought it made me feel better about myself. In truth, I was hiding and masking who I really was. I was afraid to be myself as I had been ridiculed for being myself my whole life. Most of my confidence in high school stemmed from bullying, making it all a facade.

I wish I had realized the damage I was inflicting. I recently spoke to a girl that I attended high school with named Jessie. She is a very pretty lady at this point in her life. In high school, however, she may not have been perceived that way. I am friends with Jessie now, but I wouldn't say we were friendly in high school. We were acquaintances, but that's about it. In any event, she told me that she would never go back to high school now if given the chance. Jessie said she would never want to relive those years, as she was frequently bullied and harassed by the older girls in school. By looking at her now, you would never have guessed this; it's quite stunning that she was treated this way. I never knew about her pain back then. It just goes to show that indeed anybody can be a victim of bullying.

I gained a lot of perspective from talking to her, as I think back and reflect on my past. Besides my bullying episodes, I actually had a tremendous high school experience. My popularity propelled me into a place that not everyone gets to experience. It really made me think. Here's this pretty woman as I know her to be now. However, back in high school, she was considered not pretty and certainly not popular. I realized that I had ruined many high school experiences for people just like her. There are many people that would not want to go back and relive their high school experience, all because of me. This is a tough pill to swallow. I am immensely remorseful, and I am glad she opened my eyes to all of this. I am exuberant that I was able to change the person I once was. After high school and college, I really made huge strides and began to change greatly.

It was in my mid-twenties that I truly began to change. I began to judge less, and I was also beginning to soften as a person in general. It was a slow process, but I remember a specific incident that helped me turn the corner. One of my best friends was having a party and all of my close friends were there. A couple of them had actually become good friends with Rich, the guy who dated Jaime after me. You know, the guy that had to experience my psycho stares and subsequent maniacal stalking. This was a couple years after all that, when my feelings had cooled substantially, and I was no longer a deranged lunatic. Some of my friends were still worried though, because the last time I had seen Rich, I had that demented episode. The incident where I chewed a plastic Solo cup and there was blood, saliva, and red Solo cup dripping from my fury infused mouth. I assured them, I was fine and not to worry. I was way over Jaime at this point, and I was changing as a person. I had no idea who Rich even was as a person, as I had never even given him a chance.

Then, at the party, I did the unthinkable, I pulled Rich aside to talk. A few people watched with a wary eye, but they were soon eased by the sight of me actually putting my arm around him. I told him how sorry I was and that I was over everything. I told him I was sorry that I treated him with such vitriol and never gave him a chance. I was sorry for being a crazy, outlandish lunatic and I wanted his forgiveness. Rich forgave me pretty easily and said it was all water under the bridge.

From that day on, Rich and I forged a fantastic friendship. This cemented to me even further that I had been doing things the wrong way, and I had been doing them wrong for a long time. Rich was and still is an amazing individual, truly a great guy that I'm proud to call a friend. Rich and I have had countless good times together since that day. Being stubborn and immature blinded me to the fact that he was a cool guy and an even better friend. But previously, I couldn't get past my own ignorance to see it that way. The bully in me could never have given him a fair chance. After all, he was dating my ex-girlfriend who I wanted back. I could not let that slide at the time. I couldn't let my friends see me giving Rich a reprieve. I could have been perceived as being soft and I couldn't have that. I didn't want to be perceived as weak in any way, as I was too much of a "tough guy." My macho bravado would not allow me to be sensitive or compassionate in any kind of way. Looking back, I see how ludicrous this was. If I had been more mature, I could have talked things out with Jaime and with Rich. I would have realized that Jaime wasn't in love with me anymore and that she was with Rich, who was an incredible individual. Maybe I would have forged a friendship with him sooner, but I wasn't mature enough for that.

My macho bravado often led me down the wrong path. My alpha male personality made me homophobic. I ridiculed my own cousin and I am ashamed to say this now. When we were younger, nobody knew if my cousin Joe was indeed gay, but years later, he did divulge his secret to everyone. He did not come out of the closet until later in life. It is said that gay people are in the closet to hide their true feelings. This couldn't have been truer for Joe. He was in his mid to late twenties when he finally came out. He was fearful to come out, and for good reason. Our family is old school Italian and there were many who may not have accepted this. One person could have been his own father, who was a strict old school Italian man. That was probably the hardest for him to reconcile with. Joe probably could have given a damn about the whole family, but his own father, that had to be the toughest to endure.

When Joe came out, my sister and my cousin Rose, who is Joe's sister, met to talk about the situation. They listed members of our entire family and discussed who they thought would and who wouldn't accept the fact that Joe had come out of the closet. The girls didn't make an actual list but more or less went through our family verbally. As they said the names of each family member, most seemed like they would be fine. Then they reached my father and me. My cousin Rose was slightly hesitant at first, especially when it came to me. In my mid-twenties, I was still going through changes and I still wasn't 100%

accepting. However, my sister said that we would be fine with it, especially my father who was clearly more accepting than I was. My father has an amazingly giant heart and he accepts everyone without prejudice, therefore he would be indeed fine. I guess the true question was whether I would accept this. The answer was surprisingly yes, as I had become more accepting at that time in my life. My sister was indeed correct. Ten years earlier, that may not have been the case, however, this was a new time for me. I had grown and was now more accepting than I ever had been. My father had stereotypes and negative judgments engrained in him from a young age, but was able to break away from the inherent racism he was surrounded by. My father was a better man than me in that way. He had been surrounded by hate and racism, but he had friends of color during a time when it was considered even more taboo. My issues lingered as I couldn't see past my own racism and judgements. I obviously could not replicate my father, as my feelings weren't only negative, they were extremely hateful. I was homophobic from an early age and I was somewhat of a gay basher, but interacting with gay men eventually changed my stance. I had interacted with gay men on a social level when I was a bartender. I served them as my patrons and worked alongside several of them as well. I became used to it over time and eventually I came to accept homosexuality. I am straight, and I love women, but to each his own. You do you. If being gay is who you are, then that's cool with me. Don't let anyone change who you are. Don't let the bullies suppress the true person that lies beneath the surface. Stop letting the bullies push you into anonymity and be proud of who you are.

Yes, there was a time when I would not have been accepting of a gay man. I was ignorant and I was a bully. When I was in high school, I would have never associated with a gay man. But years later, I have changed dramatically, and I am now accepting of all those in the LGBTQ community. I have zero problem with any LGBTQ person, and I support the LGBTQ community to the fullest. I think people have a right to identify with any sexual orientation that they wish and any gender they distinguish themselves as. I would never go against those rights.

The LGBTQ community often have it the toughest when it comes to being victimized. They are perceived as being different more times than not. Being different is a recipe for bullying, especially for kids. I understand why so many young people stay in the closet as they fear the repercussions. They will most likely be ridiculed and called names. I have heard firsthand that coming out of the closet is one of the hardest things some of these people will ever have to endure. The LGBTQ community is an ongoing target for bullying and this needs to stop. This is a new world and a new time. Everything and everyone needs to be accepted. We need to accept those that are perceived to be different. That perception of being different needs to be smashed as well. Being gay should just be a normal way of living nowadays. Being a gay person should be accepted more than ever now.

We live in new times and for me, when Joe came out, it was time to move out of an archaic way of thinking. There was undoubtedly some tension with Joe and his father for a while, but that eventually simmered down. Almost twenty years after, Joe's father thawed quite a bit. Unfortunately, during the time of this writing, Joe's father passed away. Prior to his passing, I had seen them in pictures together and I had heard firsthand that they were getting along great. It's a shame that they didn't have more time together. But the fact that they mended a somewhat broken relationship is beyond amazing. It certainly proves that anyone can indeed change. If Joe's father—an old school thinker engrained with hardcore beliefs—can change, we all can change.

The time for change is now. We can all try and change together. We can all try to be more accepting and make this world a better place. We live in a great time that almost everything is accepted. I say almost, because of course there are still ignorant people out there. I don't think we can ever eliminate all of the ignorance, but we can make people more aware and possibly slightly more accepting. The truth is we will never live in a perfect world.

Years after Joe came out, when I was the manager of a restaurant and bar, I hired several gay men. One of them did such a fantastic job, that I gave him a raise. I definitely no longer discriminated. So, if anyone is having doubts about me and my acceptance of the LGBTQ community, this should prove my transformation to be true. I even made friends with a gay man because I have to say, he was one of the funniest people I have ever met. It did not matter that he was gay, he was an extremely funny and likable guy. His name was Jimmy and he made me and many others laugh ceaselessly. He was constantly putting on costumes and his energy was contagious. When Jimmy was fed up at work, he would yell, *"I've had it!"* He said it with such emphasis, that the rest of us followed suit and it became a catchphrase around the restaurant. I can't say that Jimmy was my first gay friend because I had a friend in high school, Billy, who turned out to be gay. Billy, however, did not come out of the closet until years later. I probably would not have been friends with him in high school had he been forthright concerning his sexual orientation. Scratch that, I DEFINITELY would not have been friends with him, because I was closed-minded at the time and admittedly homophobic. Hence, Jimmy was my first gay friend that I truly and knowingly accepted.

I was immature in high school and would have never been friends with a gay man. Now I understand why so many gay people stay in the closet until they are older. Most children are indeed immature and cannot handle when someone is different from what they know. It is about time that kids realize that bullying others because they are different is wrong. I encourage you to be yourself and be proud of that. If you are gay, then be proud of that. If you are reading this and you bully someone because of their sexual orientation, just know what you are doing is completely wrong. Plain and simple, hurling gay and homophobic slurs at people is considered bullying and cannot be tolerated. People in the LGBTQ community are just regular people like anyone else and they have rights. They shouldn't be ridiculed for their sexual orientation.

My friend Billy from high school was probably conflicted about his sexuality at the time. We were pretty close friends, and I had slept at his house a few times. Even though we were good friends, I don't think he would have divulged his big secret to me, even if he had known it at the time. I've always been so obviously straight, as I have always talked about banging hot broads. I was always talking about this broad or that broad and how beautiful women were in general. In fact, this was learned behavior from my father who is also obviously straight. My dad was always talking about broads. My dad and I were constantly jabbering about broads. My dad was always busting me and my friends about not having any girls over at our house. He would always jokingly ask, "Where are the broads?"

For the record, I know many women may have just gotten offended at our use of the word "broads" and I want to acknowledge that we say this in jest. We do not intend this to be offensive in any manner. This is just something said sarcastically, and we do not intend to be distasteful. My father and I have high respect for women, and we are inherently gentlemen at our core. I also use the term "broads" because I love mafia movies and that's how they refer to women. I apologize if any women are offended when reading this.

The focus of this section was not on women though. I had some major homophobic issues when I was younger. I would have never been friends with Billy had he come out of the closet then. Had he come out, he would have ruined my whole precious reputation. My popularity would have crumbled before my eyes. The sordid reputation that I had built from bullying and mistreating others would have vanished. At the time, it meant everything to me. I am glad that I gained perspective over my life and realized that popularity is not really important. It's more important to have good people in your life that you can love and trust. Billy was one of those people and I wish I remained friends with him. I pretty much ousted him from my life after I found out about his sexual orientation when he came out. It was easy to distance myself from him and our friendship, as I was in college. Many people drifted apart during that time. I wasn't mature enough to handle it at the time. My friends weren't mature either as they busted my balls that I had slept at his house in high school. Even though we were older and should have been able to be more accepting, I just couldn't handle the ridicule. Even though nothing had ever happened, I felt shame for having a gay friend and for this I am sorry. Billy is a good guy and he deserves better.

My behavior was deplorable, and I know that now. The LGBTQ community has my highest respect and I will never act like the young jackass that I once was. I was utterly and completely ignorant. Coming out is hard enough as it is. Just look at my friend Billy and my cousin Joe. They may have been afraid to come out as they knew the ridicule they would endure. People like me definitely didn't make it any easier. I'm ashamed of this and I am now hoping to shine a much needed light on the LGBTQ community. Unless you are part of that community, we could never truly understand what they go through. I can sit here and say that it's difficult to come out of the closet, but I'll never truly understand that concept. But what I do know is that they endure endless bullying and it is completely unnecessary. They really need to be accepted once and for all.

I am accepting of all people now but obviously there was a time when I was not accepting. I used derogatory terms and I aimed my ire towards the LGBTQ community far too many times. I used terms that are highly offensive like "fag" and "dyke" without even thinking twice. I used these words and I cursed often. I thought it was so cool but in retrospect, it was the farthest thing from cool. Using derogatory words and cursing is never cool. I often cursed and yelled these offensive slurs at my victims and even at adults.

A major part of my transformation has been to become more accepting of the LGBQT community. I ceased using the offensive slurs, but I felt I needed to do something more to illustrate that I truly had changed. There was one year I attended a Christmas party at Joe's house. Joe had a lot of friends who were part of the LGBTQ community, so there were a lot of them at the party. My presence was a sign of my acceptance. I was in the minority of straight people to attend the party and I had no problem with it. The homophobia that once ran rampant inside of me was now quelled. I am proud to say that I am no longer homophobic. I was smashing down my own ignorant barriers. Everything inside of me was changing for the better.

The bully inside of me was finally beginning to thaw. The bully was becoming human and I couldn't be happier. My Bully Complex was slowly fading away and the feeling was invigorating. There were few times I had felt uplifted from vindicating a damaged relationship, but there was never a time in my past that I felt uplifted in this manner. Making amends first with Rich and then with my cousin Joe were both huge accomplishments, because these were signs that I had compassion and I was seeking to redeem myself. Becoming friends with Rich and attending Joe's Christmas party gave me a new sense of atonement and peace.

Atonement is something that I have been seeking since college. I have been seeking to make penance for all of the dreadful sins I have committed. I don't know if I will ever make penance, but I can seek forgiveness. Forgiveness may be the best remedy for my stained soul at this point anyway. Making all of these remarkable changes in my life is hopefully pushing me towards atonement, penance, and forgiveness.

I am constantly making changes for the better. I am continuously picking apart my sordid past and looking into my soul. All the soul searching is a continuous pursuit to change everything that was evil and wrong in my life. In retrospect, I think my changes may have all started on one specific day. The day of my high school senior class trip. In my mind that was the fateful day that facilitated a necessary change inside of me. When I volunteered to take that handicapped girl, Christine, through the theme park and assist her with all of her needs, my heart was touched forever. This was really the day that I started to become humanized. You remember her, of course?

Years later at my ten-year high school reunion I would certainly be reminded. This was an outstanding event and it was terrific seeing many old and familiar faces. Even though I'm sure there were many at the party that were less than thrilled to see my smug face. There were several people in attendance that I had previously victimized. Even though I was changing, I was still fearful of asking for their forgiveness. I wanted their forgiveness because I was a different person and I had compassion for my actions, but I still couldn't bring myself to do it. I was afraid to get rejected or even worse, have one of my victims want to fight me or something.

I also had reservations because many of my friends were there and all of my high school memories came flooding back. I did not want to be seen apologizing to anyone by the "popular" people at the party. I couldn't have that. I had allowed my Bully Complex to win over once again. Therefore, all I could muster for my victims was a fake "hello" and then we did not speak the remainder of the event. I noticed that many of my victims did not attend the reunion. I am unsure if I am the reason. Maybe they didn't want to remember high school and the unsavory memories I had given them. If that's the case, I feel remorseful that I ripped away attending the event. I shouldn't have been the reason that somebody missed a landmark occasion. This really makes me feel emotional and I want to find contrition. Those people deserved to be there, and I probably did not.

The reunion was quite surreal because, after the initial hellos and catching up, I noticed something. The subgroups that had formed in the room were just like high school. The jocks were together conversing, the other "cool" kids were in a group and the nerds were in their own world as well. It was as if we were all transported back to that time of innocence and we didn't know any better. But we should have, as we were all adults by now. There was no longer any need for the cliques that had formed. We should have all realized the dynamic and inter-mingled with each other. I had yet another chance to change things and be a bridge to band people together. However, I was still not ready to do that. Therefore, the dynamic of the party stayed the same for most, but it would soon change for me.

At one point during the party, one of my old classmates said that Christine was looking for me and wanted to speak to me. I walked over to where she sat in her wheelchair and we began conversing. At first, we had general conversation about where we were in life.

But then Christine with a tear in her eye stared at me and said, "Thank you!"

I said, "For what, Christine?"

"For our senior class trip. I just wanted you to know that you were amazing that day and I truly appreciate how you were with me. You could have paired up with someone who wasn't handicapped, but you gladly went with me. And you helped me eat and you cleaned me up. You lifted me onto the rides. I just, just wanted to say thank you."

At that moment, I was overwhelmed with feelings. Besides the fact that I had originally raised my hand in order to skip the lines, that day had touched me as well. That day changed me in a lot of ways. I knew that I had done a good deed that day, but I had no idea that I had touched her in such a way. Nor had I thought it meant that much to her. She nearly brought me to tears.

I looked her in her eyes and said, "Of course, Christine, I would do it all over again and I would choose you as a partner every time!" With that we embraced, but she had no idea the lessons that I had learned from her. She also had no clue how deeply she affected me going forward. My heart and soul were finally heading in the right direction and she was a giant part of my changes. Christine imparted infinite wisdom and goodness upon me, and I will be forever grateful. So, anybody out there that thinks handicapped people are slow, well they are not. In fact, in some ways they are way smarter than us, because they appreciate the little things that we often take for granted, and for that I thank you Christine!

Thinking about that day at the amusement park makes me realize that I had a genuinely good soul. I had used my soul for positivity and put my destructive nature aside for once. I had an array of feelings that day: euphoria, consideration, compassion, humaneness, tenderness, empathy, and satisfaction. Above all, I felt love. I had love in my heart, and it made me want to wash away all the hate from my tainted soul. I can only wonder why I had never harnessed these feelings before. Why couldn't I have done for others what I had done for Christine? The answer is, I probably could have but I was not nearly strong enough back then. I am happy to say that I am more than capable now. I am finally harnessing all of these feelings and doing something positive for this world.

After the impact Christine had on my psyche, I wanted to do more good for others. One day I was at a bar and I was trying to pick up a few broads, who were there by themselves. I made my way over to their table, when I noticed something disturbing going on just a few tables away from us. There was a local named Jeff there and he was a cool dude that everybody at the bar knew. Jeff was not only a local musician, but he was handicapped, making many people gravitate towards him; because even though he had a disability, he didn't let it hold him back. One of Jeff's legs had been severed but he walked around with one crutch. I was a big fan of Jeff, so when I saw two guys hovering over him and beginning to get loud, it piqued my attention. The two bullies were standing over Jeff and yelling profanities in his face. My original intent to pick up a broad quickly changed, especially when I saw that the two antagonizers were ready to hit Jeff. I darted over as one of them cocked his arm back. Just as the ruffian swung at Jeff, I tackled him onto the ground. His accomplice jumped on my back. My adrenaline was pumping exceptionally hard at that very moment, therefore, nothing was going to stop me. I exploded from the floor and threw the other guy into the wall. I was now in full Beast Mode, as I pinned his arms back and gave him a stiff head butt. Next thing I know, people were cheering me on, and this adrenalized me even more. The other antagonizer was now on his feet and I saw him in my peripheral vision. I grabbed the one guy I had pinned down and I hip tossed him into his partner in crime. They both tumbled to the floor and I pounced on top of them. Someone said, "The cops are here."

I kept them both pinned underneath me until officers came flying into the bar. They grabbed me off of the two perpetrators. The bartender, Jeff, and several other onlookers said that I had protected Jeff. The officers knew both of us, but because of my tainted past, they pulled me to the side in order to inquire more about the situation. After taking statements from everyone at the bar, they knew it was abundantly clear that I was not the antagonizer and I had indeed protected Jeff from these bullies.

One officer looked at me and said, "Be proud. You're a hero!"

With that the whole bar gave me a rousing ovation and a round of applause. My smile was gleaming from ear-to-ear and my soul felt like it was glowing.

Needless to say, Jeff and everybody at that bar bought me a drink that night. But it didn't matter to me, what mattered is that I had helped Jeff. I had aided someone who was handicapped and may not have been able to defend himself. I was proud that night and still am. There were many reasons I felt uplifted. Jeff may have been someone that I could possibly have tormented in my ugly past. This was something that I had done out of instinct, without thinking. This was a new me. A new me that I could finally be proud of. I wanted to do more, but at the time I didn't know what.

All these lessons helped to mold who I am now. Don't get me wrong, there were times later on in life that the bully in me came back out. I was a manager at several jobs and when somebody pissed me off, my Bully Complex would rear its ugly head. But overall, I have buried that person. In fact, that person is so far gone that I almost forgot all the damage I had caused until I dredged up all these painful memories. All the people that I had hurt were a fading memory. I was in my early thirties and I thought all the pain I had caused was well behind me. That is, until another fateful day. If the day in the theme park with Christine was my awakening, this day would be the day that forever changed me, and I have never looked back since.

On this day, I was bartending at a tavern that I had worked at for several years. This one regular, named Mark, would make frequent visits to the bar every week. He was a nice guy, a few years younger than me. We actually went to high school together. His older brother graduated with me and he had been someone that I bullied. He was one of my many targets, who I nicknamed "Sasquatch." That guy hated my guts and I don't blame him. I mean, I branded him with the nickname Sasquatch.

Anyway, I hadn't thought I had any problems with Sasquatch's younger brother, Mark. But he used to come into the bar and stare at me with hostility in his eyes. I just didn't get it. Maybe he hated me because I had been unrelenting when it came to his brother. Maybe his brother told him to come stare at me as an ominous warning that they were going to pummel me. He and his brother, Chad (I shall now refer to him by his real name), were big dudes. Honestly, I did not want to fight them.

One day, I decided to be a man and ask Mark why he leered at me with such contempt. His clear disdain prompted me to go over and ask, "Mark, why are you so angry with me?"

He said, "You really don't know?"

"No, I honestly don't."

"You were an asshole to me in high school."

"I'm sorry Mark, I don't remember. What did I do exactly?"

"You used to come around the corner to my locker and just point at me and laugh. You and your buddies would always just point at me and laugh. It was worse than any nickname you could have given me, because it was humiliating. Other kids would see you and your friends pointing and laughing, and they would join in. They thought it was funny to point and laugh at me as well."

At that very moment, my heart sank, and all the color was flushed from my face. I was genuinely befuddled and bothered by what he had just told me. First of all, because I honestly didn't remember doing that to him. Secondly, because he obviously was reliving the pain at that very moment.

I had a sudden epiphany because all in one moment, I thought of all the countless people I had hurt in my life. I remembered the countless number of kids that I had inflicted pain upon, just as I had Mark. But the only thing was, I didn't even remember bullying Mark. That's what made this incident extraordinarily eye-opening. I thought of all the people I had probably caused suffering with my victimizations and I realized that I couldn't even remember them all. How many people had I antagonized that I didn't even remember? There had to be countless victims. All at once, the guilt washed over me. I was overcome with sorrow and regret. At that moment, I looked him dead in the eye and said, "Mark, I am so sorry that I did that to you. I am a different person now and I feel terrible. I hope you can accept my apology."

Mark looked shocked, totally dumfounded, and then he muttered, "Wow, really? I thought you were just going to be an asshole. Are you being serious?"

I smiled wide and extended my hand to shake his, "I'm dead serious. I am genuinely sorry about what I did to you."

Mark was mystified. "I guess people really can change."

From that day on, our relationship changed. Mark and I were cool as hell. We even arrived at a point that we could bust each other's balls. For the record, I already clarified that busting balls is not like bullying. Busting balls is back and forth banter usually between guys or a really cool chick. Both parties razz and make jokes to each other unlike bullying which is one sided.

I really made an effort to get to know Mark over the next several years. He is a really nice guy and he knows all about sports. He was even a New York Giants fan. He shared my unbridled enthusiasm for the GGGGG-MENNN! Mark and I had a lot in common. In high school, I never gave him a chance. Now I'm proud to call him a friend. His brother, Chad, eventually came into the bar, after he heard that I was different from the insensitive jerk that he knew in high school. Chad and I would speak regularly and eventually he realized the changes that I had made. We've also made amends and now I am on a friendly basis with him.

All of this was extremely satisfying. But I know there are still a whole slew of people out there that I have made a negative impression upon. They are out there and possibly still having excruciating flashbacks. For this I am truly sorry.

I know that I undoubtedly have changed, because Mark wasn't the only relationship that I repaired over the years. Even though I never formally apologized to Bones, he and I became cool over the years. He's a funny guy and I enjoy his company. I don't know why I never gave him a chance. Bones, I wanted to say I'm sorry for everything I put you through.

Making amends is difficult as it brings up painful memories. There is someone that I have spoken to recently, and what he told me made me feel even more guilt-ridden than I already am. His name is Dan Liddell. As you might remember from earlier in the book, I used to beat on him with other bullies and he seemed desensitized to the beatings. I came to find out that, he was indeed somewhat desensitized to the beatings, because of what was going on in his home at the time. Dan revealed to me that he was abused at home, or in his own words, "If you think for a moment that what I endured in school was bad, what I endured in school was an absolute cake walk compared to what I was getting at home."

That made me detest every single thing I ever did to him. Not only did he get abused at home, but then he had to come to school and endure more abuse because of a jerk like me. This is hard for me to live with. I now see why Dan just took those beatings. I now see why he hardly put up a fight. I now see that there may be many others out there just like Dan. There are many others out there who need our help. There are kids who are getting abused at home, and school should be a safe place for them. However, most times school is not safe due to bullies like me. Bullies like me need to be stopped. Dan turned his life around because he is strong-minded and strong-willed. There are others who will go in the opposite direction and they will not turn things around. We need to reach out and help. Next time you bully someone, think about what they might be going through. You don't know about their home life. You don't know what other pain they may be suffering from. Why would you compound their pain? I wish I had known what Dan was going through, because then I would hope that would have stopped me from victimizing him.

Besides Dan and Mark, there were a few others I made amends with, but one specific person from my college days comes to mind. His name is Dave Goldberg. I had actually met him prior to college. I met him through my K-Town friends who had attended high school with him during their senior year. Goldberg was from Clark, and he had the misfortune to cross my path, because the school in Kenilworth had closed. I bullied him from the moment I met him. He was the prototypical nerdy type that I would blast. I used to make fun of him pretty badly. He also attended Monmouth University, therefore I would have met him either way. I carried on with my bullying ways in college, as I tortured him even more than in high school. We were on the college newspaper staff together. I'm pretty sure he hated me. I used to yell his last name, "Goldberg," like a popular wrestler of the time, but I used a sneering voice inflection to reflect that he was somewhat dorky. I probably had very few conversations with him, only speaking to him when necessary for the student newspaper. I was quite the douche.

Anyway, years later, Goldberg and I became Facebook friends and over time things changed. I only friended him because we were on the student newspaper together. There were times that I was forced to have civil conversations with him about newspaper affairs. But nonetheless, I still had some civility towards him.

Over time, Goldberg and I started exchanging a bit on Facebook. I started liking many of his posts. I realized we had a lot in common. We were both big fans of the NY Mets and the WWE. I came to see how well we could get along, but I had never given the guy a chance in college. I was now ready to see what he was all about. I wanted to get to know him. Our relationship grew organically over time. After I started to feel more comfortable, I frequently commented on his posts and we would have friendly banter. Eventually, the ice thawed, and we were quite friendly on Facebook. We often have friendly banter about the Mets or about professional wrestling. I genuinely appreciate his opinions and I enjoy talking with him. He's a genuinely funny guy, who has made me laugh countless times over social media. We've even spoken directly through messenger on Facebook and I can honestly say that I feel we are now friends. Recently, Dave Goldberg and I actually met up and I gave him a formal apology for what I had put him through. He was very receptive, and I am proud to call him a true friend. This is another gratifying reparation that I have made in my life.

I have recently reached out to others that I had abused, however, not everyone was quite as receptive. I really tried to speak to them and to apologize, but they wanted nothing to do with me. All I can say is that I tried. If they don't want to speak with me, I'm not sure what else I can do to try and make amends with them.

There are many others that I have not tried to contact because I am fearful of them. I have not accepted their friend requests. Not because I am the "cool" guy, but because I fear they are out for revenge. I was uncommonly mean to some of these people, and I cannot see why they genuinely would want to be friends with me. Because of my past actions, I believe there may be some people out there who may actually want to harm me. I never had a normal, civilized conversation with any of these people. I have not been in contact with them since high school, when I brutally victimized them. Therefore, I cannot imagine why they would want to be friends with me. It's a shame really, especially considering how I have changed. I am hoping to mend many of these relationships after the publishing of this book.

We live in a deranged world; it's sad but true. I should probably give some of these people that I tortured a chance. But I am not kidding, there are probably people out there that want to murder me. Unlike Dave Goldberg, I never had civil conversations with them. Our only interactions were my victimizations and humiliations of them in public. You cannot underestimate the pain that I have caused my victims. I just want them all to know, if you are reading this, that I am truly sorry. I know what I did to you can never be undone, but I am hoping we can leave it all in the past and we can somehow move forward. I would certainly give you a chance now and I would hope that you could do the same for me.

SECTION FIVE

BULLYING IN OUR

CURRENT SOCIAL CLIMATE

PART 1: VICTIMS OF AN UNRELENTING EPIDEMIC

"It doesn't matter if you're pretty, you're popular, an athlete, or considered an outcast, no kid is immune to the bullying epidemic."

During the writing of this book, an eight-year-old boy from Cincinnati and a thirteen-year-old Staten Island boy took their own lives. These two harrowing suicides have been directly linked to bullying. As tragic as these incidents are, I felt they were signs that this book needed to be written and distributed to raise awareness concerning this ever-growing, bullying epidemic. The ultimate sign came when I saw the story of the thirteen-year-old boy.

My cousin, whom I relentlessly bullied for being gay when we were younger, had posted about it. Joe posted the story on his Facebook and it was like a lightning bolt from above, that I needed to get on this and get this book out. It was also ironic that someone that I had bullied posted this story. This really tugged at my heartstrings and I felt I needed to include these stories in order to make everyone aware of these heart-wrenching tragedies. It is also important to note that I have encountered and read numerous other tragedies when it comes to bullying, however I could not include them all. I chose these stories because I connected with them in some way.

The story of Daniel Fitzpatrick is heartbreaking and tragic, yet educational. I don't like to say that this atrocious tragedy was educational, but we all need to learn from this. The following information was taken from the nydailynews.com. "Before he took his own life, Daniel Fitzpatrick, taunted and bullied, wrote a final heartbreaking letter lamenting that nearly no one tried to help him. The 13-year-old Staten Island boy, mercilessly badgered over his weight, grades and his innocent heart, pleaded to his school for help." The boy sought help from countless teachers and even the principal. "Finally, overwhelmed by the torment, Daniel hanged himself," his family said. "I gave up," the teen scrawled on two sides of a single sheet of paper." Daniel's mother blamed the adults in authority and rightfully so.

We the adults need to start recognizing bullying as a serious and continuing problem. Daniel's dad, describing the boy said, "His confidence was completely shattered." The report continued, "Daniel wrote in his letter that he felt tormented by a group of five boys who he said bullied him relentlessly. 'They did it constantly,' he wrote. His parents said the boys targeted him during gym class, often throwing balls at him. A teacher also embarrassed Daniel by calling him 'lazy' in front of the class, the boy's father alleged."

I know exactly how it feels to be humiliated in front of the rest of your class, especially in gym class. You feel like you are left out and different from the rest of the group. Daniel's father corroborated my sentiments saying, "Danny was always left out. He used to come up to me and ask me to get kids to play with him. The other kids would say they thought he was weird."

This is exactly how bullies work as they alienate their prey. In my repugnant past, I would have called Daniel weird as well and isolated him, made him feel as if he were an outcast. The fact that this boy cried out for help and nobody did anything is absolutely abhorrent!

The family said, "They and Daniel brought his concerns directly to school administrators but received no support." There was one teacher who did help, but it apparently wasn't enough. The school responded that they are "re-examining all bullying prevention policies and training."

It sounds to me like there was NO bullying prevention policy.

"Danny said that he was afraid of his teachers," his mom said. "He felt like the whole school knew what was going on and was laughing behind his back. They humiliated him." His mom continued, "The school tried to sweep the problem under the rug to preserve their image." "My son is not supposed to be dead," she concluded.

There has been another recent tragedy concerning another boy that should not have died. This was even more shocking due to the child's age. The following account was taken from the reporting of Local 12, WKRC-TV in Cincinnati where the mournful incident took place. "An 8-year-old boy hanged himself which seems to be the result of several bullying incidents. The family of 8-year-old, Gabe Taye, said that the boy was bullied to death." Bullying was common in the elementary school that Gabe attended. The report stated that violence, bullying, and intimidation were common themes at this local Cincinnati school. These are unfortunately common themes in many schools, and we need to start paying more attention to what is happening concerning these young kids. Bullying starts at a young age and it can obviously have deadly consequences.

Gabe was having a rough time when dealing with bullies at school. However, the school didn't alert the parents as to what was happening. According to the WKRC report, "There were at least six incidents of aggressive behavior, but the family was only told of the last three, which happened the same month he took his life."

There is a video that has now surfaced which shows young Gabe being bullied. Here is a quick account of that incident: "Gabe extended his hand as if to shake the bully's hand. He is yanked toward the wall, hits his head and was unconscious for 7 minutes." The video depicts Gabe passed out on the ground for a full seven minutes, while other students just walk over him or around him. This is quite a disturbing scene and it makes you wonder how these young children have been taught. Not one kid tried to help the unconscious young boy. This should be eye-opening for parents. Parents need to take note of this incident and we need to teach our children better. Of course, the main lesson is don't be a bully. But there are other lessons to be learned here. We need to teach our children to help those in need. One of these kids should have immediately gone to an adult in order to gain assistance.

The school did not alert Gabe's parents about the true nature of the incident. Instead of being told what had actually occurred, they were told he passed out. On the very next day, Gabe was bullied yet again. This time he came home and hung himself. Gabe's mother, Cornelia, said she would have done something had she known about the prior day's bullying incident. She went on to say, "He would have stayed home with me. Maybe home schooled or transferred to a different school if I had known he was going through what he was going through. It could have been prevented."

Gabe's parents say his suicide could have been prevented. They both felt like the school system didn't do as much as they could have. Their suspicions may be warranted. It was reported that, "There was a meeting concerning Gabe, 17 days before he took his own life, because the boy was punched in the mouth. Two boys admitted to it and the assistant principal called it horseplay." This is a travesty that the assistant principal likened a physical altercation to horseplay. Gabe was punched in the mouth and nothing was done. This is absolutely intolerable and the adults who knew about this should be ashamed. I believe that this tragedy had a chance to be prevented.

Gabe's dad went on to say, "They should take a lesson from my son. They should start paying attention to these kids, so this never happens again." Gabe's parents want his death to be a warning. There have been too many tragedies that have taken place because of bullying. We all need to start paying more attention and be more aware of how our kids are being treated by other kids. How many more kids need to die, before we will actually do something about the bullying epidemic?

Gabe never told his parents that he was being bullied. He kept his disheartening victimizations to himself. Cornelia thinks he didn't tell her what was going on to protect her. I can empathize with this sentiment. When I was a young victim, I didn't want my parents to know the pain I was in. I thought I was protecting them, because I thought it would sadden them to know their boy was going through that much anguish. I expressly didn't want to make my parents upset, therefore I kept everything inside. I was also embarrassed about my victimizations, so I hid them. These are hard experiences to share when you are a young kid. Bullying is not an easy thing to talk about.

His father has another theory about why Gabe never spoke out, "I'm thinking that it was normal to go to school and you know get bullied." This could be very true as well. If the school didn't recognize these incidents or report them to the parents, then this becomes accepted behavior. The adults in this situation had several chances to do something in order to help Gabe, but nobody did a thing. This is absolutely egregious, and these adults need to re-evaluate how they are running this school.

In the end, we lost an eight-year-old boy and most likely he is lost because of bullying. Gabe Taye was an innocent young boy who didn't deserve to lose his life at such a young age. This is something that will traumatize his parents for the rest of their lives. Cornelia went on to say, "To find him like that, that's with me every day." Once eight-year-old Gabe took his own life, there was nothing that could be done. We need to start intervening earlier in these cases of bullying, in order to prevent more senseless tragedies. Innocent kids don't deserve to have their life cut short. Innocent kids need to be saved and we need to be the ones who save them.

After hearing of Gabe's extremely saddening story, one athlete used his resources to shed light on bullying and its possible effects. Professional football player, Carlos Dunlap is a part of the NFL "My Cause, My Cleats" program which gives players an opportunity to lace up special cleats for different charitable causes. On week thirteen of the 2017 NFL season, players wore a cleat of their choice to represent their cause. Dunlap chose to bring awareness to bullying. There is a video highlighting his cause which can be seen on nfl.com and one child opens the video with these statements, "I make a commitment to stand up against bullying. I will treat others with respect and kindness. I will have the compassion to not be a bully and the courage to not be a bystander. I am a difference maker."

Dunlap has the children read these words and declares that they are in a "Bully Free Zone." He seems passionate, and that passion seems to stem from Gabe Taye's suicide. Dunlap speaks about Gabe, as he states in the video, "He didn't feel like he had the help or the resources that could've helped him rather than committing suicide. You should never have to feel like you have to stand up to a bully alone. Kids should know that bullying is not something you have to accept, you just have to get help."

Dunlap's anti-bullying message comes across with impact. He continues to say in the video, "Whether you're the bully or a bystander watching bullying, I challenge you to be a difference maker. Step in, get help. Help that person. Just so that we all can stop and put an end to bullying."

Dunlap shares the same sentiments that I have been writing about. All the kids out there need to speak up and be difference makers. If kids begin to realize that being a bystander and watching the bullying take place is wrong, then we are moving in the right direction. If kids can reach down and find the strength to help others, then bullying will become less and less of a problem. If kids can reach out to those who are victimized and tell them that somebody is there for them, there will be less tragedies.

In the case of Gabe Taye, nobody was able to reach him before it was too late. His tragic suicide is absolutely heart wrenching. But I think we can all agree that we need to stop tragedies like these from occurring. If bringing these stories to light prevents further loss of life, then I am glad that I included them. I am also thankful that I never drove someone to their demise. I don't know if I could live with myself if I had. Suicide is a serious matter that deserves our full attention.

Many kids who are bullied have thoughts of hurting themselves and in extreme cases like Daniel and Gabe, will go as far as killing themselves. I want the children reading this to understand that you have your whole life in front of you. Everything will get better and you will achieve much more than the ones who are victimizing you. Hurting yourself is not the answer. Taking your life is not a choice. Suicide is NEVER the answer!

Suicide is something that can be linked with being bullied. Bullying can actually encourage someone to commit suicide. Bullying can cause depression, and suicide often times stems from being deeply depressed. When someone is being bullied and is made to be a victim, this is extremely depressing. Take it from me, as I know firsthand that bullying leads to depression. I was personally never suicidal, but I am only one person. You can never know what a person is thinking deep into their own personal thoughts. We need to be especially cautious and cognizant of children, especially those being bullied and victimized. These kids are prone to suicidal thoughts more than kids who are not being bullied.

Often times, bullies even tell their victims to go kill themselves. Regrettably, this does happen on occasion in these situations. There was an instance in 2017 where a bully told his victim to kill himself, but luckily the young child did not listen. A fourteen-year-old boy, Dustin DeVaney was bullied by a classmate and was told to go kill himself. Dustin told his mother of the incessant bullying in search of an escape. His mother Lili DeVaney said the bully was relentless and told her son that nobody wanted him around. She said the final straw was when the bully told Dustin to go kill himself. She had described her son as "depressed" and "withdrawn." She also said, "His grades went down significantly...he came home crying."

Being depressed and withdrawn are classic symptoms of being bullied. Lili DeVaney knew why her son was acting in that manner, but many other parents who see their children going through similar mood swings don't always know why. Now, we can all be aware that there could be a possible bullying situation going on. Sometimes, these kids are not willing to open up about it. Recognize the signs and take action.

Lili DeVaney took action and transferred Dustin to a different middle school where the young boy's life changed dramatically. A year later, he was happy and enjoying life. He was on the school's basketball team and made new friends. However, DeVaney said she can't forget what happened. "I think people don't understand is that when your child is bullied, it doesn't just affect the child, or the parents, it affects the entire family," DeVaney has said.

The sentimental mother decided to write an open letter to her son's bully and posted it on Facebook. She wanted to raise awareness to the bullying epidemic. Off of the momentum of her poignant letter, DeVaney started a Facebook page for parents of bullied kids and has held forums where parents can come address these issues. The letter which sparked DeVaney's anti-bullying activism is one I feel needs to be highlighted. Here is that emotional letter in its entirety:

An open letter to my son's bully

Dear XXXX,

I know you are busy being a teenager, but today marks a year since you changed my family's lives forever. You probably do not remember what happened, as life went on as normal for you. However, I remember everything, like it happened yesterday. My son, your victim, remembers, as he still gets angry just hearing your name. His little brother remembers, as he also had to switch schools due to what you did.

You see, while you remained at the same school, my kids had to start over at a new one. While you are able to see your friends every day, both my sons had to make new ones. While you go about your life like nothing happened, my son still lives with the anger and frustration of feeling like he was victimized twice...once by you, and once by having to change schools to escape you and your wrath.

While the physical scars you inflicted on him faded away, the emotional ones are still very much apparent. He remembers how you told him that no one liked him, so he should just go kill himself. He remembers how you told his friends not to hang out with him anymore,

230

so he ended up eating lunch alone. He remembers how you told him you purposely picked a fight with him, to make him ineligible to try out for the basketball team. He remembers the anger and frustration he felt on this very day, when he was suspended for a fight you started, and you did not.

Even though you and your parents have denied that anything ever happened, and you received zero consequences for what you did, you might be surprised to know that I thank you. Thank you for all the lessons my son learned from you, that we did not know he needed to learn. Thank you for teaching him how life is not always fair and the adults won't always have his best interests at heart. Thank you for toughening him up, and being the main reason he started karate. Thank you for making it unsafe for him to go to your school anymore, as he has made new friends and is thriving at his new school. Thank you for showing my son that his parents will do whatever it takes to keep him safe. Thank you for showing my son that he can always go to his parents with any problem, and we will work together to find a solution.

Funny thing, your efforts to keep to him from basketball failed. You know this, as he has now played against you both in 7th and 8th grade. You gave him a fire in his belly to drive him to do his best. In addition, while we live in a city that is still a small town at heart, we know we will cross paths with you again. Even though I still get angry whenever I see pictures of you having fun at birthday parties with kids my son used to call friends, I know my son is in a better place. I know my son is now happy. I know my son will grow up to be an amazing man. Maybe you will too. Maybe you will one day wake up and realize how many people you hurt with your bullying ways. Maybe your parents will have enough of putting their heads in the sand, and will teach you about consequences. Or maybe I am now the one in denial.

Just know this, young Mr. XXXX...life goes on for us. I thank God every day that my son came to me, instead of taking your suggestion to heart and taking his own life.

My son will not be a statistic, and because of you, I will continue to fight for other victims like my son. So, thank you for showing me my purpose.

Sincerely,

Lili DeVaney

The "Antibullying Mom"

That letter speaks to me in more than one way. Instantly, you can feel the emotions of the distressed mother. The letter runs a gamut of emotions as you can feel that DeVaney is relieved and now happy that the bullying ordeal her son went through is now behind them. Of course, having a bullied child is going to affect a parent, but DeVaney really took everything to the next level. She now has become a bullying advocate. The "Antibullying Mom" has said about the letter, "This was my way of letting other kids and families know that if you've been through bullying, you can come out on the other side OK." DeVaney, although unsure if the bully has seen the emotional letter, said that ultimately the experience has made her family stronger. In the closing of her letter she wrote, "I will continue to fight for other victims like my son, so thank you for showing my purpose." Well, DeVaney has lived up to that promise. Her work as an advocate led her to start a group in her town called "Parents of Bullied Kids" where parents can speak out against bullying incidents that their kids are going through. A common theme from those who speak, is that they feel like the district and schools are not addressing the bullying. This seems to be an all too common and disturbing theme that schools and teachers aren't doing enough. DeVaney also formed a Facebook group called "Parents of Bullied Kids." Parents of bullied children are encouraged to join and share their stories with other parents, who have been through similar experiences. DeVaney has truly found her purpose and is making the most of it. We need more people like her to fight this great fight.

At one point, I felt like that letter was written directly to me. One particular sentence hit me and affected me greatly. *"Maybe you will one day wake up and realize how many people you hurt with your bullying ways."* I believe that everything I have been through has finally made me aware. I do realize how many people I have damaged with my bullying ways. I need to find a way to make my amends to all of them.

Even though I've hurt many people, nobody has taken their own life because of my hurtful ways. As I've stated, I'm glad that nobody I victimized ever went to this extreme and actually committed suicide. I am now a totally different person and I couldn't imagine having to bear that burden. Even though I did inflict major damage upon many victims, I guess it could have been much, much worse.

Thankfully, none of my victims have committed suicide and that has helped me move on. As part of my transformation from Super Bully to sensitive, caring human being, I have taken my past head on, trying to make amends for what I have done. I have changed my lifestyle and I make time for others like I never have before. I decided to dedicate my life to helping others.

One day, one of my good friends named Dai brought her son over to the house I was staying in. We were having a barbeque on a beautiful summer afternoon. He was a friendly young boy and he started asking me questions. I could tell that he might be different or something, but I couldn't quite put my finger on it. At first, I thought he might be slow, but he was rather intelligent. It didn't matter to me that he might be perceived to be a little different. As a matter of fact, it made me want to listen to him more and show him special attention. Besides, I didn't care for outside perceptions any longer, as he seemed like a perfectly normal young man to me. He was expressly excited and exuberant when he spoke to me, and I found his charisma to be contagious. His name is Clayton, and we continued to engage in conversation. He asked me if I liked the band Rise Against, which I do, and he instantly loved me for it. I know all of their songs and I am truly a fan. He could tell that I was genuine as he asked me what my favorite songs were. With each answer, his face lit up even more and this endeared him to me. I gathered that he was a smart young man from all of his thorough knowledge of the band. He recalled dates of concerts and he knew when every album was released. The band Rise Against helped us forge a bond and after that day, Clayton and I would grow closer and closer over time.

I came to find that Clayton has autism, which made me want to be there for him even more. At the time of this writing, he is a sixteen-year-old high school student. Although many may find it strange that I have forged this friendship with him, let me assure you, it is not. Clayton will often refer to me as his "best friend" or his "number one homie." At first, I was highly flattered by his affection. I just thought he was a highly affectionate and loving kid, which he actually is. I didn't think Clayton could look at this older man, who is old enough to be his father as his best friend. But the more we talked on the phone, through Facebook or text messages, I came to learn that he truly meant it. We have an extremely special relationship and I have come to cherish it. Everybody that knows about our friendship says that Clayton is lucky to have me. But I say that I am lucky to have him, as he's changed me forever. I've never had a friendship this rewarding in my entire life and I can't even put it into words sometimes. That's why when I see people being mean to him, it makes me angry.

Because Clayton is autistic, some kids are flat out mean and perceive him to be different. Let me tell you that he is indeed different. He is kindhearted and loving, unlike the kids who ostracize him and make him feel like he doesn't belong. During the early phase of our friendship, he revealed to me that he didn't have many friends. That has changed because he has gained many friends since. As Clayton and I became best friends, he started opening up to me more and more. He told me he didn't have many friends at that time, because he was frequently being harassed and bullied by the other kids in school. Hearing that he had a hard time in school, and making friends, really broke my heart. This made me want to be his friend even more as I knew he needed me. Our friendship is definitely the forever kind, as I know that I will always be there for him.

Clayton was perpetually called stupid and mocked for being different. This infuriated me, but also made me realize what a horrible person I had been in my past. Although I never mocked the handicapped (for the most part), I still hurt many who were defenseless and that's positively shameful. This made me want to help Clayton even more. This made me want to be his friend more than I can express. He needed me in his life and he still does. I am happy and extremely lucky to have him in my life. I have changed for the better as he has made me a higher quality person. I am there for him whenever he needs me, because I genuinely want to be. I don't care what anybody thinks about it. There was a time when I would have never made time for him. I would have only worried about where the next party was or what broad I was going to chill with. I would have never given this kid the time of day. I am proud that I am becoming a better person day by day. I truly care about Clayton and everything I do for him is absolutely from the pureness of my heart. We've even gotten to a point that we say, "I love you," to one another. I have to say that I truly do love that kid with all of my heart, and I would do anything for him.

The closeness of our friendship has made me especially invested in being there for Clayton when he opens up to me. Sometimes it's difficult though, as some of the stories he has told me are positively disgraceful. Several years ago, he called me almost on a daily basis to tell me how several bullies abused him. He'd been punched in the face, pushed to the ground, and choked. The worst of it brought me to tears. He called and recounted to me how five kids held him down and they drew on his face with marker. The nefarious bullies would go on to draw a penis, a middle finger, and an "L" on his face. The kids told him the "L" stood for "Loser." I choked back my tears to be strong for him. I remained as calm as I could, even though I was shaken by his obvious agony. I continuously told him not to listen to these kids, that he's better than them and he is an amazing kid.

But when I hung up the phone that day, I cried. My heart felt like it had sunk into the pit of my stomach. All my senses were tingling, and I wished I could do something more for him. I was horrified by his story. But I think I was also feeling remorse for the horrid things I have committed in my sordid past. All of it congealed together into an emotional salad that I couldn't just toss to the side.

Clayton called me soon after that incident to tell me yet another insufferable story. One kid called him ugly and retarded in class and the whole class started laughing at him. He stood up to defend himself, but the teacher barked at him to "sit his butt down!" Clayton said, "But the kids are making fun of me." The teacher didn't care and did not address Clayton's pleas. So, the bewildered boy did something wrong and called his insensitive instructor stupid. Clayton was sent to the Dean's office and was reprimanded, as opposed to the kids who were administering the bullying. My little buddy has told me about similar incidents where he told his educators he was being bullied and each time he was ignored.

Clayton attended a new school his junior year of high school, as he had moved. In the beginning, the situation seemed to be better, but over time, the bullying reared its ugly head again. My homie still had to endure the wrath of many imposing bullies. He was even bullied by girls at the school. Although, it seemed he did have more friends in this new school, he also seemed to be enduring more bullying. He would call me and tell me that he wanted to be home schooled. He said he hated it and hated being bullied. My heart would wrench every time I spoke to him and he was upset over it. You see, Clayton is mostly a happy, loving kid. The only time I see him down is because of these constant bullying episodes.

Even though Clayton was in a new school, there was a glaring similarity to his last school. The teachers in this new school did not help him in any way either. He often asked for help but would never receive any. He often went to the principal, who sounded like a despicable person. One girl was harassing Clayton to no end, which prompted him to speak to the principal about it. The principal responded, "The reason why you're upset is because nobody wants to date you and you always get rejected!" When I heard this, I wanted to march down to that school myself, but it wasn't my place. What kind of

Principal would say this? The adults in these situations have had deplorable behavior.

What kind of world do we live in? This resonated with me so much, especially after that thirteen-year-old boy killed himself due to similar circumstances in Staten Island. None of the adults listened to that boy's pleas, and look what happened. Now I'm not saying Clayton is suicidal, because I believe he is not. In fact, he is such a happy and loving kid that spreads extreme amounts of joy to others. I'm just saying that hearing about these adults and their lack of concern is quite abominable. None of them have taken any actions to help a sixteen-year-old autistic boy, who is constantly being bullied. They don't know if Clayton or any other student they are ignoring has suicidal tendencies or not. As I've said, Clayton does not, but some other kid who is being victimized might be having negative thoughts. The educators of our society don't realize the power they have to help these children and it is extremely alarming. The fact that they didn't help Clayton is seriously horrendous and if any of them are reading this, I think you should be ashamed of yourselves!

The oblivious adults are a big reason why I am writing this. It is time to be more aware of what is going on right under your noses. If you can stop bullying in one way or another, you could actually save a young child's life. You could actually make a difference! You might help with the victim's self-confidence and you may even alter their whole life trajectory in a good way. Many of these victims are scarred for life and you can help end the vicious cycle.

The other glaring abomination about Clayton being bullied, is the fact that he is autistic. I know he is not on an island either. There are many children with autism, mental illnesses, or physical impairments being bullied. Kids with special needs require our assistance the most. According to the website, stopbullying.gov, "Children with disabilities—such as physical, developmental, intellectual, emotional, and sensory disabilities—are at an increased risk of being bullied." This is quite alarming. These children are amongst the most helpless. These children need our help. It is time that we started listening to them and take the bullying they receive especially seriously. If you are bullying someone like this, you should be ashamed. You need to re-evaluate your life, recognize that what you are doing is exceptionally wrong and is absolutely disgusting. You need to make a change for the greater good. You need to stop your bullying ways. These kids that you are victimizing cannot fight back and that makes this the worst kind of bullying. I am here to fight for those that cannot fight for themselves. Hopefully, others are joining me with each word that I write. We will be watching you and we will shut down your bullying ways!

Autism has impaired Clayton's ability to discern what is happening to him sometimes. Kids have been beyond cruel to this amazing young man. One day, my #1 Homie called me, and he couldn't hide his excitement. He told me he had a girlfriend. I was elated for him. But I came to learn it was all a farce. Another day I watched as my little buddy called his so-called girlfriend. I observed and saw that the girl was just pretending to be his girlfriend, in order for her and her friends to get a good laugh from it. The girls all sat around in a circle and the FaceTime call quickly became a joke to all of them. They giggled as they mocked the oblivious autistic boy. Clayton was laughing as well, as he thought he was laughing with them. When the phone call ended, I didn't have the heart to tell him that this was all a cruel joke. The next day, he said the girl had broken up with him and he was heartbroken. I was sad for him, but I was relieved because the farce had ended.

What happened to Clayton is not uncommon in bullying. There are often times a popular kid will pretend to be friends with someone just to bully them even further. They gain the victim's trust and then make them do unsavory things, in order to impress the popular group. These victims have yearned and dreamt of being part of the popular crowd. Sometimes they are willing to do anything. This can lead to dangerous situations. Initiations are common with this form of bullying. This could include many precarious activities. Many times, kids are forced to drink alcohol heavily, or perform extremely risky stunts like jumping off of bridges into water. These initiations can result in injury or even death. Please do not engage in this type of bullying.

A rather disturbing story has recently surfaced concerning the bullying of a seven-year-old boy named Jackson with special needs. His father, Dan Bezzant, had a Facebook post go viral after he asked people to educate their children about special needs and compassion. It has been reported that "Jackson has Treacher Collins syndrome, a rare condition that affects the development of bones and facial tissues. He is nearly deaf, and the condition has also affected his eyesight. He has undergone major surgery already and will eventually need to have several more."

Dan Bezzant's Facebook post was impassioned, but I will let it speak for itself: "My heart is in pieces right now...my soul feels like it's ripping from my chest...this beautiful young man, my son Jackson has to endure a constant barrage of derogatory comments and ignorance like I've never witnessed. He is called ugly and freak and monster on a daily basis by his peers at school. He talks about suicide...he's not quite 8! He says he has no friends and everyone hates him. Kids throw rocks at him and push him shouting these horrific words...please, please take a minute and imagine if this were your child. Take a minute to educate your children about special needs. Talk to them about compassion and love for our fellow man. His condition is called Treacher Collins. Maybe even look it up. He's endured horrific surgery and has several more in the coming years. Anyway...I could go on...but please educate your children. Please...share this. This shouldn't be happening...to anyone."

Bezzant is precisely on point with his statement. This should not be happening especially to a child that is so young and clearly defenseless. What happened to this seven-year-old boy is absolutely reprehensible. The fact that kids were throwing rocks at him and pushing him is completely unacceptable. Jackson having thoughts of suicide makes this the most gut-wrenching part of this heartbreaking story. The parents of the kids in this school need to start educating their children immediately before another tragedy occurs. Bezzant's plea is undeniable as it shows that we do indeed need more compassion and love for our fellow man.

I am sure that Jackson already feels different from other kids. If only he was made to feel accepted, then maybe he could live some semblance of a normal and happy life. The kids in this situation are making that an impossibility. Jackson needs special attention and people need to make him feel loved. The Facebook post has had some impact as there have been countless positive responses, however, this just isn't enough. Kids in situations like Jackson are in dire need of our assistance. The adults who are near these situations need to intervene and help try to prevent any further tragedies. There has been enough damage done due to bullying. These innocent kids should not be taking their own lives. Do something, take action and you can possibly save somebody's life. Every child deserves a chance to live.

All kids who are being victimized need our help, but especially kids with special needs and disabilities. They often already feel different and they should not be made to feel as such. These kids deserve to be accepted like any other. These kids have special qualities and talents just like other kids. Even though they feel limited, we have to let them know that they can indeed do anything they put their mind to.

Although my friend Clayton has autism, this doesn't hold him back. I spend time with him as I watch him play instruments, we use the computer, play video games or we sing and dance together. We always have a good time! Becoming close to Clayton has been both gratifying and heartbreaking. What's most gratifying for me has been watching his development. I've known him since he was sixteen. He is now approaching twenty years of age! I watched this young man graduate from high school. I have watched him grow so much over the years. He has developed more and more confidence over that time. When I first met Clayton, he didn't have many friends. That has changed, as he now tells me he has many friends. I am elated and extremely proud to hear that.

His mother Dai has done a tremendous job raising this jovial young man and she has a lot to do with his budding confidence. She often tells him what an amazing young man he is. I know that instills confidence in him. I'd like to think that I also played a role in Clayton's growing confidence. I was always there to give him pep talks when he was feeling down. I was there to talk to him on the phone whenever he had a rough day. Most importantly, any time he was bullied, I reassured him that everything would be all right. I reinforced what his mom would always tell him, that he was an amazing and wonderful kid. That he shouldn't let anybody bring him down, no matter what! As he blossomed from an unsure kid into a more self-assured young man, he began to exude confidence. His newfound confidence translated into more kids being attracted to his greatness. He made more friends than ever, and even more kids became further accepting of him. I couldn't be happier than to see Clayton making all these new friends.

Despite all these new friends though, he did continue to have an altercation with a bully here and there. This is the heartbreaking part of our friendship, as I have to stand by and listen to his horror stories about being bullied. All of his pain has dwindled though, as the bullying used to be on an almost daily basis, but has thankfully slowed down. However, that doesn't make it OK. The worst of it is that I actually witnessed him getting bullied. No, not at his school. I witnessed this bullying online. This type of bullying is referred to as "cyberbullying" and has become another avenue for bullies. Now anyone can bully another person from anywhere in the world using the internet. This is a horrifying trend that is going to be hard to stop and to regulate. Cyberbullying is trending and is happening more and more. It's quite scary.

According to Stopbullying.gov, cyberbullying is "bullying that takes place using electronic technology. Electronic technology includes devices and equipment such as cell phones, computers and tablets as well as communication tools including social media sites, text messages, chat and websites. Examples of cyberbullying include mean text messages or emails, rumors sent by email or posted on social networking sites and embarrassing pictures, videos, websites or fake profiles."

As I've mentioned, Clayton is an avid Rise Against fan. He loves the music so much so, that he started playing guitar and the keyboard as well, in order to emulate the rock stars that he worships infinitely. Clayton tried his hardest to learn the catalog of songs by Rise Againstand he practiced relentlessly. He did not let his autism slow him down. However, like most sixteen-year-old boys, he was not an expert player by any means. Clayton often posted videos of himself playing and singing the songs of Rise Against on a Facebook group page created by Rise Against fans. It was on these posts, that Clayton was often bullied, put down, and flat out called names for his renditions. Often times, he was bullied and demeaned by adults, which infuriated me even more. I have come to his defense on several occasions, as people can be excessively cruel. There are some good souls out there as well, as there have been a few to come to Clayton's defense alongside of me.

Most times the bullies backed down when I said he was a sixteen-year-old boy just having fun, and what they were doing wasn't right. A few times when the perpetrators persisted online, I had to private message them, tell them that he has autism and then they finally stopped their bullying. There were rare occasions when the bullies actually did not back down. One jerk went as far as to say that this was the internet and Clayton should get used to the criticism. He was an adult and I was extremely fired up that he would not back down. This person was chastised and berated by me and a few others. This man should be ashamed of himself for bullying a sixteen-year-old boy with autism, no less.

Those incidents occurred to Clayton on Facebook and Instagram as well. I told him to contact me immediately or tag me when it occurs, therefore I can intervene. I always immediately come to his defense. What about the kids that don't have someone like me to come to their defense? Those kids will continue to be cyberbullied without consequence. The internet is not school; there will be no detention, suspensions, or expulsions. The internet predators will continue to roam freely without a care in the world. In some cases, they can actually hide their identity, and this is extremely scary. These predators can go undetected without fear of being caught, which is a highly dangerous premise.

Kids are affected tremendously by cyberbullying and the effects can be very similar to being bullied in person. Bullying is bullying whether it's in person or happening from behind a computer screen or texting through phone messages. Bullying of any form is extremely damaging to a child, but cyberbullying could in fact, be even more dangerous.

I have encountered another extreme case of cyberbullying and this story hit immensely close to home as it involves a family member. I have been talking to many adults about the subject of bullying since I began writing this book. During the time of this writing, I had a conversation with my cousin, Jackie, and I came to find out that her fourteen-year-old daughter, Noel, was the victim of bullying. I am not just putting her story here because she is family, but because I think her story is extremely powerful. When it comes to bullying situations, many people would consider her case quite rare.

Noel is a strong-willed, confident, and likable young girl. She is highly intelligent and has many talents including singing and athletics. In fact, I've heard her sing and she is phenomenal. She's extremely talented and her singing can bring you to tears. She is a highly touted, state-ranked track athlete as well. I know what you're wondering, but what does she look like? This is the most surprising element of her story. Noel is a very, very beautiful young lady. I am not just saying this because she is family. I was actually shocked to hear that she was bullied because she is exceptionally pretty. Her mom, Jackie, said it best to me, "Her situation wasn't the 'norm' of what I think most people believe goes on with bullying, because she isn't perceived as the nerd or ugly. It's actually quite the opposite."

I have spent a good part of this writing telling you stories of how I bullied others. I can tell you straight out that I never bullied anyone who was considered to be a pretty girl or a popular person. Every last one of my victims were considered to be an outcast in some way, whether they were considered nerds or freaks or whatever. This is why I think Noel's story is paramount and necessary to tell. It has to be noted that Noel was a high school freshman at the time and as I've illustrated, freshmen do usually have to endure some type of abuse or hazing.

Noel started to receive verbal lashings in the hallways, and she says she didn't understand why. A group of older girls consisting of two ringleaders who are twins and at least five others would continually harass her. It started with the girls yelling at her about Noel possibly liking their boyfriend. Noel says she had zero interest, but the bullies were insistent that she did. One girl screamed at her, "I'm gonna smash your face in the pavement and make you bloody."

The twin ringleaders led the other girls in the frequent harassment of Noel. The posse of bullies would shoot Noel constant dirty looks and deliver ominous messages through perpetual phone calls. The bullies told her that she needed to know her place and that she was "nothing" and "she better watch out!" The perpetrators continued to send nasty tweets for all to see on Twitter.

One night, Noel was out with friends at a local Applebee's. They were just having a normal weekend routine, where many of the kids go to enjoy half-priced appetizers. On this particular night, Noel was asking around to see if she could get an upperclassman to give her a ride home. She accidentally stepped on the foot of an upperclassman girl and she quickly said she was sorry. The upperclassman just shot her a dirty look, but said it was fine.

A couple days later, Noel's friends tagged her in an Instagram post. There she could see the cyberbullying that was aimed in her direction. The sisters posted, "We should just fight her." The girl who had her foot stepped on, said she was going to shove Noel in a locker and beat her up for stepping on her foot. Numerous upperclassmen began chiming in all with negative sentiments. One stated, "We're gonna make her freshman year a living hell." The girl whose foot was stepped on continued, "She stepped on my foot at Applebee's, that's hands! Let's get her!" ("Hands" is young person lingo for fighting, like we're going to throw fists.) Not only were all the comments negative, but some were posting the laughing emoji, as if it were all a joke, but it was not a joke to Noel. In fact, all of the persistent abuse caused Noel to break down and cry.

Her mom, Jackie, describes Noel as tough and strong-willed, but said that she still broke down due to all the girls ganging up on her. Noel is adamant that she was not interested in any of the bully's boyfriends, but the harassment continued on about the subject. One girl said, "She better stay away from my boyfriend or I'll strangle her in gymnastics practice!"

Jackie was pretty much clueless in the beginning and was unaware of her daughter's constant victimizations. Then one day Noel broke down after gymnastics practice. The downtrodden young girl began crying during the car ride home. She sobbed and said, "I don't know why Mom, but everybody hates me!"

Although Noel did the right thing in telling her mom, she didn't want to for a long while. She didn't want to appear as weak. She didn't want to look scared telling "mommy." But she was fed up and needed to tell someone.

Jackie took immediate action and contacted the guidance counselor. Jackie did not like what she was told. The counselor said there's nothing that could be done without evidence. At this point in time, Jackie did not see all of the cyberbullying, which meant she did not have access to the actual evidence. The counselor, however, also made it clear that the sister's names had been involved with bullying before, but nothing had been done. Jackie was somewhat dumbfounded and asked why nothing had been done. The counselor reiterated that Noel had to show or provide concrete evidence. The counselor then ended the conversation by saying she would forward the information over to the anti-bullying counselor and that Jackie would hear from him shortly. The bewildered mom never heard from him.

Jackie took further action as any good mother would, and she contacted the mother of the main perpetrators, who she had known for some time. The mother of these two bullies didn't say much, except that the girls needed to work it out on their own. I personally believe she was in bully denial, as no parent wants to believe that their child is a bully.

Jackie told me that the bully's mom was friends with people in the guidance office and she feels that's why nothing was done. She feels like there was favoritism shown towards the bullies. Jackie said, "I felt like the school wasn't on my side."

Even though the sisters were the ringleaders, they recruited many others to join them. There were kids in every grade from seniors to juniors to sophomores, who all ganged up on Noel. The bullying trickled down through grade levels and had become engrained in the fabric of the entire school. Noel, just a young freshman girl, must have felt isolated and alone.

Jackie tried one more time to help her beaten-down and victimized daughter. She decided to have lunch with a mutual friend of the bully's mom. She told the mutual friend what was going on and Jackie was told to be quiet, because "people might hear." Jackie said that she didn't care who heard because her daughter was being traumatized. Jackie couldn't be sure, but thought the lunch meeting did wonders. Shortly after the lunch meeting, things seemed to simmer down considerably for Noel.

Two weeks after the lunch meeting, Noel received a text from one of the sisters which read, "Why is your mom telling everyone we are bullies?" They had a back-and-forth exchange, which Jackie watched over to ensure nothing would get out of hand. Noel responded, "I can't speak for my mom, but it must be based on the things that you're doing to me." The girl asked what exactly they did. Noel then sent screenshots of the incessant cyberbullying posts. The girls claimed they were only jokes. Noel persisted, "Can I ask you a question? What did I ever do to make any of you hate me so badly?" There was never any answer back. The bully then became seemingly worried as she texted back, "I have track and a scholarship to worry about." Noel retorted, "Well, you should have thought about that before you started all this with me." The bully ended the conversation by saying, "Well, you do you and we'll do us."

Everything had calmed down for a while, but Noel soon had to encounter some of these girls on a daily basis at track practice. She was dreading it and for good reason. Noel is a top performer on the track team. In fact, she was ranked #1 in the state of New Jersey and #55 in the entire nation at the time. She continued to get bullied, because of her athletic talents. Upperclassmen were mad that she had taken spots from them. Noel's success had pushed them down the depth chart. Therefore, this rekindled all the bullying that had subsided for a short while. Even though she continued to get bullied, I can see she is a strong girl, as she told me that she would endure the awkward situation.

Noel's mom and her family were her only support during this troublesome time. The school was not there for her in any capacity. As illustrated over and over, school systems are flawed, especially when it comes to bullying. Schools need to intervene more often. The school had heard these sisters were synonymous with bullying, yet they never did anything about it. The school did not even bother to follow up. The school did nothing, probably in hopes that this would all just pass.

You might be asking about Noel's friends, because she does after all have many friends in her own grade. She is a popular girl. So why didn't any of them come to her defense? Well, Noel's very best friend was actually pulled away by the bully's influences. Her best friend since grade school left her and became friends with the menacing bully clan. Noel was extremely upset over this, but her mom tried to help her once again saying that, "She wasn't your true best friend if she left you that easily."

What was most shocking to Jackie besides the fact that Noel was bullied in the first place, was that no one stuck up for Noel. She said, "I couldn't believe that nobody had Noel's back. They were more concerned with being liked than sticking up for one of their best friends." Noel's friends just wanted to fit in and not be hated. This is how a majority of kids feel; therefore, I will not condemn these girls. Many kids are afraid to stick up for somebody who is being victimized. We just need to educate them and make them feel safe. We need to make them feel as if they can go to somebody and get help. It is obvious that nothing is being done at this school, so how could these girls be expected to reach out to the school for help?

Noel's other friends admit to not standing up for Noel in fear of being bullied themselves. They wanted to be liked and not hated like Noel. Even though they remain friends, they would not do anything to jeopardize being made into an outcast like Noel. Kids are afraid to tell someone if they witness a bullying incident, because they are fearful they will be targeted next. This is a sentiment that needs to be highlighted. I have said that kids are fearful to say anything. This happened to me as well when I was younger. My friends never said a word when I was being bullied, as they did not want to endure the same fate as I had. We need to teach kids to stick up for each other, tell an adult and take action! Then the adults need to be held accountable. The adults need to take action as well and actually do something. Ignoring the situation is only making it worse. The bullying is not going away, it's only intensifying.

It is hard to speculate what started all the bullying towards Noel. Jackie has a few ideas though, as she told me that Noel has been a bonafide track star for a while. Prior to her current state and national ranking, she came in first place in the county. One of the bully sisters had previously placed second. Jackie believes the other girls are threatened by her daughter and her success. Jackie wrote such on a Facebook post which read, "When people are hating on you, you have something they want." One of the bullies retorted on Twitter, "Listen honey, nobody wants what you've got."

Another theory, which I believe could be a problem occurring frequently in these situations is that the boys are contributing to the girl-on-girl bullying. Boys could have a lot to do with it. If the boys are looking at the younger girl, even if the girl doesn't look back, this could cause a problem with the boy's girlfriend. If the boy goes as far as to flirt with the younger girl, then the upperclassmen will take it out on the younger girl. They usually will resort to name-calling and making up rumors. Since the bullies are often upperclassmen, the names and rumors usually spread throughout the school. This was proven by my own stories, because any nickname or story I concocted spread throughout my high school like wildfire. Adults need to keep an eye on situations like these, as someone could be made out to be a school-wide outcast, which could lead to devastating consequences for the child.

Children who are singled out and made to feel different, begin to act differently. They often isolate themselves. I asked Jackie if she had noticed anything different about Noel during the time that the bullying was unknown to her. She said she noticed that Noel was being a little bit more introverted. "She seemed quieter than normal and was home more. She didn't go out as much."

These are tell-tale signs of being bullied. Many kids become more introverted and keep to themselves. When I was bullied, I tried to avoid social situations with other kids as much as possible. The more you avoid other kids, the less you are bullied. Jackie was unaware that Noel acting like this was a sign of bullying. Now, we can all be aware.

Jackie tells me that the whole situation was completely shocking, because she had no preconceived feeling that this would ever happen to Noel. She thought since Noel was pretty, popular, and athletic, that she would do just fine in high school. "I would have never believed it." Jackie went on to say that if Noel was a weaker person, then she may have had a lot more to deal with. She is thankful that Noel is indeed strong-minded and would not commit suicide or hurt anyone else in a grave manner. Noel would not retaliate, because she knows it is wrong to strike back. Many other parents cannot say the same as illustrated, we have lost lives due to bullying and this needs to stop.

Noel was extremely courageous in this case, but a person can only take so much. Jackie said of the situation, "Even the strong break down. She cried a lot. She cried herself to sleep often."

This story has numerous elements to it. Once again, most of the adults in the situation didn't do anything to help Noel's cause. In fact, the mother of the bullies was in severe bully denial. Many parents are in denial when it comes to their own children. I get it, nobody wants to believe their child is a bully. However, we need to wake up and realize that this could be the case. Denying it only exacerbates your child's actions. So many parents are quick to say, "Not my kid!" "My kid would never do that!" Parents are quick to jump to their child's defense. I understand, but after your initial reaction, maybe it's time to take a step back and analyze what exactly the circumstances are. Maybe you need to play devil's advocate and say, "What if my kid really is being a bully?" Being in bully denial will not help your child break away from these tendencies. You need to step up as a parent and confront your child. You should talk to them about exactly what is happening. If talking to your children doesn't work, then maybe you need to seek professional help. Bully denial is a serious issue that needs to be addressed.

There are more elements to Noel's story, but I feel the most important is to illustrate that nobody is immune to bullying. It doesn't matter if you're pretty, you're popular, an athlete, or considered an outcast, no kid is immune to the bullying epidemic. Noel's bullying should show people that anyone can be a victim.

Truly anyone can be bullied. Even if you're popular, there's always someone who thinks they are more popular, or they are older than you or bigger than you. Even people destined for greatness have been victimized. There are many people who go on to be famous, but at some point, they were just regular people. Regular people who may have been abused or bullied in their past. Demi Lovato is one of those people. This now famous singer was once a victim of bullying. Her story is heart wrenching, but needs to be told. In Lovato's documentary *Simply Complicated*, she speaks about how she was victimized. "I developed a social anxiety where I didn't trust other girls my age. Then one day, this girl who was popular started saying, 'Demi should kill herself. She should slit her wrists.' It resulted in a suicide petition that got passed around and she had other classmates sign it. When I asked them why, nobody could give me a specific reason why they were treating me the way they were. I had no friends, I was alone."

This is one of the worst kinds of bullying. Sadly, this is common for kids to bully others by telling them to kill themselves. This type of behavior is immensely destructive, as it can end in someone getting extremely hurt or even someone's death. Lovato would resort to a form of coping known as "cutting." Cutting is a form of self-inflicted injury where the person literally makes small cuts on his or her body. This is a difficult coping mechanism for many people to comprehend, but for many kids, cutting helps them with their emotional pain and issues. I explicitly do not condone cutting, as it is an unsafe way to attempt to ease your pain. If you or someone you know is cutting, you need to seek help immediately.

Lovato resorted to cutting because she felt all alone. She identified with what she was being called in school. She started to believe she was a "whore" and she was "fat." She went on to say, "Growing up I had been bullied in school and I felt like an outsider. I felt like an outcast." This is perfectly summed up by Lovato, as many kids are made to feel like outcasts and outsiders. This is what bullying does. Kids are excluded from the group and they develop complexes and emotional issues. Lovato developed an eating disorder as a result of her bullying. In an interview with Good Morning America, she said that bullies constantly teased her and called her fat. "From when I was bullied until now, I've suffered from an eating disorder from the things that were said to me." She said all the bullying led to depression and a self-described dark period in her life.

Fat shaming anyone is absolutely vile and wrong, especially a fourteen-year-old girl. Unfortunately, I have a lot of personal experience with fat shaming. My friends and I would stay at beach houses every summer during college and beyond. The Jersey Shore was a place where some of us objectified women, especially the bigger ones. I must say that not all of my friends would partake in these activities and that they are all good guys. Even the ones who played along with my demented games, they were indeed goodfellas. I led them down a dark path, as I was always the ringleader. There were only a select few of us who did fat shame women. I even made a game out of it. We would try to see who could have sex with the biggest female each summer. We joked that we were going to bring a scale to the house and weigh girls in. I even nicknamed one unfortunate girl "Tugboat," because she was the biggest of them all. Every time she entered the bar, I would motion my arm and pretend to "tug" on a horn, signifying that the Tugboat had arrived. These vicious games were disgusting and beyond deplorable. You would think I would know better than to partake in these vicious defamations, after I was ridiculed for being overweight when I was younger. I knew better than anyone how it felt to be fat shamed, yet here I was dishing it out. How could I sink this low?

I cannot say enough how sorry I am for my detestable actions. I am sorry to every woman I ever disrespected. I am elated that I have become an advocate and that I am someone who will fight for those who are being fat shamed.

Lovato has also become an advocate for those who are in the situation she was once in. She and I both have become advocates for anti-bullying all around. We both are trying to get our story out there in hopes of helping those who are being victimized, as we both were. Lovato has said, "People believe that words don't really mean that much, and people are just saying this or saying that, and it doesn't mean anything. But words can be really powerful. It caused a lot of problems for me to this day that I still struggle with."

Lovato has strong messages for the bullies out there: "If you're bullying someone, I would say to put yourself in the victim's shoes, because you would never want someone saying those things to you and even if they are being said to you, remember how hard it feels and how much it sucks. So, don't do it to other people."

Growing up when Lovato did opened her up to the new ways of bullying as she was cyberbullied in middle school. "Somebody's older sister had said that I looked heavy and that I should start throwing up." This must have been terrible for a fourteen-year-old girl to have to endure. After going through this, Lovato has a strong stance on the new way to bully, "With cyberbullying, it's a whole different world and that is the scary part is there's no teachers, there's no parents to put their foot down and say you can't post this about so and so. Most of the time, they're not even watching. So, I think it's up to the kids and the teenagers that are on these sites, to take the responsibility to step up for one another and really make sure that none of this happens." She continued, "If you see something going on in front of you that's not right, you should stand up for what you believe in. You could be a hero for somebody if you stand up for someone."

Cyberbullying is indeed a scary new development. Kids cyberbully more than ever, especially considering that social media and texting have become a constant part of their everyday lives. There are other dangers when it comes to cyberbullying as adults can now bully young kids. Adults have more access to children, more than they ever had before, therefore we need to be aware of predators. It makes me sick when I see an adult cyberbullying a young kid. In fact, being a mature adult now and seeing these adult cyberbullies, makes me even more proud of how far I've come. I could have easily fallen into being a cyberbully. It would have been a natural continuation of what I was doing in high school and college. I am ecstatic that I broke away from that trajectory. I finally matured and realized the error of my ways. I became self-aware and now I am here to battle those who are still ignorant to the bullying epidemic.

There are many new trends that contribute to bullying. Computers and phones have given bullies easier access to find their prey. Another new practice in many school systems has also made it easier for bullies to not only find their victims, but to keep them nearby for an extended period of time. A new practice called "Looping" has allowed bullies to have access to their victims for multiple years. Looping refers to the practice of a teacher remaining with the same group of students for more than one school year. For example, a teacher would have a class of third graders and teach the same exact group of kids in the fourth grade. This has been a new trend in education systems implemented to promote familiarity between teachers and students. On the surface, this seems like a positive practice. However, victims of bullying in these classes have found that they cannot find an escape. There have been many instances of continuous bullying in these situations. Parents have been left with little to no options, as school systems are not making it easy for kids to switch classrooms. The education systems have steadfastly stood by their looping programs. Most have refused to budge for the parents of distraught and victimized children.

One particular case became a brimming news story and slowly mushroomed into something massive. So much so, that a mom sued the public school district over the continuous bullying of her nine-year-old daughter. The story of young Emma Spektor started in her elementary school, located ironically in Springfield, NJ. You remember, don't you? That's the town where I famously harassed countless Jewish people. I was a notorious bully in Springfield. Now, a young girl is having her own troubles in that very same town. Emma's mom, Irina Spektor filed a lawsuit in 2017, because the district refused to move her daughter to a different classroom. According to NJ.com, "The federal lawsuit filed last week, claims the district is rejecting requests to move the student to another class at Thelma L. Sandmeier Elementary School as retaliation for bad press and in defense of 'looping,' a practice it uses to determine students' classrooms."

Irina has been widely outspoken to news outlets regarding her recent dealings with the Union County district and the bullying of her daughter. According to NJ.com, "The bullying started last school year, when four girls in Emma's class made fun of her appearance, called her names, took away her school supplies and told other students not to be her friend," the lawsuit claims. According to tapinto.net, Emma "was made fun of because of her freckles and birthmark, and was called stupid and an idiot and told she did not belong in the class."

In another article posted by nj1015.com, Irina had said, "I was quite upset by the fact that she didn't say anything to me when it was happening. At the same time, I do understand why she did what she did." The article continued, "Spektor said her daughter told her she didn't want to tell her mom what had happened because she was afraid it would make things worse." According to NJ.com, "After Emma's teacher told her she was 'a smart girl and can handle it herself,' Emma did not tell anyone about the bullying." The young girl finally broke down and she revealed it to her mom over the summer, according to the lawsuit. "The family then learned Emma would be put in the same class with the same teacher for fourth grade, a practice known as looping," the lawsuit says. "Emma told her mom the previous year had been 'pure torture' and she doubted she could bear it again, the lawsuit claims." According to the nj1015.com report, Irina said, "When my daughter learned about that, she was absolutely mortified because this meant she was now going to be in the same class with the exact same people who bullied her for a year."

When the school year started, trouble continued for poor, young Emma. Irina has said, "We did this for a period of two weeks where she would be hysterical both the night before she had to go to school and also in the morning, crying and asking me to not make her go," according to nj1015.com.

"The school's principal declined to change Emma's classroom and encouraged Spektor to file a bullying complaint with the district, according to the lawsuit. The principal, Michael Plias, later told Spektor the school's investigation had failed to verify the bullying claims and Emma would stay in the same class, the lawsuit says. Spektor was not satisfied with the school's investigation which was asking eight and nine-year-old girls what they had remembered from the year before. The frustrated mother said in the nj1015.com article, "To nobody's surprise, nobody remembered anything." She continued, "The principal called me and said we concluded our investigation. We're not saying that this did not occur. What we are saying is that this cannot be substantiated. As such, we don't really see a reason for concern, so we're done." Spektor then decided to stop forcing Emma to go to school, the lawsuit alleges. District officials continued to deny Spektor's request to put Emma in a different class, despite letters from Emma's pediatrician and her therapist saying the bullying was hurting her health, according to the lawsuit. One of the letters stated that the symptoms that Emma was experiencing, including headaches and sleeplessness "are the direct result of her anxiety pertaining to her class placement."

I have to disagree with how the school handled this investigation and the issues at hand. Most bullies are not going to willingly admit that they are victimizing others. More often than not, you are going to have to take the word of the victim and parents in these situations, especially when a young girl is clearly shaken. Emma was obviously in fear and did not want to attend school. These feelings are not just conjured out of nowhere. Young children arrive at these feelings one way or another. You have to ask, why would this young child not want to attend school? She was apparently a good student otherwise. The answer is fairly obvious, and one would have to ascertain that these victimizations most likely occurred. Therefore, I feel the principal and the corresponding district should have made an exception in this case and granted young Emma a change to an entirely new classroom.

The district did offer Emma home instruction and a transfer to a different school altogether. The district's refusal to change Emma's class only elevated her depression and anxiety. In fact, the whole ordeal caused her to miss two months of school. Although the district is providing home instruction, they hoped Emma would return to a regular classroom. Emma would not go back to that same classroom. Irina also rejected the offer to move Emma to another school.

According to NJ.com, "Other Springfield parents have been raising concerns about alleged bullying in the district at recent school board meetings, multiple news outlets had reported. One group of parents had been lobbying for the district to allow parents to opt out of looping and place their children in a different classroom than they were in the previous year." According to tapinto.net, another town resident, Lisa Reilly, said, "her two children were bullied in Springfield schools and the bullying did not stop until they were moved out of township public schools." The mother of the bullied girls "felt the situations could have been improved, if her daughters did not have to attend class with certain classmates and she couldn't understand why the district would not grant a class transfer to Emma Spektor." Reilly "also credited one guidance counselor with helping her daughter Chandler to overcome some of her situation when teachers and other officials pretty much told her to deal with it on their own." As documented previously, this is a disturbing trend in the educational field, where teachers and other administrative members are turning a blind eye to bullying. It seems that they rarely intervene and just hope the problems will go away on their own. However, ignoring the bullying only exacerbates the issue.

The lawsuit has since been dropped as both sides reached an agreement. Specific terms were kept confidential, but Emma has since returned to the public school system in Springfield. Although most of the investigations by the Springfield school district did seem shoddy, I will give the district some form of credit, as they have been implementing some programs to deter bullying. There was a program already in place called "Bullies 2 Buddies." They also had a licensed social worker administer two programs in 2019 to the staff and two in 2020 for students about the essentials of HIB situations. HIB stands for Harassment, Intimidation or Bullying. The Department of Education in the state of NJ developed this term and also an "Anti-Bullying Bill of Rights Act" in an effort to fight back against bullying. As illustrated by the events of this story though, there has to be even greater efforts in the fight against bullying. There is an immense amount of work to do especially from the adult perspective. The adults need to make changes first, or young children like Emma will continue to feel powerless. Emma Spektor was a victim who needed help and luckily, she had one person in her corner. If not for her mother intervening, who knows what could have developed for her. Removing the child from the bullying situation is of paramount importance.

If only my victims could have been removed from the torment I was putting them through. If only they could have been removed from the situation. If switching classrooms would have saved them, I would say it should have been done, but I would have found them. If I couldn't bully them in a classroom, I would have found them in the hallways, in the lunchroom or off school premises. So even though I do condone being able to switch classrooms in a bullying situation, it's not always the solution. If a bully wants to victimize, they will find a way.

PART 2: FINDING A VOICE

*"I certainly could have driven someone
to the point of committing murder."*

Nowadays, it's funny because people find it hard to believe that I was a bully. I have been opening up and letting people know about my bullying past, in order to start conversations and try to promote change. Most people are shocked, because I seem to be an all-around nice guy. My story is a prime example that we never really know what someone has gone through. Yes, I was a bully for a large portion of my life, but I was also bullied early on. I endured punishment and mental torment. People also would have never guessed that. But all these experiences have shaped who I am and brought me to this point. Even though I regret all of my offensive actions, I cannot say that I wish I hadn't done them. Well, maybe some of them as there were times I went way too far. But without everything that has happened to me, I would not be here trying to make a change. I wouldn't be trying to make people aware that there is a serious bullying problem and we can all take steps to stop the bullying epidemic.

The biggest reason I needed to write this, is to try and change the bullying culture that is dreadfully pervasive in our current society. I've unquestionably affected people's lives in negative ways. Maybe if they read this and see that I've changed, they can forgive me, and we can both find peace. I also realize it could be too late. Maybe I've affected people to the point that I cannot help them any longer. I can honestly never make things right or forgive myself for it, but I can maybe give myself some inner peace. If I can help to change things in this world just a little, then maybe I can feel free of all the pain and suffering I have caused. If I can somehow help to reverse this course that the bully train is on, I can perhaps feel absolved to some degree. I feel like the bully train will never go off its tracks though. Bullying will always be around as long as we are human. It's in some people's DNA to be a bully. I was a rare breed. I think I am inherently a good person and I am not naturally a bully. I was originally submissive to the bullies. But I received a taste of what it was like to be a bully and I became intoxicated. I loved the feeling and it took a long time for me to relinquish it. When I finally realized the error of my ways, I came back to reality and the person I really am. I am really just a sensitive, soft hearted man, without a bullying bone in my body. I am exhilarated to be back to my normal self. Part of me wants to go back to being that innocent young eight-year-old boy who used to cower in fear every day in the school yard. To be honest, I wouldn't want to go back that far, nor would I want to feel that pain again. I am just glad to have back my sense of right and wrong, which I had back then. My sense of humanity had left me for so very long. Now, I feel bad when I see people being bullied and I even try to help them. I have already helped some, but there are countless others that need help. I am elated to have made these exemplary changes and have this chance to help those who are being victimized.

The importance of stopping the bullying epidemic cannot be understated. There have been countless tragedies which have been linked to bullying. One of the most infamous incidents occurred on April 20, 1999, when two students orchestrated what became known as the Columbine High School Massacre in Columbine, Colorado. Thirteen people were murdered in total: twelve students and a lone teacher. Immediately in the aftermath of the tragedy committed by two teenage boys, it was speculated that the boys had been bullied. This terrible mass shooting had been attributed to other students bullying the two boys. Now this has come under some debate in recent years, as some are saying there was no bullying involved. However, I spoke to someone that actually lived in the same county where the incident occurred. She lived just a few towns over, and she told me that it was well known that these kids were bullied. I say without a doubt that there was some form of bullying involved, because it had been reported that those students felt like outcasts and felt isolated. That is a form of bullying, even if they weren't name-called. Making someone feel isolated and not part of the group is indeed bullying. When kids don't feel accepted, sometimes they act out in vicious ways. That's why we need to make all kids feel accepted.

Acceptance is the first step in preventing these tragedies. When parents, teachers, and other adults who deal with children see isolation occurring, we need to step in. Intervening and communicating could help make the isolated child feel like someone is there for them. These are vital steps to try and prevent something tragic from happening. We as a society need to start examining these tragedies and need to start administering steps to prevent them. It's a sad reality, but often bullying and isolation are the spark.

Bullying has become such a prevalent part of our society. It has been woven into our culture and for some, has become second nature. We need to put an end to these trends. Shining a light on what has become an ongoing problem will help to prevent similar tragedies like the one at Columbine High School. Even if the Columbine shootings weren't totally attributed to bullying, there are certainly situations where kids do think about killing others, because they are being bullied. Sometimes it just comes down to whether or not the child is in a sane frame of mind. Children who are unstable often times have been brought up in a violent environment. This tumultuous environment could foster psychotic tendencies and these kids could possibly snap and become killers.

There have been many incidents where bullying has led to mass shootings at schools. We need to intervene *before* these tragedies occur. Adults and other kids witnessing the bullying need to speak up. We need to intervene and stop the bullying. We need to get the victims help and get them immediate counseling. The victims need someone to talk to. We can start to cut these tragedies off at the source, if bullying or isolation in any form is detected. Teachers and administrators need to recognize when students seem to be withdrawn and not part of the crowd. Then they need to ask the students questions. They need to find out the child's state of mind and the reason behind their withdrawal. If it seems their behavior is off in some way, perhaps it's time to suggest counseling.

I am relieved that I never drove someone to come to school with a gun or another weapon intending to hurt people. I certainly could have driven someone to the point of committing murder. I am thankful that I never pushed anyone to that breaking point. Killing others is never the answer, even if you are being victimized. If you are reading this and are having thoughts of killing others, then please reach out to someone. Talk to someone and try to recognize that this is the absolute wrong thing to do. I implore you to reach out to someone. Talk to a friend, a parent, a teacher, or anybody you trust. Please go and find the help that you so desperately need.

I understand you are being victimized and being bullied, but there are other ways to fight back rather than taking someone's life. Killing others would also end your life, as you will spend the rest of your days in jail. Think about your actions. Think about the countless lives you would affect. You will rip families apart and give them a lifetime filled with sorrow. Killing will leave a permanent stain on your soul. There are a multitude of other answers and alternatives. There are people who will help you. I promise you that everything will eventually get better.

We all need to start recognizing when kids are being victimized. This heightened awareness could help put a stop to school shootings. If we spot a troubled child before they make a deadly choice, we could save lives. It is time for us all to change. I am calling for a change! I want our society to start speaking out against bullies and to stand up for those who live in perpetual fear. We also need to tell those getting bullied, that it is OK to stand up for yourselves. However, they need to retaliate in less abrasive means. Killing someone is never the correct path to follow. Speaking up, and in some rare instances fighting back is the answer.

I hate to condone fighting, but sometimes that is the only answer to the problem. I would tell you that it is certainly the last solution. Only fight if that is your only recourse. If a bully has pushed you into a corner and is unrelenting in their assault. If a bully is pounding on you and beating you, then and only then, is it OK to fight back. You should first use words to try and talk the bully down. The next step would be alerting a teacher, a parent, an authority figure, or any adult that you trust that the bullying is taking place. Fighting is always the last resort. Killing is NEVER the answer!

Sometimes killing others isn't a victim's answer, but their answer is to take their own life instead. I have documented two specific suicide cases already. Before the Columbine incident, the band Pearl Jam unleashed a video for their single "Jeremy" in 1992 that caught the public eye. The song was inspired by a newspaper article that lead singer Eddie Vedder had read. The article was about a high school student, Jeremy Wade Delle, who shot himself in front of his English class on January 8, 1991. The video depicts a child neglected by his parents and a class of students pointing and laughing at the boy. Although nothing was ever confirmed in the suicide of Jeremy, there was much speculation that part of his pain stemmed from incessant bullying. The manner of his suicide seems it was no doubt intended to traumatize his classmates, some of whom could have been his bullies. Jeremy was described as quiet and shy. Sometimes children are quiet and shy because they feel as though they don't fit in with the crowd. Most kids just want to fit in and feel accepted. Kids don't want to be perceived as different or weird, because that is what attracts the bullies. Bullies often feast on the quiet and reserved, as they view it as weakness. I have been there. I've sat by silently in a group of children and just hoped nobody noticed me. Because if they did, I became a target for bullying. I felt if I spoke up or was seen by others, I was susceptible to the constant barrage of harassment that would be hurled my way. But if I remained reticent, sometimes I could squeak by under their radar and go undetected. Now, I am not saying that this was the case with Jeremy, but we will never truly know.

Amongst all the horrid and horrifying tragedies, there has been some light. One such positive story struck a chord with me so much so, that I took it as a sign that this book needed to be written. I feel there have been countless signs that I need to get my story and message out as soon as possible. All these signs were swirling around me, and they all pointed to my anti-bullying message. Bullying has always been a persistent problem and needs to be highlighted. People need to start to open their eyes to its horrors. We need to stand together united, ready to combat bullying and change the ugly culture.

The positive story I encountered was a beacon of light amongst a sea of darkness. There was one particular person that gave me hope; there was one person who was such a shining star, that he brightened the black hole known as bullying. That one person, a football player on the Florida State Seminoles 2016 team, started what could hopefully become a positive trend. Travis Rudolph, a former wide receiver for the Seminoles, visited Tallahassee's Montford Middle School in early September 2016. While eating pizza in the cafeteria, Rudolph spotted one boy sitting alone and went to join him. "I asked if I could sit next to him, and he said, 'Sure, why not?'" Rudolph told multiple news outlets. He continued, "I just felt like we had a great conversation. He started off and was so open. He told me his name was Bo, how much he loves Florida State and we went from there." "I feel like maybe I can change someone's life or I can make someone a better person or make someone want to be great or be like me, or even better," Rudolph went on.

Bo's mother, Leah Paske, shared some thoughts saying, "Sometimes I'm grateful for his autism. That may sound like a terrible thing to say, but in some ways I think, I hope, it shields him. He doesn't seem to notice when people stare at him when he flaps his hands. He doesn't seem to notice that he doesn't get invited to birthday parties anymore. And he doesn't seem to mind if he eats lunch alone. It's one of my daily questions for him. Was there a time today you felt sad? Who did you eat lunch with today? Sometimes the answer is a classmate but most days it's nobody." Leah also posted on Facebook, that most days he sits alone but it doesn't bother him. "I'm not sure what exactly made this incredibly kind man share a lunch table with my son, but I'm happy to say that it will not soon be forgotten," Paske wrote on Facebook. "This is one day I didn't have to worry if my sweet boy ate lunch alone, because he sat across from someone who is a hero in many eyes."

After that fateful day, life changed for Bo Paske, especially during lunch. The following day Bo had a table full of kids sitting with him. And every day after that, Bo's mother has said that the middle schooler is having no problem finding people to sit with. It seems that Bo now has a different group of people sitting with him almost daily. "Yesterday in the cafeteria he was sitting at a table full of girls, he was definitely the most popular kid in the room," Leah said. "Everyone was cheering for him and applauding."

Travis Rudolph is most certainly a hero and deserves the highest of praises. If more people would make an effort like this, we assuredly could change the culture of bullying. Now I am not certain that Bo was bullied, but I am sure he received some form of mistreatment. The boy was sequestered at a lunch table alone. Making people feel reclusive and shut off from normal functioning society is a form of bullying. When you isolate someone and make them feel like an outcast from the group, this is categorically a form of bullying. It's like saying you are not good enough to sit with us. You are strange. You look different. You act different. You don't belong with us. You're weird. You're a nerd. You're a dork. You're a geek. I could go on and on. I know all this because these are all the deplorable things I would say to isolate someone that I didn't deem worthy. I decided they weren't "cool" enough to hang with all of uscool kids, therefore I bashed and ridiculed them. I would never let one of my targets sit with me at lunch. I sat with the popular kids, and if you weren't one of them, then you weren't good enough to sit with us. I was a bully in every conceivable way, as I hounded kids in the hallways, in the classrooms and especially in the lunchroom. I made kids do my bidding in despicable ways, as I made them eat repulsive items. I made them carry my lunch to my table. I would trip them as they passed by my table. I made them stand and sing songs in front of the entire lunchroom. I publicly humiliated many victims in the cafeteria.

There is a considerable amount of bullying that takes place in lunchrooms everywhere. Playgrounds and busses often have minimal supervision as well. These areas are usually not very well monitored and are havens for bullies. Many kids suffer from victimizations here, often without consequence. The adults in the lunchrooms, on playgrounds, and driving the busses, need to be more aware of what is going on in their designated areas. I wish somebody would have intervened and saved those who I tortured, during what is meant to be a peaceful meal or a fun break on the playground. I never rode the bus, but I'm sure I would have victimized kids there as well. Too bad none of my victims had a hero like Travis Rudolph to sit with them at lunch and make me see that the ones I constantly tortured were not too much different from myself. In fact, what *was* I doing? How could I turn around and do this to others, after I had endured extreme amounts of trauma and pain from being bullied? Why didn't I help instead of hurt? I knew the pain of being victimized firsthand and I should have been the first one to know better, than to bully others. I should have used my popularity for good and set a shining example. I could have been somebody's hero, just like Travis Rudolph.

All of the bullying I endured gave me no chance of becoming a hero. Instead, I turned evil and I became the villain. After being victimized for so long, the first time I was able to bully someone was like an aphrodisiac. I couldn't get enough. I was addicted to the power. I think I was somewhat of a rare case. I am not sure, but from talking to numerous adults about the subject of bullying, it seems they were all on one side of the spectrum or the other. They were either bullied or the bully. I somehow transformed from being the feeble prey into the ultimate hunter. I realize that there are many who actually do make the same transition that I did and become bullies after being the victims. After all, I am not the only one with a Bully Complex. Many turn to bullying as I did after being bullied, as it is a learned behavior. But I do feel that I was an extreme case. Did others actually convert the way that I had? I was one of the biggest victims without many friends and somehow transformed into the biggest bully with a plethora of friends. I was at the bottom end of the social pyramid and somehow I became Mr. Popular. My complex led me to believe that I was the King of the school, even though in reality I was far from it. I didn't care if I really had a crown on my head or not, I was extremely popular and people followed my every move. This was everything a former victim could ever want. I was finally accepted, and my social status was elevated to the very top. People loved me, and when I bullied others, they would come watch it firsthand. All of this perpetuated an inflating ego and turned me into an unrelenting monster. I had come full circle and I was no longer the victim. It seems a little strange that I went from one polar extreme to the other.

What's strangest is that I used to be surrounded by people who were fellow bullies, but now, I have become friends with more people that have *been bullied*. It's crazy because I'm now friends with people that I would have never been friends with during my jaded past. I now have several friends that would probably be considered the nerdy type. They are certainly people that I would have victimized, but I am different now and I am undeniably a better person for it. Now, I make friends without judgement, prejudice, or stereotypes. I have friends that I would have never given a chance in my past. I'm proud of that. They are some of the most amazing people that I have ever met. I am grateful to have changed and have friends that I would have never had before. It's almost like I've come full circle back to where I started. I have found the people that I turned on, the ones that I would have bullied and victimized in my sordid past. I am now friends with them, when I probably should have been all along. All those years ago, if I had only realized what I now know, that I was turning on myself. I, too, was a victim and maybe, just maybe, I could have helped others that were like me. But I was not strong enough to help anybody else, and for that I am sorry. Looking back and reflecting has my insides twisting with guilt and remorse.

Reflections. All around me, I see reflections of who I was when I was that bullied little boy. I can still hear those chants ringing in the auditorium. I can hear kids yelling "Fat Chink" at me with malice. I can feel the pain that I felt, every day on that desecrated playground. I also feel the pain that I have personally caused to all of my victims. I want to take that pain away from all those that I mercilessly tortured. I know what it's like to be in that pain. I prayed and wished somebody would take away my pain, from all the times I was bullied and beaten down. I now see kids getting bullied on social media, I see stories on the news, and I hear stories from kids that I know personally; all of them make me reflect back to a place when I felt that pain. This book has me reflecting and all I can think is that things need to change.

Reflections. Putting my victimizations into words has me reflecting back on all the horrible and horrific things that I have done. I am reflecting back to a time when I was not a good person. I have tried to bury these thoughts into a remote place in my mind and erase them from my memory. I tried to bury these recollections and pretend as if they had never occurred. But they certainly did. Now, I reflect on a daily basis and think how I can possibly change things for the better. What I did in my past can never be undone, but I can certainly help shape the future. I can certainly aid in opening everyone's eyes and show them that we all need to make changes.

Reflections. I reflect back on all the people I hurt, and I yearn for their forgiveness. I reflect back on everyone that I never gave a chance and I think about how I altered the trajectory of their lives. My thoughts are always drifting towards everyone I damaged. Drifting to them and trying to touch them, reaching out to them. I wish I could touch their souls and give them the spirit back, that I may have taken away. I wish I could take their memories of me being a monster and wash them all away. I wish I could show them how warm and inviting my heart has become. I wish I could show them my glorious transformation.

Reflections. Reflecting back to a time when I was a complete monster. These are not easy memories to dredge up. I know I need to find redemption. I know that some people may not forgive me, but I can only try. I can only reach out and hope they are better people than I once was. I can only pray they have sympathy and compassion, even though I never had any for them. I can only hope to give them a glimpse of the inner peace that I have found for myself. Well, as much inner peace as I could possibly find for myself at this juncture. I am not sure I will ever truly have 100% inner peace. How can I, after everything I have done? The pain I have inflicted may never wash away.

Reflections. Every day I want to find my victims. Every day, I want to say "I'm sorry" to each and every one of them. I want to reach out and shake all of their hands, embrace them, and give them their spirit back. Every day I want to, but I don't, because I am a coward. I am afraid that they have extreme hate in their hearts, that they will rebuff my apologetic advances.

Now you see I am vulnerable. Now you see that I actually have a heart and am not the heartless villain that victimized you, am I able to reach out to you? Now, am I able to make amends? Now, can I give you the inner peace that I so tragically disrupted? Now, will you give me the chance to get to know you? Even though I may not deserve it, will you speak to me once again?

As you can see, my heart and soul have been affected greatly from reflecting on all of my memories. My memories take me back to places that I've tried to block out. I have plunged into the depths of my mind and I am reliving many horrors that I had locked away. I wish I could go back and fill my ears with wisdom. If I could go back to the time when I was being victimized the most in the fifth and sixth grade, I would have a great deal to tell myself. Here is what I would say to that bullied little boy:

"You are stronger than these boys who are tormenting you. You are better than them. They are weak for picking on you. You are a strong person and you will persevere. Just hang in there and be tough. You will overcome all of this. You can get through this. Be strong, I promise you can fight through this. You have to rise above this. You need to stand up for yourself and fight back. If, after you fight back, the bullying doesn't stop, then you need to tell somebody. Don't be afraid to tell your parents. Your parents are there for you. They want to be there for you. They will help you. Don't be afraid. Be courageous. Make your voice heard."

The kids who are being bullied need to be courageous. We all have inner-courage and it can be harnessed. We can all rise above bullying. The bullies should fear what is coming their way. All the beaten down and abused, are about to stand together. I encourage you all to channel that inner courage. Be brave! Be courageous! Be valiant!

I was anything but courageous and valiant when I was nothing but a cowardly high school bully. I had no compassion for anybody, and I only worried about my self-image. If I could go back and give myself a tongue-lashing, I most certainly would. Here is what I would say to my cold-hearted high school self:

"What you are doing is wrong. You need to stop victimizing all these helpless kids. How could you do this to others, especially after you had endured being bullied for so long? Think about what you are doing. I mean really think long and hard. You are hurting innocent kids and they don't deserve this. Remember all the pain that you endured when you were younger? Why would you want to put others through that? You are doing this to look "cool" and to fit in, but you can be popular without being a bully. People will like you, for you. You are a funny, likable guy. You don't need to do this. Showing off for others is only hurting people. Those kids cannot fight back, and you know it. Why are you picking on the weak? This only makes you a coward. You're popular for the person you truly are. Stop being insecure. Your insecurities are encouraging you to be a bully. This is not true confidence that you are feeling after victimizing someone. This is not making you a tough guy. *You* are the one who is weak, not your victims. You are headed down a dark path and acting this way will not end well. You need to shed this Bully Complex you have developed. You are a better person than this. You are better than this!"

If only I could actually speak to my younger self, it would have hopefully led me in a better direction. When I was being bullied, I was immensely beaten down that I became withdrawn. Maybe I could have given myself some much needed confidence. When I was a big bad bully, I was developing my Bully Complex. I was fixated on being "cool" and popular. This drove me to show off and make countless kids my unwilling victims. Being bullied and being a bully, impacted my life tremendously. Both affected my psyche remarkably. Bullying has affected everyone to one degree or another. We need to change this never-ending bully mentality.

If only one day we can find a middle ground. No bullies, no victims, just people. We are all just people. You don't have to like everyone you meet, but just respect them. If you dislike somebody, then just stay away from them. I'm not saying we all have to like each other, because that is an impossibility. I'm just saying we can respect each other enough to not taunt, mock, and belittle others. You're not going to like everyone in this world, but you also don't have to interact or even have those people in your life. We are all people and we are all equals. We all deserve to be treated with respect.

Are there times now when I revert back to being a bully? Of course, as those tendencies are engrained within me. But now I stop and think about what I'm doing and how it's wrong. I know that bullying isn't right and is NEVER the answer. It never was OK, and it never will be OK. I need to stop myself and recognize what I'm doing. I realize we are all human and although I have changed, we are all a continuous work in progress. I am persistently working on who I am, and I have indeed come a long way, but I also have a long way to go. Nobody is perfect in this world and we all need to work on ourselves. Obviously, I am far from perfect, but I have also recognized my wrongs. I am hoping that all my mistakes can be turned into a positive. I hope that by reading this book, people will understand how drastically wrong bullying is and we can all try to eradicate it from our society.

Bullying is an emotional roller coaster. The lows you feel when you are being bullied make it extremely difficult to open up and tell someone what is going on. Children are often embarrassed to talk about it, as I was, and they just hold their feelings inside. Just because your child doesn't speak up about bullying, does not mean that it isn't happening. There are many signs to be aware of, as I exhibited many of the tell-tale signs myself. I would not tell my parents the horrors I endured for many years, as I was embarrassed. I screamed and cried in an attempt to get sent home from school, almost on a daily basis as a young child. I wanted to avoid the kids that were bullying me on a frequent basis and the only way to do that was to avoid going to school. I was withdrawn from other children and social activities, due to my fear of being bullied. I eventually turned to bullying as an outlet and I developed a Bully Complex. I admittedly was addicted to the high I felt from being popular and gaining acceptance. Once you reach the top of the roller coaster, everyone knows what's next. You must go down and that's where I went after victimizing countless undeserving people. Especially after nearly killing Teddy, I had hit new all-time lows. My feelings of guilt and shame had me free falling into an emotional state of heartache and regret.

My Bully Complex was the ultimate response to my early victimizations. All the pain and hurt that other kids inflicted upon me, I would eventually inflict onto others tenfold. It was as if I was transferring my scars to other victims. I wanted them to feel the pain that I had felt every day, for so very long. Now that I'm older, I have reversed my way of thinking. Now I don't want people to feel that anguish. I want to prevent that pain. Hurting others is not a good measure of revenge or a measure of relief. I realized how wrong I was, as doing this to others will not take your pain away! This was severely wrong, and everybody needs to recognize this. Hurting another person because you have been hurt is the incorrect emotional response. This compounds the wrongdoing and causes a dangerous domino effect which might not be stopped. Before you know it, your Bully Complex is spiraling out of control. The bully train starts racing at uncontrollable speeds and eventually crashes causing a titanic train wreck.

Nobody is immune to the bullying epidemic. If you are a kid reading this book and experiencing bullying behavior in any fashion, you must speak out to a parent, relative, teacher, counselor, or any adult you are comfortable with. Please do not be afraid to speak out. USE YOUR VOICE! Do not be afraid of what will happen next. The only way to stop this is to give yourself a voice. Let me be clear: YOUR VOICE MATTERS! Let somebody know about the situation you are in. Nobody can help you if you don't speak up and give them the chance. Don't make the same mistake I did. Maybe if I had spoken out, my life would have been drastically different. Instead of telling an adult, I decided to bully others to let out my pent-up aggression. I began bullying others and I never looked back. I regret my bullying past, but I cannot fully regret it, or I would not be writing this and trying to make a change. I would not be here, telling you that you need to speak up, and that together we can make a change.

Making a change will not be that easy, as bullying is excessively pervasive in our current society. I felt like I needed to tell my story in order to help initiate change. The anecdotes and nicknames were all factually accurate. The things I did in the stories I told directly inflicted copious amounts of pain and suffering. I have referenced several times in this book that there are people out there who still may want to hurt me for the anguish I caused them. I was truly that gruesome of a person and I understand why some have held a grudge. They have scars that cannot be undone. All I can say is that I am genuinely sorry for all of my damaging and insensitive actions. I hope my victims read this and realize that I have indeed changed for the better. I hope some of the scars I left will begin to repair. Mostly, I hope that they can find forgiveness in their hearts for me, as I have become a better person.

Since I've recognized and acknowledged the damage I've done, I have been trying to better myself. If anyone still has any hate or negative feelings towards me, I want them to realize that we were young kids. I now know what I did was wrong, but at the time, I didn't think about people's feelings or the damage I might be causing. I never thought about the pain I was inflicting. I only thought about my evil-minded intentions, how I could humiliate someone and the high I attained from doing so. All I ever thought about was being popular and how doing these heinous things would make me look "cool." All I ever worried about was how I appeared in front of others or my tough guy image. I never worried, had care or compassion for any of my helpless victims. I could have stopped and initiated change. I know I could have done more. I had an innate strength that emanated from my inner-being. I had real power and I'm not talking about the false confidence I attained from bullying. There was always a leader inside of me that I could never harness in a positive way. Now that I have channeled those true inner leadership skills, I want to use that influence to give others hope. I want to prove I am truly a strong person by lifting others up, not putting them down any longer.

If you are someone who is witnessing bullying, then you too need to display leadership skills. You need to speak up and let the bullies know you are going to do something. First, if you are strong enough, try and intervene. If you don't want to interact with the bully any further, that is understandable, but you absolutely need to report the bullying to an authority figure immediately. You can also try to let the victims know you are there, and you will do everything you can, in order to help them. Your words could possibly lift them up and make them feel their self-worth again. If you can lift the victims' spirits after a bully has oppressed their broken will, you could possibly save them from further mental anguish. You might even save their life. A caring word can go a long way. You can definitely make a difference if you try. When it comes to saving someone, you could BE the difference!

If only I had recognized my wrongs sooner. I could have tried to make amends long ago. Hopefully, it is not too late for me. Hopefully, I can be reunited with some of my victims and lift them up, like I never would have before. I want to show them my extraordinary changes and that I truly deserve their forgiveness.

In some cases, like with Teddy, I may not even deserve forgiveness. Therefore, all I can do now is extend my hand out and tell you that this is my way of trying to change things. I am hoping that bullies read this and realize that what they are doing is wrong. I want kids to see the error of my ways. I want them to know that all the pain I inflicted was unnecessary and wrong. I want kids to try and make changes to themselves and to the bullying nature that has been cultivated. I also want the victimized to see that I was doing things wrong as well. They need to speak up and use their voices. If I can start a change in the bullying culture, then I will feel somewhat vindicated. Maybe I can finally find the penance that I so desperately seek.

There may be many of you who decide to seek your own atonement after reading my story. I can only hope that some of the bullies reading this are considering a change. I know that sometimes, when you're the bully you don't think about what you're doing and how you're hurting others. You don't think about the consequences or how you might affect someone's life. I can tell you that you may be changing someone's life in an extremely negative way. I want you to realize what you are actually doing. I hope that I have assisted you in realizing that your actions are grotesque. Bullying someone could drive them to their demise, and you do not want that on your head. You will never be able to cleanse yourself if a tragedy occurs. If one of your victims takes their life due to your actions, you will never wash that from your soul. You are no better than the person sitting next to you and it's time for you to change your hellish and abhorrent ways. The bullying and victimizations that occur by your hands, will only lead to your own downfall. This path is dark and will lead you in the wrong direction. I promise that if you continue to bully in life, you will not be a winner. Bullies NEVER win! Your victims now have a voice and they will stand up to you. Let this serve as a warning, because one day soon, the ones you are bullying will finally stand up for themselves!

I hope I have given the victims strength to stand up and use your voices. Stand up to your perpetrators and let them know that you will no longer be a victim to their abuse. Be someone who is respected and powerful! BE A VOICE!

Using your voice and speaking out will help slow down the bullying epidemic. We can start to save these innocent kids, even if we do it one kid at a time. Every child matters. Every child deserves peace and deserves to be bully free. Help set them free!

If you are a victim and reading this, I want you to understand that you have done nothing wrong. You have done nothing to justify what is happening to you. If you are being bullied for being different, don't hide from who you are. Be yourself and be proud of who you are. What makes you different is what makes you special. I truly believe you are all special in your own way. I believe in all of you. I urge you all to believe in yourselves. Don't let bullies take away your identity.

Sometimes being victimized takes away more than your identity. Sometimes, these victimizations take your pride and your dignity. Sometimes, all you want to do is cry. It's OK to cry once in a while, but sometimes crying only makes things worse; it can make the bullying worse. Learn to try and stand up for yourself. Try to hold back the tears as best as you can. Use what you're feeling and try to turn those desolate feelings into something positive. Try not to cower in fear. I understand that you may be afraid but try and summon your inner courage. Try summoning some intestinal fortitude! Dig down deep and you'll find an inner strength buried way down. Unearth your fighting spirit. Hold the tears back and put on a strong face. Your perceived strength will give the bullies pause. They will think they cannot overpower you. You can truly overpower them with a tough mindset.

If you continue to get victimized and abused, you need to understand that you have a voice. Use your voice to speak out in an attempt to try and end the victimizations you are enduring. The pain will subside, I promise you. Do not try and hurt others as a coping mechanism. You should never hurt others in an attempt to numb your own pain. You should never turn to becoming a bully, as I did. Victimizing others to escape your pain is not the answer. Do not hurt others, as there are other alternatives. Especially do not go to the extreme and try to kill those who are tormenting you. You will ruin your life and the lives of many others. Killing others is beyond wrong and is NEVER the answer! It is also equally important for you to never intentionally harm yourself. Inflicting pain on yourself is not the answer, either. If you are having thoughts of hurting yourself or committing suicide, then it is time to speak up and tell a trusted adult. Don't ever give up. Suicide is NEVER the answer.

Thankfully my experiences have never led to me harming myself or someone else hurting me in a fatal manner. I have learned an extreme amount from my experiences as both a victim and as a bully. My Bully Complex has taken me on a tumultuous journey. I have finally transformed into a caring, kind, and loving person. I am no longer the Super Bully. I have shed the bully and I have shed all judgements! I want you to know that you can change, just as I have. I have recognized all of my despicable, deplorable, and downright evil actions and I want to make reparations for all of them. I would love to make amends to all the people that I have hurt along the way. If I can change and transform from being a big bully, we can all do it. If my world of bullying has transformed into a world of peace, love, and tranquility, then so can yours. If I can strive to become the best form of myself that I can possibly be, then you can as well! Stop and think about your actions and the consequences of what you're doing, as this will lead you away from bullying.

If you are an adult reading this and your child is acting out in ways like I have described throughout the book, then you need to pay attention. If your child is lashing out in school, resisting authority, or displaying anger towards others, there is most likely a problem. If your child is acting withdrawn or doesn't seem to be interacting with other kids, then something is wrong. Your child could be suffering from being victimized. You need to speak with your child and be more alert to their interactions in school. Many kids will hide their pain from you, just as I had. Bullying can directly affect your child's behavior. These kids are not problem children, as they are just finding a way to release their own personal misery. Try to catch what is happening and maybe you could put an end to their victimizations.

In the end, I think we can all see that bullying is wrong and there is no tolerance for these actions. The question is, will we start to do something about the bullying that we see on a daily basis?

Will you, the bully, take what I have said and realize that what you are doing is wrong? Will you make a change in your lives and stop victimizing others?

Will you, the adult, start intervening more when you see bullying occur? Will you start to become more educated and be more verbal concerning the bullying epidemic?

And last, but certainly not least, will you, the victim, finally speak out and fight back? Will you stand up for yourself and believe in yourself? Because in the end, that's what this book is all about. I want you to know that you are all amazing people, no matter how much somebody puts you down and makes you feel otherwise. No matter how different you may feel. Even if you feel like you don't truly fit in. If you don't feel accepted, I will tell you, there is a place for you. You do fit in somewhere, I promise you! Be who you are! OWN IT! You have your own individuality, your own personality and that's what makes each and every one of you special. I hope I have helped you from being judged and ridiculed. You all deserve to feel special, and you are to me. In my eyes, you are all ROCK STARS!

The time is now to use your voice. I hope I have given any victim out there a voice. I want to give a voice to the voiceless! I want to give power to the powerless! Take my words and use them to be brave! Stand up to those who are putting you down! The time is NOW!

This world can be a bully-free world, if we all work together. Let's band together and stand up for what's right. Let's join hands, open our arms, and accept everyone. Everyone deserves to be accepted. We are all equal, after all. Let's start to eliminate all the hate and learn to respect each other.

The time is now to let bullies know that we will not let them continue with their victimizations. It's time to let them know that somebody is watching. It's time to let them know that things are going to change. Let's stand up and show bullies that their actions are wrong. Let's show bullies that no matter what they do, how much they put us down, that they will never win!

Your life matters. Your voice matters. You matter. Together, we can stop bullying. Together, we can change the world. Together, we can change lives.

SECTION SIX

ANTI-BULLYING RESOURCES

IMPORTANT ANTI-BULLYING ORGANIZATIONS

"Be a STAR": WWE's anti-bullying initiative

Growing up I was a huge fan of professional wrestling. I watched these larger than life athletes in awe. My earliest memories are of my favorite wrestlers coming down to the ring in grand fashion. I would cheer vigorously, as the maniacal Ultimate Warrior raced down to the ring and he shook the ropes, as if he were having convulsions. When Ric Flair cut a promo, he had me yelling "Wooooooooo!!!!!" at my television screen. A promo is when a wrestler speaks to the audience or to the camera and tries to attain a reaction. As the years went on, other generations of wrestlers continued to keep me engaged with their promos and entrances. My heart raced every time Stone Cold Steve Austin's music hit and I waited with bated breath for him to race down to the ring. He would always give the Stone Cold Stunner to a ring full of wrestlers. I was glued to the TV for every single one of the Rock's captivating and hilarious promos. I was enamored with the storytelling and I have been hooked ever since. I have continued to follow professional wrestling, and my passion is for the king of all wrestling organizations, the WWE. I have remained a fan to this very day, and I continue to watch on a weekly basis. I am a devoted fan and an ardent follower of the WWE. Therefore, the fact that the WWE has an anti-bullying organization really hits home with me.

Even though the WWE is a world where our reality is suspended, they take the time to engage in real matters. I understand that it is a world based on imagination and characters. I am saying this because one of their most divisive Superstars is a man named John Cena. Now I am going to be completely honest, I am not a fan of Cena's on-screen character. However, I am huge fan of John Cena, the actual person.

Cena has done some great things for kids especially through the Make-A-Wish Foundation, where he holds the record for granting the most wishes by a celebrity, with over 500 wishes granted. Cena also has amazing catchphrases for his WWE character. There are two in particular that I am fond of. They are "Never Give Up" and "Rise Above Hate." These messages are important for people of all ages. No matter how bad things are, there is no reason to ever give up. If you are feeling depressed, just remember that life takes us through ups and downs. Things may seem bleak at the moment, but everything will change in time.

Besides all his work for Make-A-Wish, Cena has also teamed up with the WWE in an anti-bullying initiative. They are doing their best to help as many kids as they can. According to the WWE website, "Be a STAR, WWE's anti-bullying initiative, has the mission to encourage young people to treat each other with respect through education and grassroots initiatives. Be a STAR promotes positive methods of social interaction and encourages people to treat others as equals and with respect because everyone is a star in their own right."

This mission statement says a remarkable amount in only a few words. These are points that I have been trying to drive home. I want to see kids have more positive interactions, rather than the bullying and victimizations which so often occur. I have been preaching to treat everyone with respect, because we are all indeed equals. Finally, I agree that everyone has some form of talent or shine to them. Everyone indeed is a star in their own way. I love this mission statement and I stand by it wholeheartedly.

The website continues to state, "over 30,000 people from all 50 US states and from 91 international countries have taken the pledge to end bullying through WWE's Be a STAR program." We should all take their pledge and join their lauded efforts to end bullying.

What a phenomenal effort WWE is making with this campaign. I hope that I can join them and strengthen their magnificent efforts. WWE has their superstars visit schools and community centers several times a month and I hope that I am invited to join them at some point.

Thank you, WWE, for being a major part of my youth and now my adulthood. WWE should be lauded and recognized for their anti-bullying endeavors.

STOMP OUT BULLYING

One of the biggest current anti-bullying campaigns is called "STOMP Out Bullying." They aim to "Change The Culture" and that's what I've been lobbying for, too. This is exactly what we need: to change the culture of bullying. Bullying has become a common way of life in many areas and this is completely unacceptable. Surely, there are many areas where there are tremendous anti-bullying preventions in place throughout school systems, but there are still far too many that are lacking. Many more prevention programs need to be put in place throughout school systems nationally, if we are to achieve our lofty goals.

According to their website, "A pioneer on the issue, STOMP Out Bullying is recognized as the most influential anti-bullying and cyberbullying organization in America and beyond. STOMP Out Bullying is dedicated to changing the culture for all students. It works to reduce and prevent bullying, cyberbullying, sexting and other digital abuse, educates against homophobia, LGBTQ discrimination, racism and hatred, and deters violence in schools, online and in communities across the country. In this diverse world, STOMP Out Bullying promotes civility, inclusion, and equality. It teaches effective solutions on how to respond to all forms of bullying, as well as educating kids and teens in school and online. It provides help for those in need and at risk of suicide, and raises awareness through peer mentoring programs in schools, public service announcements by noted celebrities, and social media campaigns."

This organization seems to cover the gamut. STOMP Out Bullying addresses not only bullying but cyberbullying which has become the latest disturbing trend. They also focus on the LGBTQ community which are often one of the biggest categories of victims of bullying.

They focus on suicide which is a subject I touch on that we probably should put the limelight on more.

One of the most important factors that STOMP Out Bullying focuses on is that they "teach effective solutions on how to respond to all forms of bullying." That is one of my main messages. I want to give a voice to the voiceless. Kids need a way to help themselves from these victimizations. These victims need to know where to reach out for help and STOMP Out Bullying is doing a tremendous job in aiding them.

SHRED HATE

X GAMES

Another high-profile anti-bullying campaign is called SHRED HATE. This was founded by a group of X Games athletes. Many of these athletes, believe it or not, have experienced isolation from participating in non-traditional sports. They identify with those of us that feel isolated and often times not part of the group. I have touched on this and said that when you make someone feel isolated, that is a form of bullying.

According to an article on espnfrontrow.com "For more than 20 years, the X Games has represented individuality in sport and progression, with our athletes often taking the non-traditional sports event route in their lives. The individualism of these athletes often isolated them during their growth. Bullying has become a widespread issue around the globe with nearly one in four students reporting instances of bullying."

This is eye opening when hearing that many of these athletes were victims of bullying. Athletes primarily seem like the opposite type that would get bullied. Therefore, the fact that these athletes felt isolated is really telling. This goes to show you that anybody could be a victim to bullying and nobody is immune.

The SHRED HATE website opens with this statement, "Ten million students are bullied each year in the U.S. We want to change that, which is why we launched SHRED HATE, an initiative to end bullying in schools."

Ten million is an astounding number and it needs to be reduced. There are countless kids being bullied and need our help. I stand behind this campaign and all these campaigns listed for that matter, in our fight to end bullying of all types!

RACHEL'S CHALLENGE

Rachel Joy Larry was the first person killed in the Columbine High School shooting on that fateful day of April 20, 1999. Immediately in the wake of her death, a non-profit organization was formed in her honor which is called "Rachel's Challenge." According to the website, "After her death, many students that Rachel reached out to shared stories with the Larrys about the profound impact her simple acts of kindness had on their lives; even preventing one young man from taking his own life. They soon realized the transformational effect of Rachel's story and started the non-profit organization that is Rachel's Challenge today."

I am hoping to team up with this organization in an effort to raise awareness. Approximately 160,000 students skip school every day for fear of being bullied. I was once a part of that group in my early youth. Then later on I am sure I caused some students to miss school due to my presence. I remember many of my victims purposely trying to avoid me in the hallways. They would duck and some would even run. In college, after I had beaten the living daylights out of Teddy, he too ran in fear when he saw me months after the beating I had administered. I am not proud, as I have hopefully made abundantly clear, but I am just illustrating how powerful bullying can be. Bullying changes lives as it can alter a student's academic experience. The victims miss school and often lose their focus on schoolwork, causing a slip in grades. This is a vicious cycle that organizations like Rachel's Challenge are aiming to put a stop to.

RachelsChallenge.org goes on, "It doesn't have to be this way. Creating a school climate less susceptible to harassment, bullying and violence is possible. We see it happening in socioeconomically and demographically diverse schools across North America every day."

This organization has raised a massive amount of awareness as the website also states, "In the seventeen years since we lost twelve innocent lives, including Rachel, her legacy had touched 22 million people and is the foundation for creating programs that promote a positive climate in K-12 schools. Her vision to start a chain reaction of kindness and compassion is the basis for our mission: *Making schools safer, more connected places where bullying and violence are replaced with kindness and respect; and where learning and teaching are awakened to their fullest.*"

Now that's a mission statement! My goals are very similar in writing this book. I too have a clear mission statement and I am hoping to start promoting change. I want to help students who are victimized and give them a voice. I want to help the fight against bullies. I want to make schools safer. I want children to learn that bullying is wrong and to ultimately try to end the bullying epidemic altogether. I want to help save lives and this is why I'm aiming to team up with Rachel's Challenge in their fight. I stand by their mission statement 100% and together we WILL make a difference.

This organization is also bringing awareness to adults, which I am a huge advocate of doing. Many tragedies have occurred because of the ignorance of the adults involved in the situations. Many adults failed to use their authority and interject themselves, when there was bullying happening right before their eyes.

The website further states, "Rachel's Challenge programs provide a sustainable, evidence-based framework for positive climate and culture in our schools. Fully implemented, partner schools achieve statistically significant gains in community engagement, faculty/student relationships, leadership potential, and school climate; along with reductions in bullying, alcohol, tobacco and other drug use."

The programs run by Rachel's Challenge are comprehensive, and the "objectives of these programs are all the same; to continue Rachel's legacy of kindness and compassion and to: Help schools and businesses become safer, more connected places to live and learn. Stimulate real culture change by actively involving the entire community in the process. Change lives by providing culturally relevant social/emotional training. Increase achievement and ensure results by engaging the participants' heart, head and hands in a continuing improvement process. We are hopeful that you will decide to continue Rachel's legacy by helping us get her message to more students and adults. As Rachel wrote in her final school essay: 'I have this theory that if one person can go out of their way to show compassion, then it will start a chain reaction of the same. People will never know how far a little kindness can go.' Thank you for starting your own chain reaction."

All in all, this is an influential endeavor that I am proud to bring to your attention. Please join in the fight with Rachel's Challenge and start your own chain reaction. The more people we can reach together, the more awareness we can spread and ultimately save lives together.

THE BULLY PROJECT and STAND FOR THE SILENT

The Bully Project is one of the fastest growing anti-bullying organizations. According to their website, thebullyproject.com, "Over 13 million American kids will be bullied this year, making it the most common form of violence experienced by young people in the nation." This is quite a staggering number to digest. The Bully Project was founded off the strength of a documentary called *Bully* which according to the site, "brings human scale to this startling statistic, offering an intimate, unflinching look at how bullying has touched five kids and their families."

The film gives a compelling look at bullying and I was instantly pulled in when I watched it. Several kids and families are highlighted throughout the heartfelt documentary. The most poignant being two families, where their child committed suicide, as a direct result of bullying. This is something I have touched on and is a problem that we need to be focused on. Bullying can drive children to want to end their lives if they are being victimized relentlessly. One kid retaliated by bringing a gun onto a bus where she endured bullying. This is another extreme result of bullying that we need to pay attention to. Kids are sometimes driven to a place where they want to hurt their perpetrators. All the victims want is to put an end to the bullying. Most times these victims aren't even intending to cause harm. Luckily, that was the case in the instance the film documents and nobody was hurt. However, there have been countless cases that turn into tragedies and result in fatalities.

Bullying occurs everywhere, but a lot of the victimizations captured in the documentary occurred on the bus. Buses seem to be a haven for torture and torment. There is little to no supervision and there is rarely any proof. This is something to keep a keen eye on, as bullying on the bus seems to be escalating. Schools need to put bully prevention programs in place that target these bus routes. Something needs to be done to reduce these incidents.

Bully also highlights a movement started by one of the parents who lost their child to suicide. The organization is called "Stand for the Silent" and is spreading its anti-bullying message around the world. According to their website, standforthesilent.org, "Stand for the Silent has fast become one of the leading and most effective anti-bullying organizations. Our mission is simple: bring awareness to bullying and the real devastation it causes."

Bringing awareness to bullying is the most important message that we can spread. I for one am joining this heroic crusade and hope to help spread their message. The website continues, "Stand for the Silent has heard from the bullies, the bullied, schools, teachers, and parents. Everyone says they're making a change to stop bullying." Making a change in the bullying culture is exactly what we need to do. We need to reach out to all of the bullies and to all of the victimized. We need to make them aware and try to put an end to the bullying epidemic.

The Bully Project has done a tremendous job in bringing the Stand for the Silent organization to our attention through their heartfelt documentary *Bully*. I feel it is something that all kids should see, as the film gives a jarring perspective on bullying and victimization. The Bully Project is focused on educating kids, but they aim to teach adults about bullying as well. Bringing awareness to adults is also one of my main focuses. Many adults are ignorant to the bullying epidemic and we need to open their eyes. The website continues on the subject, "When we started, our primary goal was to educate kids, and we aimed our materials at teaching them the lessons of the film. But we soon realized that we were missing a bigger opportunity to impact the adults in the school community."

Bully documents how adults can frequently ignore the bullying that is going on right under their noses. Many of the educators and authority figures depicted did not do much to deter the bullies. As a matter of fact, a couple of teachers actually bullied the kids themselves according to the film. The adults were in a position to do something, but often times did nothing to help. This is a disturbing trend and something we need to reverse. Teachers and authority figures really need to take bullying as a serious matter. Bullying can actually be a matter of life and death. You could help save someone's life or prevent them from taking lives.

The Bully Project also spreads its convincing message on social media platforms. On a recent Facebook post, the organization highlighted a new application called "Sarahah" which can be extremely dangerous for children to use. According to the post, Sarahah "is an anonymous feedback app that teens are using to pass anonymous digital notes to each other. Drawing upon the contact list on your phone, it lets you connect with friends and send anonymous messages to them as well, even if you don't know them."

This is a dangerous app because people can navigate social platforms anonymously, therefore there could be undetected cyberbullying taking place. The post continued about how the questionable app works, "Sarahah is a very simple app. Once you register with a username and password, you can share your profile link on any social platforms and ask that people use the link to give you feedback. People can type anything anonymously and it will be delivered to you through the app or site."

This certainly seems like a breeding ground for cyberbullying, and The Bully Project is lending a warning that this app may not be appropriate for children. The post continues on saying, "Sarahah is easy to use, so kids won't have any trouble figuring out how to operate the app. But because all comments are anonymous, it's very easy for people to say mean and hurtful things without any repercussions. Reviews on the App Store indicated that Sarahah is being used as a cyberbullying tool. For these reasons, Sarahah is not appropriate for kids."

We need to be aware of such applications like Sarahah and make sure our children are not using these apps. They are dangerous breeding grounds for cyberbullying. The anonymous nature of the app makes it nearly impossible to catch possible perpetrators. The Bully Project does a tremendous job of shining a light on this precarious application and cyberbullying. The movie *Bully* also has exceptional insight and I feel we can all benefit from watching it. The Bully Project is such a well-rounded organization and the work they do should be commended. I am firmly behind their strong messages and I am hoping to join in their amazing efforts.

LOVE IS LOUDER

A PROJECT OF THE JED FOUNDATION

Love is Louder is another anti-bullying project. Their website has an abundance of information to help kids that are being victimized. The site offers an action kit that kids can download. The action kit "gives you ideas for programs and events that you can bring to your campus or community to inspire people to take those actions."

The action kit is spectacular, and I suggest that kids download it, especially those who are being victimized. There are many amazing ideas for kids to find positivity, which include expressing themselves through art, photography, writing and more. The kit suggests doing random acts of kindness and so much more. It's positively worth taking a look at.

The site has different programs, and during Bullying Prevention Month, they featured rock band From Ashes to New. Their hit song, "Broken" has a powerful message. The singer bellows the main lyrics with a determination, "I was standing in the dark. I was damaged from the start. But I knew it in my heart. That I won't be broken." The message is that no matter how damaged you are, you can't be broken. Don't let a bully break your spirit.

The website loveislouder.com is full of impeccable content. Their message continues, "In 2010, we started Love is Louder with The Jed Foundation to amplify a simple message — love and support are louder than any voice that tries to bring us down. Our movement started at a time when there was a lot of anger and confusion online after a series of tragedies involving bullying. Six years later, hundreds of thousands of you have grown the movement around the world. We've relaunched Love is Louder as a community because we want to turn our message into action. We want individuals and communities all over the globe to commit to taking actions that make us all feel more connected and supported. Now feels like a good time to reinvigorate and amplify the Love is Louder message. Once again, we find ourselves in a time where tensions are high on and offline. Conversations have become a war of insults. Instead of celebrating and embracing our differences, we've let them divide us. Some days, it feels like we've forgotten the power of communicating with kindness and taking the time to really understand each other. It's time for us to use our voices and actions (on and offline) to support and look out for each other."

Love is Louder has seen the rise in bullying and heinous incidents that I have been witnessing recently as well. It certainly is a perfect time for this project to become reinvigorated. The bullying epidemic needs as many people fighting against it as possible. Their message is highly prevalent in today's climate. The site continued with its current message, "We will be sharing ways that we can all tune out some of the negative noise, turn our social media accounts into positive forms of expression instead of speaker systems for harmful words and actions, and to help us better understand and respect each other...even if we don't always agree."

The best part of that statement is that we all need to respect each other even if we don't agree. That couldn't have been said any better. Teaching our youth to respect everybody no matter what, is a major key in this fight. Respecting everybody no matter their race, religion, skin color, social status, sexuality, or anything that sets us apart is paramount.

This project continues with the positive messages on their exceptional website, "Love is Louder is all about taking simple actions that make us feel more resilient, connected and supported. What happens when we take actions to strengthen our emotional health and look out for each other? We turn down the volume on those negative internal and external voices that cause us pain. And we amplify the good stuff that improves our lives...and our communities."

This is an uplifting message that kids need to try. Kids need to try and shut out the negativity. As Love is Louder says, "turn down the volume" on the negativity and focus on the positive. Kids need to try and see the good no matter how difficult it may seem. Maintaining positive thoughts will help combat the pain. Loveislouder.com is a tremendous place for kids to visit if they are feeling down. The Love is Louder project emanates positivity and I hope we can link up at some point in our aligned fight against bullying.

JAYLENSCHALLENGE.ORG

One powerful and courageous young man has made a serious dent in the bullying epidemic. This young man has been bullied since he was a young boy. Jaylen Arnold was diagnosed with complex Tourette's syndrome at a young age. As a young boy with this rare disease that causes "tics," he was bullied for being different. This prompted Jaylen and his mom to start a foundation called Jaylen's Challenge that would blossom into one of the biggest anti-bullying causes out there today.

According their tremendous website, jalenschallenge.org, this is their purpose:

"Jaylen's Challenge Foundation, Inc. is a non-profit, charitable organization dedicated to promoting awareness and prevention of bullying through education and community service."

The website tells all about young Jaylen's story as it reads, "At the tender age of 8 years old, Jaylen Arnold wanted to make a difference. In response to bullying, he wanted to fight back with words and experience — rather than with fists or name calling. Jaylen had suffered at the hands of bullies in school due to his disabilities making him an easy target. Bullies don't like different."

Jaylen goes on to explain how his condition interrupts his daily living. "I have complex Tourette's, which means I have vocal 'tics' and motor 'tics' pretty severely. They interrupt my daily living and are quite troubling."

According to a CBS 2 News Report, reported on by Adrianna Weingold, "Jaylen was born with Tourette's syndrome, a neurological disorder that causes repetitive involuntary movements and sounds called 'tics.'" Because of these 'tics,' "Jaylen has himself been a target of bullying."

Jaylen said in the news report, "I got bullied in school at a young age and it hurt me a lot. And I wasn't the only one being bullied. My friends were too."

The report continued, "But instead of letting the bullies get the best of him, Jaylen is fighting back by educating other kids about the pain bullying can cause."

Jaylen continued, "There were kids getting bullied worse than me and they're taking unthinkable ends to themselves just for what someone says or does."

Jaylen's foundation and his movement picked up steam especially with celebrities. Lebron James even posted Jaylen's message on his personal Instagram account for a 24-hour period. Ellen DeGeneres has also worked with Jaylen. Another celebrity actor Dash Mihok traveled with Jaylen as he was helping him spread a message of acceptance. Mihok also has Tourette's syndrome. Mihok had stated in the news report, "I was bullied, but I never had the courage or the fortitude to speak up and so Jaylen was an inspiration to me. I looked up to him and I wished I had been that brave when I was a kid."

The news reporter continued with the story, "Jaylen has made it his life's mission to save others from becoming targets and help bullies see how their actions and words profoundly impact other kids."

Jaylen then said, "Life is too precious for you to want to commit suicide or to hurt yourself or to feel worthless just because of one or two other people's words on you."

Jaylen has been traveling across the country spreading his message since he started the foundation. "Jaylen has made it his own personal challenge to battle bullying," were the words from yet another news report on the young anti-bullying advocate. This report was from WFLA TV news channel 8 and reported on by Jennifer Lee.

Jaylen said in this report concerning his Tourette's, "If you ignore it and just accept it, and just don't pay attention, I don't 'tic' as much. I barely 'tic' around my friends and they forget that I have Tourette's, because I don't do it all because I'm relaxed, and I'm accepted."

Acceptance is something that I have been preaching about this entire book. This is a wonderful example of acceptance. Jaylen, when feeling accepted by others, had infrequent 'tics' and thought about his condition less. "But acceptance isn't something Jaylen has always enjoyed." Four years prior to this report, "at a different school, he encountered vicious verbal bullying from other kids."

Jaylen went on to say, "I was never punched or kicked but to me, verbal is the worst."

His mother Robin Eckelberger continued, "He was mocked. If his body made a sound, that sound was copied by several students over and over." Jaylen's mom Robin who has chronicled his Tourette's over his lifetime said that in 2009, "verbal bullying, (and) mocking inflicted such extreme stress on Jaylen, he endured heartbreaking, near daily physical and neurological meltdowns."

This is definitive proof that acceptance has positive effects on our children. When Jaylen was accepted, people barely noticed his Tourette's. However, when he was mocked for it, he was having daily meltdowns.

The news report continued, "That time in Jaylen's life inspired his mission now. He and his mom created an organization called 'Jaylen's Challenge.'"

Jaylen said of the foundation, "I describe it as a big anti-bullying awareness."

Robin said of her son's efforts, "He didn't want anybody else to experience what he experienced. He has a soft heart and he wants to help others. That's his gift. That's his purpose."

Jaylen continued talking about kids who go to extremes and "making sure nobody wants to attempt suicide, because it's a horrible thing for somebody to be bullied to the point where they want to stop their own life."

Robin said that Jaylen's work has already saved lives; she says that kids write to Jaylen and have said, "I was a bully, I stopped. I was getting bullied and because you came to my school, the bully stopped. I was gonna kill myself but because of you, I didn't."

That's extremely powerful that this young man had the power to help other kids in that way. He is helping to save lives. When it comes to bullying, Jaylen said in the news report, "It's all something that you have to work through. It's a big obstacle course and we can all do it together. Nobody says you have to be alone during this."

Jaylen is clearly a brave young man who has set a shining example of what our kids can be. He is a leader and hopefully will continue to lead in this never-ending fight against bullying.

TYLERCLEMENTI.ORG

The story of this young man is gut wrenching and inspired many advocates to join in the fight against bullying. Many of these advocates are celebrities and I will speak about them later on. The reason many of them were inspired by this story was because Tyler Clementi was a gay man. According to the website, "The summer after his high school graduation, Tyler was learning to embrace his gay self. He had just begun the important journey of coming out to close family and friends. Tyler was brave and honest about who he was, but this was still a difficult, vulnerable time for him."

Shortly after coming out, Tyler began attending Rutgers University in August of 2010. He was excited to learn, grow and to finally have the freedom of living as a gay man.

According to the website, "Smart, talented and creative: Tyler Clementi was deeply loved by family and friends for his kind heart and bright spirit. At the young age of 18, he became a victim of a horrible act of cyber-harassment and humiliation. His story puts a human face on the consequences of cruelty, which has been faced by millions of others suffering in silence in their schools, colleges, teams, workplaces, or faith communities. Tyler's story has inspired tens of thousands of youth and adults to be 'Upstanders' in the face of bullying, harassment and humiliation across the globe."

The website has come up with a definition of what an "Upstander" is and a pledge that goes with being one. Here is how it reads:

I pledge to be an Upstander:

I will stand up to bullying whether I'm at school, at home, at work, in my house of worship; whether I am speaking in the digital cyber world or out in the real world with friends, family, colleagues or teammates.

I will work to make others feel safe and included by treating them with kindness, respect and compassion.

I will not use insulting or demeaning language, slurs, gestures, facial expressions, or jokes about anyone's sexuality, size, gender, race, any kind of disability, religion, class, politics, or other differences, in person or while using technology.

If I realized I have hurt someone I will apologize.

I will remain vigilant and not be a passive audience or "bystander" to abusive actions or words.

If I see or hear behavior that perpetuates prejudice:

I will speak up! I will let others know that bullying, cruelty, and prejudice are abusive and not acceptable.

If I do not feel safe or if my intervention does not change the poor behaviors, I will tell a trusted adult or person of authority.

I will reach out to someone I know who has been the target of abusive actions or words and let this person know that this is not okay with me and ask how I can help.

If I learn in person or online that someone is feeling seriously depressed or potentially suicidal:

I will reach out and tell this person, "Your life has value and is important, no matter how you feel at the moment, and no matter what others say or think."

I will strongly encourage this person to get professional help.

This is something that I truly love! This pledge and its inspiring messages need to be spread. If we all would stand up to bullying and treat others with kindness, respect, and passion, this world would be such a better place. I have been preaching to respect everybody and not make others feel like outcasts. Another point I have tried to make in this book, is that if you see someone being bullied, do something about it! This "Upstander Pledge" couldn't be more spot on. I think we all need to sign it and adhere to its poignant messages.

The paragraph that lists off everything we shouldn't insult people about, is extremely eye-opening to read. Sadly, I have mocked and taunted every single thing on that list in my despicable past. I wish I had a wakeup call and realized that picking on people's differences is by far the worst thing that we can do to each other. If someone had realized that picking on Tyler Clementi for being different was wrong, he still may be here. According to the site, "Tyler became the victim of a horrible act of cyber-harassment, a type of bullying or cruelty that takes place using the internet. One night, Tyler asked his dorm mate for some privacy because he had a date. His dorm mate agreed, but what Tyler didn't know was that his roommate was planning a horrible act of humiliation; he secretly pointed his computer's webcam at Tyler's bed, and then left. The camera captured Tyler in an intimate act, as his dorm mate invited other students to view it online. Many students at the university contributed to this invasion of privacy by not reporting or stopping what was happening to Tyler. Tyler discovered what his abuser had done when he viewed his roommate's Twitter feed. He learned he had widely become a topic of ridicule in his new social environment. He also found out that his roommate was planning a second attempt to broadcast from the webcam. Several days later, Tyler Clementi ended his life by jumping off the George Washington Bridge. He was eighteen years old."

Clementi took his life due to his roommate's horrific and uncalled for actions. His suicide sparked an outrage in the LGBTQ community as it should have. This cyberbullying incident also sparked the comprehensive website tylerclementi.org. You can find programs, actions, and resources there that will help anybody struggling with bullying, cruelty, or harassment. There is a plethora of information as well about Tyler Clementi's heartbreaking story. Let's all try and learn a lesson from this tragic death. Let's all pledge to be an "Upstander" and stop these types of harassments before we lose even more lives.

IMPORTANT ANTI-BULLYING ADVOCATES

ELLEN DEGENERES

Ellen DeGeneres is a comedian, television host, actress, writer, and producer. She is obviously a multi-talented and charismatic woman. Besides her obvious talents, her most important role may actually come as an activist and advocate. DeGeneres is an activist for the LGBTQ community as well as an anti-bullying advocate. These roles have spawned from her past, where she too was bullied for coming out. There was an article written about the bullying she endured and how you don't have to be a child to be bullied. DeGeneres was bullied as an adult, and according to the article taken from goodhousekeeping.com she has said, "The bullying I endured [in Hollywood] after I came out made up for the lack of it during my childhood." Her sitcom was canceled, and opportunities vanished. "I moved out of L.A., went into a severe depression, started seeing a therapist and had to go on antidepressants for the first time in my life," she has said. "It was scary and lonely. All I'd known for 30 years was work, and all of a sudden I had nothing. Plus, I was mad. It didn't feel fair — I was the same person everyone had always known."

The multi-talented star never gave up on herself as the article highlights, "Eventually I started meditating, working out and writing again, and I slowly started to climb out of it," she has said. Her perseverance helped pull her out of a severe depression. Many of us should be inspired by this and hopefully you can find your own inner perseverance to overcome what you are going through.

DeGeneres has strong messages to be proud of who we are and not change for anyone. She says to love who you are. The article continued, "When I was coming out, someone gave me the Martha Graham quote, 'There is only one of you in all time.'" DeGeneres continued, "You're unique, and you're supposed to be." She added, "It's not up to you to try to change it or question it. You're supposed to be exactly who you are. I took in that message. I always remember it. It's not up to me to question why, who or how I am. I just accept who I am, and I don't judge myself."

The advocate says there will be times in your life when people will tell you that you have to change to be successful — dress another way, act a different way, be like someone else. She has said, "Don't do it!"

These are wise words, and I agree—what makes you different makes you special. I am also with her as far as changing who you are. You should never change for anyone. Don't ever conform to the crowd or compromise yourself. Be proud of who you are.

Unfortunately, not everyone is proud of who they are, especially some who are struggling with their sexuality. I've highlighted how coming out can be especially difficult. For some, it was actually life ending like in the case of Tyler Clementi. Shortly after the suicides of Clementi and several other teens that were linked to bullying and homophobia, DeGeneres released a heartfelt video speaking on the matter. "This needs to be a wakeup call to everyone that teenage bullying and teasing is an epidemic in this country and the death rate is climbing. One life lost in this senseless way is tragic, four lives lost is a crisis. And these are just the stories we hear about. How many other teens have we lost? How many others are suffering in silence? Being a teenager and figuring out who you are is hard enough without someone attacking you."

There have been countless deaths that have been linked to bullying and harassment. When will it all end? When is enough, enough? DeGeneres speaks the truth, as she wonders how many others we may have possibly lost. We need to stand together before more lives are lost. These struggling kids need our help as DeGeneres continued to say in her video, "These kids needed us, and we have an obligation to change this. There are messages everywhere that validate this kind of bullying and taunting and we have to make it stop. We can't let intolerance and ignorance take another kid's life. I want anyone out there who feels different and alone to know that I know how you feel and there is help out there."

If someone like this mega-star knows how it feels to be different and alone, then no one is immune to feeling that way. At one point or another, we all feel that way. Let's stop alienating others and let's try to accept everyone. I hope these messages are getting across. If not, I know I will continue the fight and it's great to know that people like DeGeneres will never stop the fight either.

JONATHAN DAVIS

#BeDifferent Brand

Jonathan Davis is the lead singer of the legendary metal band Korn. I have documented how big of a Korn fan I am. Therefore, when I saw that Jonathan was launching an anti-bullying T-shirt campaign, I was extremely excited. He was already a part of my book, as I recognized that he was a victim of bullying through his lyrics. I wanted to document that people in many walks of life have been bullied. Jonathan Davis is a hugely successful lead singer of a highly touted heavy metal band, yet he was victimized by bullies in his painful past. He is an inspiration to me in immeasurable ways. Korn's debut album grabbed ahold of me, and I never let go.

In 2017, Johnathan Davis teamed up with Merchful to create the #BeDifferent brand with his "Freaks Do It Better" shirt. It has been reported that, "The brand is designed to 'show that it is OK to be a freak, an outcast or just a tiny bit normal/abnormal.' In a post on his Facebook page, Davis continued, 'Hey guys, I'm launching a 2-week T-shirt brand campaign with Merchful to help those that are suffering from bullying or suicidal thoughts. As you know, bullying is something a lot of people have to deal with and many times that type of harassment leads to suicide.'"

Davis has an obvious passion for helping those that were bullied like him. He went on to say, "Let's help shine a light on this crap, let's be weird, let's be different, but always be yourself. Let's see how many people we can get behind this movement."

I agree with Jonathan on so many levels. People need to learn to be themselves and be happy with who we are. If we are a little different or a little weird, who cares? People need to respect the fact that we are a little different or a little abnormal in their eyes. After his first campaign, Jonathan released another anti-bullying shirt which displays the words, "Stay Weird."

Although I was a popular kid, I would have to say that I have always been slightly eccentric in a lot of ways. But that's what makes me who I am, and I am proud of my eccentricities. What is it to you if I'm different? Why do you feel the need to victimize others if they are different? Bullies prey on those that they deem to be different. I know this all too well. As an Asian person in a sea of white people, I stood out and was mocked for it. I was obese and this also alienated me from the other kids. Being different from other kids is what bullies will target and later use in their victimizations. When I later became a bully, I picked on other kid's differences and made them feel like they didn't belong. Jonathan Davis was made to feel this way, making him the perfect advocate to help eradicate this pervasive bullying culture. Davis is an amazing role model for anyone who feels different, weird, or abnormal in any way.

MR. RAY

ANTI-BULLYING/KINDNESS PROJECT

Mr. Ray is another musician, and he grew up in West Orange, New Jersey. Being from my home state makes me extra proud of his anti-bullying efforts. Mr. Ray wrote an album titled "NO ROOM FOR BULLIES," which is a fun, different ways for kids to talk about the subject. According to the website, mrray.com, "Ray's newest collection of songs is now available on iTunes...called NO ROOM FOR BULLIES.

His videos have been featured on Ellen DeGeneres' site, EllenTube.com. It's a music/video/live show project that addresses non-bullying while inspiring kids to be tolerant of each other's differences. NO ROOM FOR BULLIES is a cross-promotable new vehicle in driving a message of love to kids, tweens and teens. In this time of change, NO ROOM FOR BULLIES is an imperative theme of kindness that the world is ready to embrace."

According the site, Mr. Ray started working on the anti-bullying project in 2011. He was prompted to start the project after a suicide due to bullying and the bullying abuse of a close family member. Unfortunately, suicide and bullying has become a common theme and one we need to start to reduce. People like Mr. Ray can help save lives with their efforts. The album that he wrote has amazing themes and lyrics which could help save somebody. Here are some of the inspiring lyrics from the title track "NO ROOM FOR BULLIES" taken from the album:

Walkin' down the hallway, he called me a nasty name

Tried to make me feel like I should walk around ashamed

I won't take it anymore, 'cause I like who I am

There'll be no room for bullies anymore

You won't come around my door, I'm proud of my life

There'll be no room for bullies anymore

The lyrics send a simple but powerful message to bullies, and the album has other relevant themes, too. Some of the song titles include "Hey Hey Bully," "Be Who You Are," "Accept Me" and "Don't Keep It to Yourself." The lyrics could help the mindset of any kid, tween or teen as Mr. Ray puts it. He sings about being who you are and not changing for anybody. He croons about no one being able to take your dignity away.

The song "Accept Me" was one that really resonated with me. These lyrics will strike a chord with many kids who are being victimized:

There was this boy who walked around so sad

So different like a color never seen

This kid at school would always beat him down

What makes somebody wanna be so mean?

Can't you accept me for what I am...

Accept me, I do the best I can, accept me, this is who I am

We're not all the same...

You'll never put out the flame of my soul

These lyrics ring exceedingly true. Almost every single victim of bullying just wants to be accepted. They don't want to be made to feel different. This is how we can start to combat the bullying epidemic, by making kids feel more accepted. I am not telling kids that they have to be friends with everybody. I mean, it would be nice. I am just saying that all kids should be respected. There is no need to alienate someone and make them feel as if they don't belong. Let's accept each other no matter how different the person may seem to be. I've said it before that what makes us different is what makes us special. Mr. Ray seems to have tapped into that concept and hopefully he continues to spread his inspiring music and heartfelt message against bullying.

OTHER CELEBRITY ANTI-BULLYING ACTIVISTS

Lady Gaga, Ke$Ha, Taylor Swift, Justin Bieber, Selena Gomez, Christina Aguilera, Demi Lovato, Jessica Alba, Chris Rock, Justin Timberlake, Jennifer Lawrence

Bullying has obviously been a problem long before today's social media climate where everything goes viral. Now, we see everything that happens in an instant. We can keep track of nearly all the bullying incidents that occur in today's world. Before the social media age, we wouldn't hear as much about bullying. Bullying was somewhat hidden, and many people wouldn't even acknowledge its existence. Some would even condone it and consider it a rite of passage. The world has come a long way since those archaic times. More and more people are stepping up and not only acknowledging bullying, but becoming advocates against the practice. There are a slew of famous celebrities who have become advocates because of what they have been through personally. These celebrities were bullied in their past and they have shared their stories in order to try and change the bullying culture. Because they have gone through it firsthand, many of these celebrities have now begun to speak out against schoolyard cruelty. Bullying hits home for many of them, and they didn't have much support when they were going through it. They certainly wanted or needed support when encountering these victimizations, but there was nobody there to stand up for them. Now, these celebrities have been sending their support to fans through anti-bullying campaigns, songs, and more. They want to be the ones to stand up for all the kids being bullied, who have no one to stand up for them. These celebrities are now high-profile ambassadors and advocates against the bullying epidemic.

I have already touched on several celebrities who have had issues with bullying. One of those celebrities is Demi Lovato. Her story is included in the main content of the book, but I also listed her here, as she was part of the article I quoted. Besides Lovato, there are many other celebrities who are also part of the anti-bullying culture. Many of these other celebrities have also become anti-bullying advocates. There are many more celebrities who have joined in the fight against bullying and if I wrote about them all, this book would never end. Therefore, here we are highlighting seven pop singers,who are at the top of the list when it comes to their efforts. They are all seemingly determined to end bullying and continually advocate for victims of bullying.

The following list and accompanying quotes are taken from an article titled "7 Pop Stars Bravely Leading the Fight Against Bullying" taken from mic.com and written by Laura Donavan.

LADY GAGA

Lady Gaga started the Born This Way Foundation several years ago and the organization promotes a more accepting society. The Foundation wants a world where differences are embraced, and individuality is celebrated. Gaga's organization is dedicated to creating a safe community and the wellness of young people. There is an effort to build kinder communities and improve mental health resources. Ultimately, the Born This Way Foundation wants to build a kinder and braver world overall.

Lady Gaga, who has been known to grab attention with her unconventional style choices and extreme performance art, wanted to put a stop to bullying before she launched her organization. Her attention on anti-bullying came into focus after a fourteen-year-old Gaga fan, Jamey Rodemeyer committed suicide. The young fan fell victim to anti-gay bullying, and the recording artist expressed immense heartbreak about the death on Twitter: "The past days I've spent reflecting, crying, and yelling. I have so much anger. It is hard to feel love when cruelty takes someone's life. Bullying must become illegal. It's a hate crime."

Lady Gaga has had her own experiences with teasing and taunting, therefore it makes sense that she'd want to do everything in her power to prevent it. She has told MTV in a video interview that a bunch of guys once hurled her into a garbage bin on the streets of New York during high school.

She said all the other girls from the school could see her in the trash as they left school. Nobody did anything to help and instead just laughed. She recalls holding back the tears as she didn't want anybody to see her that way. Gaga recalled one of the girls even looking at her like 'are you about to cry? You're pathetic.'

At the time, Gaga never told anyone about the trash can incident, because it was too embarrassing for her. This is a common theme in bullying as many kids are embarrassed to tell others what is happening. I can tell you firsthand you will regret not telling anybody. Internalizing the pain only makes things worse. Telling someone will help you release some of the pain you are feeling. Also, someone may be able to help you. Please let someone know if you are being victimized.

KE$HA

'TiK ToK' singer Ke$ha shares the same sentiments as Gaga as she doesn't tolerate anti-gay bullying. The twenty-five-year-old has said in an issue of Seventeen, that she is all about standing up to gay/lesbian/transgender bullying. That is not the pop singer's only focus however, as her little brother who is thirteen, gets made fun of because he has a stutter. She has said, "I just have zero tolerance for people making fun of others." Ke$ha says she remembers every person who told her that she couldn't do something or that put her down. She was on the receiving end of insults, including that she was ugly or too fat. She remembers all the people who were in her words "soulless and judgmental."

Previously, I included the story of Tyler Clementi, a young man who took his life in the fall of 2010, after his college roommate posted a video of him engaging in sexual acts with another man. After the incident, Ke$ha uploaded a video of her own to encourage bullied or abused folks not to give up, stating, "I just want to tell you, it will get better. It will." She continues to say, that no matter what life you choose to live, if you are gay, lesbian, bisexual, transgender, that the life you choose to live is beautiful. Ke$ha lends her full support and love. She continued, "When people are mean for no reason it's horrible, but I swear to God it will get better so please don't ever give up."

This is an immensely beautiful message. No matter how badly you are feeling now and how much bullying is beating you down, everything will eventually turn. Ke$ha is spot on here, just don't ever give up!

TAYLOR SWIFT

Before Taylor Swift had her mega-success, she didn't have much of any star power in middle school, which she has publicly spoken about many times and still seems to haunt her to this day. Swift has said that Junior high was difficult because she got dumped by a group of popular girls. Swift told Teen Vogue in 2009, "They didn't think I was cool or pretty enough, so they stopped talking to me."

Once the Pennsylvania native became a big deal, her past harassers came to one of her performances where they suddenly were showing full support, as if they'd never victimized Swift in the first place. The girls showed up, wearing her T-shirts and they asked Swift to sign their CDs. The songbird went on to tell Teen Vogue, "It was bittersweet, because it made me realize that they didn't remember being mean to me and that I needed to forget about it, too."

After her experiences, Swift decided to release a powerful anti-bullying hit, "Mean," in 2011. The lyrics have an anti-bullying sentiment and you should listen to it. I have said several times that kids can be mean and the ones that are on the receiving end of their meanness, need to overcome it.

JUSTIN BIEBER

The Biebs allowed the highly-publicized documentary *Bully* to include his song, 'Born to Be Somebody' in its trailer. The documentary sparked an entire foundation called "The Bully Project" which is included in the "Important Anti-Bullying Organizations" Section of this book. The Biebs lent the song to the documentary in part because he's had firsthand experiences with harassment. "I was bullied," the Canadian has told Showbiz Tonight. The pop star continued, "Most people in their lifetime have been bullied at some point. I think that it's about time that people start making a change."

The successful pop star is definitely calling for a change and doing his part to make those changes. He clearly has his finger on the pulse of bullying and the effects it has on our society. Bieber saw something disturbing which prompted him to reach out to Australian, Casey Heynes, a young student who received worldwide praise after body-slamming his persistent bully. The clip had gone viral on the internet and that urged the Biebs to meet up with Casey.

The Biebs was amazed when he saw the clip on TMZ. Bieber told the young Aussie. "It shows everybody else that you have to stand up for yourself and you can't just take it." Bieber went on to say that the first thing you should do if you are being bullied is go tell someone. He continued to say that you might have to hit back, because unfortunately sometimes you have to. Biebs thought Casey had to in his particular situation. Biebs was clearly proud of the young man as he went on to call Casey "a kid who stood up for himself against bullying. A real-life hero."

Indeed, if you are being bullied, you should try to tell someone first. Speak up and use your voice. This is always your first course of action, but if you are pushed too far, then it is OK to fight back. This young man was a shining example of fighting back only when completely necessary.

SELENA GOMEZ

Not only is the Biebs doing his part, but his on again, off again, girlfriend, Selena Gomez has had her own encounters with being bullied. The singer had told Ellen DeGeneres in 2011 that "she hopes her music can help others through hard times."

Gomez has said that she realizes everybody gets picked on and made fun of. She continued saying that she was still dealing with it at eighteen-years-old. Gomez said, "It's already hard enough being eighteen and figuring out who you are and what you want to be, and people constantly want to take you down."

Gomez wrote an upbeat tune called "Who Says" that addresses this plight with its lyrics. The lyrics are extremely heartfelt:

You made me insecure, told me I wasn't good enough,

but who are you to judge ...

I'm sure you got some things you'd like to change about yourself,

but when it comes to me,

I wouldn't want to be anybody else,

I'm no beauty queen, I'm just beautiful me ...

Who says, who says you're not perfect, who says you're not worth it,

who says you're the only one that's hurting?

These lyrics really hit home as they demonstrate that everyone should just be happy with themselves. As hard as it sounds sometimes, you have to love yourself for who you are. Who is anyone to judge you, if you are happy with who you are? Even if you are happy with yourself, there will be people who try and tear you down. Don't allow others to tear you down; stay strong. Always believe in who you are. Gomez has been helping to spread this much needed message.

DEMI LOVATO

Demi Lovato has had quite a full life at a young age. At only eighteen years of age, she quit the Jonas Brothers tour and entered herself into a treatment center to resolve what was described as emotional and physical issues. Sources close to the singer told People magazine that the young lady was still dealing with the effects of bullying. Lovato, who struggled mightily with bullies, would eventually discuss her issues with bullying. Later down the road, she revealed all the pain and victimizations that she had to endure. This led the talented singer to become a spokesperson for an anti-bullying campaign.

"I had a really tough time when I was in middle school," the former X Factor judge divulged to People magazine. Other kids would write 'hate petitions' directed towards Lovato which they sent around and had signed. They continued the harassment with CD-bashing parties, destroying her demos. They would come to her house, stand nearby and yell things. She was a constant target.

Now an anti-bullying advocate, Lovato visited the New York City's Young Women's Leadership School in 2012, where she suggested the students rise above bullying by painting their pinky fingers blue. This was to symbolize 'pinky promising' in order to fight harassment. This, in my eyes, was a powerful technique and a sign of solidarity amongst the young girls. The singer has become quite the role model, and you can read more about her story in the main content of the book."

CHRISTINA AGUILERA

"The Voice" judge Christina Aguilera knows what it's like to be bullied and victimized. Before the Mickey Mouse alum was a singing sensation, she faced mean girls in her hometown. The mean girls slashed the tires on her family's car and laughed at her talent show performances. Christina released an uplifting song called "Beautiful," which is about feeling "beautiful no matter what they say." The singer expressed that she has definitely experienced forms of bullying, and that's why it was so important for her to write songs like 'Beautiful' and 'Fighter.'

Music isn't her only channel to combat bullying either. Several years back an eleven-year-old girl named Harper Gruzins received nationwide criticism for singing the "worst ever rendition" of "The Star-Spangled Banner," Aguilera sent words of encouragement to the young girl in a note: "Harper, you had the courage to sing in front of thousands of people and I applaud you. Keep your head up high and keep trying. You have nothing to be ashamed of."

Sometimes all it takes is an uplifting message to lift someone's spirit. I am willing to guess that Aguilera's message went a long way to lift this young girl up. The amount of criticism towards an eleven-year-old girl was completely outrageous and uncalled for. The world we live in now is a scary place. Hopefully, Aguilera gave this girl some peace of mind, after all the unwarranted harassment she received.

The following list of celebrities and accompanying quotes are taken from an article which appeared on thetalko.com

.

JESSICA ALBA

Jessica Alba is a star who has thanked her high school bullies for the fame and success she has attained as a businesswoman. She encourages young girls to try and take the bullying in a positive manner. According to the article, Alba was a victim of bullying, as "she was ridiculed by her peers because of her outfits." Alba did not come from a family of means and couldn't afford luxury clothing or accessories. This sounds familiar, as I too targeted kids who were impoverished.

Alba had a rough time in school, which prompted her dad to walk her to class, to ensure she didn't get attacked. The article continues, "She was so scared that she ate her lunch in the nurses room to avoid encounters with the mean girls." Alba has shared her story to raise awareness of the bullying epidemic. She is focused on giving bullied children, especially girls, a fair chance to escape their tormentors.

This is tremendous because I think a lot of time, we focus on young boys getting bullied. Young girls can also feel the wrath of bullies. Girls are sometimes more defenseless as well. Alba's focus will help raise awareness that girls are not immune to the bullying epidemic. We need to help all kids who are being victimized.

JUSTIN TIMBERLAKE

Justin Timberlake has confessed that the same qualities which he was bullied for, are the same ones that made him famous. Timberlake was bullied for his singing when he was growing up. He has called on rising singers and told them not to be afraid of their talents. He has said, "being different means, you make the difference."

That is a profound statement made by the multi-talented singer and actor. I love that Timberlake is encouraging kids to be different. It's similar to my motto, "What makes you different, is what makes you special!" I am glad that I am on the same page as a global icon. I hope kids can grab these messages and realize that it's OK to be different.

JENNIFER LAWRENCE

Jennifer Lawrence has a famous slogan when it comes to bullies. She has said, "ignore 'em or forgive 'em." Sometimes that is easier said than done, but I love the sentiment behind it. According to the article, "She confessed to having been bullied several times by mean girls in elementary school. One even had her hand out invitations to a party she was not invited to." Even at her young age, Lawrence was bold, as she went on to throw the invitations into the trash.

That is such an inspiring story and hopefully there are kids who can summon the same inner-strength. If kids start taking action and standing up to the bullies of the world, that will be the first step in stopping this epidemic. Standing up to the perpetrators can mean several things. Let's remember, your first action should be to try and talk the bully down. If the victimizations continue, then it is time to tell a trusted adult. Do not resort to physicality unless absolutely necessary.

CHRIS ROCK

"The comedian literally took the bullying and made a career out of it." Rock attended an all-white school, where he was a target of bullying on a daily basis. I know how it feels to be bullied every day firsthand. During one of the BET awards ceremonies, "the comedian thanked all the boys who used to bully him for giving him the drive to become who he is today." Despite all the harassment, Rock has said that he received all the love he needed as a kid at home.

Having a good home life is essential. If you are worried about your kids and whether or not they will get bullied, it's important to put them in a positive mindset. Parents must stay positive, even if their kids are getting bullied. Kids usually reflect the attitudes of their parents.

The same goes for kids who become bullies. This is usually learned behavior. These bullies either learn it from other kids who have bullied them, or from an abusive home. Even if you don't abuse your kids physically, verbal abuse can transform a child into a bully. Parents, please be aware how your home life is affecting your children.

The world we live in is indeed a scary place now. We live in a world where an eleven-year-old girl received relentless harassment and harsh criticism. I understand that she sang our nation's anthem, but she was just a little girl. If the bullying can extend this far, there is no telling how far it can go. I don't want to imagine a world that is comfortable with these types of harassments. Neither do these celebrities who are now proud anti-bullying advocates.

We should all agree that all of these celebrities need to be commended, as they are all doing their part to join in the fight against bullying. Everyone has been affected by bullying in one way or another as these celebrity stories show. Nobody is truly immune to the bullying epidemic. The celebrities are doing their part, now it is our turn to do something and join them in their courageous efforts!

LGBTQ YOUTH and BULLYING

As illustrated by the celebrities listed, the LGBTQ community is amongst the most bullied group according to many statistics. There's a reason why Ellen DeGeneres, Lada Gaga, and Ke$ha are focused on in this group. The youth in the LGBTQ community have it even tougher, as they are victimized more often. According to mentalhealthamerica.net: "While trying to deal with all the challenges of being a teenager, lesbian/gay/bisexual/transgender (LGBTQ) teens also have to deal with harassment, threats and violence directed at them on a daily basis. LGBTQ youth are nearly twice as likely to be called names, verbally harassed or physically assaulted at school compared to their non-LGBTQ peers. Their mental health and education, not to mention their physical well-being, are at-risk."

The LGBTQ youth have an even harder time than other kids, which is saying something. They are more likely to hurt themselves because of the victimizations they are subject to. The website mentalhealthamerica.net continues with the following statements:

- *Self-Harm:* With each instance of verbal or physical harassment, the risk of self-harm among LGBTQ youth is two and a half times more likely.

- *Suicide:* Gay, lesbian, and bisexual youth are four times more likely to attempt suicide than their heterosexual counterparts.

- *Education:* Gay teens in U.S. schools are often subjected to such intense bullying that they're unable to receive an adequate education. LGBTQ youth identified bullying problems as the second most important problem in their lives, after non-accepting families, compared to non-LGBTQ youth identifying classes/exams/grades.

As you can see, the LGBTQ youth needs as much assistance as possible when it comes to bullying. They are frequent targets of harassments and victimizations. We all need to make a more concerted effort to monitor how people of the LGBTQ community are being treated.

We live in new times where everybody should be accepted despite their race, color, religion, gender, sexual orientation, or lifestyle choices. I have an ample amount of remorse for the way that I bullied my cousin, Joe, when we were younger. I am happy to have cultivated a healthier relationship with him over the years. I now accept him wholeheartedly and would never mistreat him. Accepting him was all a part of my exceptional transformation. I am glad to have taken personal inventory and made the changes that I needed to make. I am now accepting of all people and I am a better person for it. We all need to make changes in order to facilitate a world where we are all equals. The LGBTQ community especially deserves to be treated equally and with respect. We are all just people after all.

MENTAL HEALTH AND BULLYING

Bullying can affect mental health in a multitude of negative ways. According to stopbullying.gov, "Bullying can affect everyone—those who are bullied, those who bully, and those who witness bullying. Bullying is linked to many negative outcomes including impacts on mental health, substance use, and suicide. It is important to talk to kids to determine whether bullying—or something else—is a concern."

Bullying affects all that are involved and more often than not leads to negative consequences. Kids can go from being bullied to becoming the bully just as I did. They can turn to substance abuse which I also had some issues with. Kids may start drinking and doing drugs at an earlier age if they are being abused.

Kids can even be driven to the brink. Kids who are victimized might have thoughts about ending everything by taking their own lives. Suicide is a serious subject when discussing the bullying epidemic. I have illustrated several instances where kids have taken their lives because they just couldn't take the pain any longer. Mentally they were driven to their breaking point. We need to prevent kids who are being victimized from taking their lives. Suicide is the ultimate consequence of bullying.

Kids are struggling with mental health due to abuse. According to stopbullying.gov:

"Kids who are bullied can experience negative physical, school, and mental health issues. Kids who are bullied are more likely to experience:

- Depression and anxiety, increased feelings of sadness and loneliness, changes in sleep and eating patterns, and loss of interest in activities they used to enjoy. These issues may persist into adulthood.

- Health complaints.

- Decreased academic achievement—GPA and standardized test scores—and school participation. They are more likely to miss, skip, or drop out of school.

A very small number of bullied children might retaliate through extremely violent measure. In 12 of 15 school shooting cases in the 1990s, the shooters had a history of being bullied."

That last statement is eye-opening, and this is yet another catastrophic effect of bullying. Many kids who are victimized feel like they want to retaliate and hurt those who have hurt them. Some kids just turn to bullying like I did. This is not a very good consequence either, but it is infinitely better than killing. We need to identify these kids and talk to them before they retaliate in a deadly manner. Their mental state is fragile, and these kids need to be stopped before more lives are taken. We need to make sure that kids understand that violence and killing others is never an option. If you see your child is becoming increasingly angrier and possibly violent, it is time to sit them down and see what is going on in their life. The signs may be right in front of you. We need to do everything in our power to stop these school shootings. Putting an end to the bullying epidemic will go a long way towards doing that.

The kids who get bullied are not the only ones who suffer mentally. Kids who bully others also will have some mental health issues and could have problems later in life as well. According to stopbullying.gov:

"Kids who bully others can also engage in violent and other risky behaviors into adulthood. Kids who bully are more likely to:

- Abuse alcohol and other drugs in adolescence and as adults

- Get into fights, vandalize property, and drop out of school

- Engage in early sexual activity

- Have criminal convictions and traffic citations as adults

- Be abusive toward their romantic partners, spouses or children as adults."

Kids who bully others can have just as many problems as those who are bullied. Kids become abusive towards others and can display violent tendencies. I even became abusive towards teachers as a result of my Bully Complex. If it comes to light that your child is a bully, you need to speak to them and make sure they know that what they are doing isn't right. You must try and intervene. In order to help the mental health of your child, the bullying must cease immediately.

There has been an abundance of research done concerning bullying and mental health. Here is some important information taken from the US Department of Health website:

"Bullying can affect physical and emotional health, both in the short term and later in life. It can lead to physical injury, social problems, emotional problems, and even death. Those who are bullied are at increased risk for mental health problems, headaches, and problems adjusting to school. Bullying also can cause long-term damage to self-esteem.

Children and adolescents who are bullies are at increased risk for substance use, academic problems, and violence to others later in life.

Those who are both bullies and victims of bullying suffer the most serious effects of bullying and are at greater risk for mental and behavioral problems than those who are only bullied or who are only bullies.

NICHD [National Institute of Child Health and Human Development] research studies show that anyone involved with bullying—those who bully others, those who are bullied, and those who bully and are bullied—are at increased risk for depression.

NICHD-funded research studies also found that unlike traditional forms of bullying, youth who are bullied electronically—such as by computer or cell phone—are at higher risk for depression than the youth who bully them. Even more surprising, the same studies found that cyber victims were at higher risk for depression than were cyberbullies or bully-victims (i.e., those who both bully others and are bullied themselves), which was not found in any other form of bullying."

Overall, bullying can have countless negative effects on mental health. Kids are at high risk to have mental health problems in the short and even the long term, on both sides of the bullying spectrum. Kids are more prone to depression and can have social problems. These are not even the most severe issues that kids can have. Suicide is one of the most dangerous consequences, and killing other kids is the deadliest and most gruesome repercussion from bullying. When it comes to the mental health of children and the effects of bullying, this is something that must be taken with the utmost seriousness. Let's try and promote a happier life for these kids—a life without bullying and a life with stable mental health.

CYBERBULLYING

According to Stopbullying.gov, cyberbullying is defined as: "Bullying that takes place using electronic technology. Electronic technology includes devices and equipment such as cell phones, computers and tablets as well as communication tools including social media sites, text messages, chat and websites. Examples of cyberbullying include mean text messages or emails, rumors sent by email or posted on social networking sites and embarrassing pictures, videos, websites or fake profiles."

I am thankful that I grew up in simpler times because I am sure I would have been cyberbullied as well. When I was younger, I was an easy mark for bullies, and I know that cyber-predators would have tracked me down. Now, I see this new form of bullying firsthand all over social media. If this type of technology was available when I was in high school, I certainly would have been a cyberbully as well. I undoubtedly would have used it to terrorize my prey. Cyberbullying is the new way of terrorizing others and is a disturbing trend in bullying. It is the hardest to monitor, therefore I have included some information here.

According to Stopbullying.gov:

"Kids who are cyberbullied are more likely to:

- Use alcohol and drugs

- Skip school

- Experience in-person bullying

- Be unwilling to attend school

- Receive poor grades

- Have lower self-esteem

- Have more health problems."

Whether referencing cyberbullying or bullying in person, kids are experiencing the negative effects from the victimization. Cyberbullying is something that we are going to have to self-regulate as I've stated. It's OK and important for adults to ask kids questions. Find out who your children are talking to, in person and on social media platforms that are harder to keep track of. It's imperative that adults monitor what apps their kids are using. That goes for all adults, parents, and teachers alike. Kids are using these apps in school as well.

Parents need to be more aware in order to help prevent cyberbullying. Teachers need to be mindful of internet and phone activities that their students engage in as well. There are ways to help prevent cyberbullying. According to Stopbullying.gov, you should:

"Talk with your kids about cyberbullying and other online issues regularly.

- Know the sites your kids visit and their online activities. Ask where they're going, what they're doing, and who they're doing it with.

- Tell your kids that as a responsible parent you may review their online communications if you think there is reason for concern. Installing parental control filtering software or monitoring programs are one option for monitoring your child's online behavior, but do not rely solely on these tools.

- Have a sense of what they do online and in texts. Learn about the sites they like. Try out the devices they use.

- Ask for their passwords, but tell them you'll only use them in case of emergency.

- Ask to "friend" or "follow" your kids on social media sites or ask another trusted adult to do so.

- Encourage your kids to tell you immediately if they, or someone they know, is being cyberbullied. Explain that you will not take away their computers or cell phones if they confide in you about a problem they are having."

These steps are crucial for adults to take in helping to prevent cyberbullying. This will be the hardest bullying to stop, but the easiest one to monitor as most of the time, cyberbullying will come in message or post form—with the exception of certain apps like Snapchat and Sarahah in which content either expires, or is anonymous. For the most part, adults can see who is doing the bullying and can stand up for their children, or in my case, stand up for my number one homie Clayton. If we all stand together, we can help reduce this trend known as cyberbullying!

The bullying epidemic is something we must all band together to fight. I hope to have enlightened you and I hope even more that I have instilled in you a will to help stop this bully train! We, the adults can do the most damage in combating the bully epidemic. So please join me in this fight and let's end all forms of bullying for good!

RETHINK ANTI-CYBER BULLYING APPLICATION

ReThink is a cutting-edge, brand-new technology developed by Trisha Prabhu which can be downloaded to a smartphone or tablet. This application is a true breakthrough when it comes to combatting cyberbullying. According to their website, rethinkwords.com, "ReThink is an award-winning, innovative, nonintrusive, patented technology that effectively detects and stops online hate before the damage is done."

The site highlights how the application actually works with the following bullet points:

- Teen tries to post offensive message

- ReThink technology detects offensive message

- Second chance to ReThink with an alert

- Teen declines to post offensive message

- Online hate is stopped. Lives are saved!

The technology interrupts the person sending the message, when it is deemed offensive and asks if they are sure if they want to post that message. According to research that Prabhu administered using 1,500 valid trials of data, kids changed their minds 93.4% of the time when asked to "ReThink" their message. Also, according to the site, "the overall willingness of an adolescent to post an offensive message reduced from 71% to 4%." These statistics are eye-popping.

The story of how Trisha Prabhu invented this application is one that needs to be told. Prabhu is a young woman herself being only eighteen-years-old at the time of this writing. In 2013, when Prabhu was only thirteen she read a news story about the suicide of a twelve-year-old girl who had been cyberbullied by her classmates. That girl's name was Rebecca Ann Sedwick and according to cbsnews.com, she was told that she should kill herself. The news report continues telling how her classmates were relentless and said such things to the victim like, "You haven't killed yourself yet" and to "Go jump off of a building." Sadly, the young girl listened to her antagonizers. The news story recounts, "After nearly a year of bullying by as many as 15 girls, authorities said Rebecca climbed a tower at an abandoned concrete plant and hurled herself to her death."

This is both stunning and tragic. Prabhu was deeply affected. According to her own website, trishaprabhu.com, "She was shocked, heartbroken, and outraged. She wondered — how could a girl younger than herself be pushed to take her own life? She immediately knew something had to change. Deeply moved by the silent pandemic of cyberbullying and passionate to end online hate, Trisha created the patented technology product ReThink."

Prabhu soon researched the link between bullying and suicide and she found that there have been countless instances, as I have illustrated in this book. According to her research, 38% of kids who are cyberbullied have suicidal tendencies. Kids are also ten times more likely to commit suicide when cyberbullied than when not. Prabhu said, "I wish more than anything that I could re-write those stories. I wish I could make every perpetrator ReThink what they did. But what if I could do that? What if I could stop the damage before it was done?"

She continued as she highlighted the flaws in today's social media climate in a speech available on the ReThink website, "What social media sites are doing is really nothing. Their mechanism is a stop, block, tell method. You stop what you're doing if you're the victim. You block the cyberbully and you immediately go tell a parent or guardian. Sounds pretty reasonable but here's what actually happens. Adolescents — we're kind of afraid to tell people that we're being cyberbullied." The young advocate is totally spot on as nine out of ten kids do not tell their parents they are being victimized.

This application is truly revolutionary because it could change the whole culture of cyberbullying by making the perpetrators think about their actions. There is so much wrong with the stop, block, tell method that Prabhu brings to light. She said in her speech, "Why are we putting the burden on the victim to block the cyberbully? Why aren't we changing the behavior in the actual cyberbully? What if I gave them a chance to think about what they were doing?" This young lady is absolutely correct as we need to try and change the thinking of bullies and that of course includes cyberbullies. They are the ones who are victimizing others. We need to get through to them and the ReThink application is a giant step in that direction.

This amazing young advocate is now helping combat cyberbullying more than anyone could have ever imagined. She summed what the application is all about in her impassioned speech, "ReThink before you type. ReThink before you post. ReThink before the damage is done." She truly has come up with a unique concept to put a stop to cyberbullying at the source.

IMPORTANT INFORMATION FOR ADULTS

This book is an important teaching lesson for adults, just as it is for the children that we are trying to save from bullying or prevent from becoming bullies. The adults are the ones with the authority and should be intervening when there is a bullying situation. In fact, as an adult, you have most likely encountered bullying in one fashion or another. Whether you have been a victim, the perpetrator or just a witness, you probably have experience with this important matter. This should give you a better perspective if you have a child who is a bully or being bullied. You might notice the warning signs more effectively. If you do recognize a bullying situation, you must intervene and attempt to rectify it. If you are an adult and you are ignoring persistent bullying, then you are perpetuating the problem. Please, I hope after reading this book, you will take bullying more seriously. You have seen how it can have tragic consequences when ignored.

It is important to pay more attention to our children. There will be many signs if they are being victimized or abused. By being more diligent and monitoring children more closely, we can all recognize the signs. Here are ten warning signs your child is being bullied according to Stompoutbullying.org:

1. Withdrawal

It's normal for kids, especially teens, to put some distance between parents. But keep an eye on if your child is disconnecting from previously enjoyable social situations.

2. Mood swings

We're not talking about talking back typical teenage angst. If your child is experiencing mood swings, appearing depressed or teary, or is uncharacteristically angry, this could be sign of a bigger problem outside the home.

3. Begins bullying siblings or younger kids

Bullied children can sometimes flip roles and become the bully, especially with younger siblings, in order to feel empowered and in control.

4. Makes up excuses for missing school

This includes students who frequently visit the school nurse or ditch school, too. Take a look and see if there is a pattern to the absences. It could be a way your child is trying to avoid a particular person or situation.

5. Complains of headaches, stomach aches and fatigue

Depression can often cause physical pain. Chronic stress and anxiousness can also lead to sleep problems, nightmares and even bedwetting in some children.

6. Changes in eating habits

Suddenly skipping meals or binge eating can be an indication that something is wrong. Bullies also tend to extort other children by stealing their lunch or lunch money.

7. Shuts down social media

This could be a sign of cyberbullying. Ask your child why they are avoiding their computer or cell phone and pay attention if they get tense or uncomfortable when answering the question.

8. Damaged or missing property

Ripped clothing could be a sign of physical bullying. Missing toys, school supplies or money may indicate your child is being pressured to give up their possessions unwillingly.

9.Unexplained injuries

Immediately notify school officials if you notice new or unexplained cuts, bruises and scrapes.

10. Fear of being left alone

Be aware if your child is suddenly clingy during drop-off, before leaving for the bus or asks for you to be there immediately after school dismissal.

There are many different kinds of bullying. Some of it's obvious, and some of it's more subtle. Bullying is always an intentional, aggressive and repeated behavior that involves an imbalance of power or strength."

I have personal experience with a lot of these warning signs when I was bullied. I was often withdrawn and didn't want to engage in many social activities with other kids. I knew that I would be bullied, therefore I tended to shy away from group activities.

My mood swings leaned toward the angry side. I illustrated many instances where anger had built up inside of me and even led to me being a bully. Bullying younger kids is a clear sign that your kid has been bullied or is currently being bullied. I turned to bullying the first chance I could. I felt that I had to unleash onto others what had been done to me. This is a vicious thought cycle that needs to be eradicated. Through education and verbal communication, we can teach our children that bullying is never the answer. Bullying isn't right in any form and even if they were victims, it does not give them the right to inflict pain onto others.

SAY GOODBYE TO BULLYING

I hope you have connected with me during my entire journey that I have documented. I hope my stories have been eye-opening, educational, and heartfelt. I hope that you are not overly offended by many of the things that I have said or done in my despicable past. I want you to really dive into my story and recognize the exceptional changes that I have made. I feel writing my story has really dredged up feelings that I needed to sort out. I needed to rectify my wrongs and attempt to make amends.

I hope you all realize that the bullying epidemic is a no-nonsense issue that needs to be taken seriously. I hope that I have opened your eyes, and there will now be a light shining on the bullying tendencies that are often ignored in our society. Now that we all see it, we all need to come together. I want us all to band together. We need to join forces and attempt to eradicate this epidemic that has poisoned our society for too long. Bullying is a problem that is never going away unless we become more proactive about it. Therefore, I implore you to join me; let's fight this growing bullying epidemic together. Together we can make changes and end bullying.

If you're a kid and still reading this, I want you to know that there is hope for you. You have to be strong-minded and stand up to those who are victimizing you. You have to report what is happening to you and USE YOUR VOICE! I want you to be as strong as you can, and remember to Be Brave! Be Courageous! Be Valiant! You can overcome anything you put your mind to. Together we will overcome bullying.

I want all the kids to know how important you truly are. I want you to know the value you give to this world. You are the future. You are all amazing human beings and shining stars. I want to leave you with these words as I want you to believe in yourselves. I believe in you and I know you can achieve success. Be a Rock Star! Be a Winner! Be a Champion!

The adults, the bullies, and the bullied must all come together. Let's all galvanize and join forces. The time is now to realize how wrong and dangerous bullying actually is. Together we can put a stop to all of the pain and victimizations. Together we can use our voices for good and fight the evils of bullying. Together we can stop future Bully Complexes from developing. Together we will make changes. I can see hope. I can see people treating each other with respect and as equals. I can see change on the horizon. I can see the day is coming when we all band together and join the fight. Let's combat this bullying epidemic once and for all. Our efforts may lead to a day when we can all finally say goodbye to bullying!

ACKNOWLEDGEMENTS

I hope you all enjoy my book in some capacity. Hopefully, I provided you with at least a modicum of entertainment in one form or another. Whether I made you laugh or cry, angry or sad. I am just happy to have made you feel something.

I hope there isn't anybody that is too offended by what I have written. If you are offended, please remember the context of what I've written. I was in a close-minded frame of thinking as I was a totally different person. I am a new man and I would like to apologize for anything that anyone finds offensive or hurtful.

I am ecstatic to finally bring you the published product. Even though this was a childhood dream, I almost never followed through. I let myself get in the way of myself for so very long. I am extremely happy to have finally woken up. I am finally seeing clearly.

For the first time in my life I believe in myself more than I believe in anything else and that's more powerful than anything. Part of that belief came from all of you, so thank you all for believing in me and supporting me!

First and foremost, I want to thank my parents collectively. Without you, I wouldn't be here and wouldn't be the man that I am today. I have fallen off the path many times and you were both there to pick me up. I've made many mistakes, yet you were both there for me when life was toughest. I can't thank you both enough for your unwavering support. I love you both and hope I have made you proud!

I would like to personally thank my father, Albert Lospinoso. Thank you for being brave and understanding. I know some people may misconstrue the things I've written. People may twist my words. But let's not get this twisted, my dad is a caring, loving, and wonderful man. He doesn't have a racist bone in his body. The opinions I formed had nothing to do with how my parents raised me. I formed these opinions elsewhere. My dad loves and respects everybody. Please really read the words that I have written, and you will see that what I am saying is absolutely the truth! Thank you, dad for letting me write this story the way it was intended to be written.

I would like to personally thank my mother, Sonia Lospinoso. Thank you for being tough and honest. You raised some questions about some of the questionable things that I have written. I'll be honest, I needed to hear them. I did lighten certain areas of the book because of your concern. I understand there are still some tough things for you to read. I just want you to know that you made me a strong, tough willed man. That is why I wrote the book the way I did! You taught me to be fierce and not to hold back when I believe in something. Mom, you always loved me so much that you made me a mama's boy. I can't wait until you see the success that is coming to me. Then I can finally return the favor, by spoiling you. I hope I have made you proud! I finally wrote a book like I always said I would.

Next, I would like to thank my younger siblings. My sister played a role in this book. I could never write my life story without including her. Thank you, Jennifer Lospinoso, especially for letting me use you as a part of my story. I know you're a very private person and I appreciate you letting me include you. As you've said to me on several occasions, "It's not only my story." It certainly isn't. But as always, you put things into perspective and kept me in check. You've been an amazing sister my entire life and an even better friend. You've supported me throughout the years, and I had you to lean on. I felt like I failed you as an older brother, because I leaned on you so much. For that I'm sorry and I thank you for always being there. Without you, I wouldn't have survived this long. Seriously, I wouldn't be where I'm at without you. I would probably be in jail or dead if it weren't for you. Thanks sis, I'll always love you!

To my younger brother, Michael Lospinoso, thank you for being an amazing man! You have a short role in this story, but it was an important one! During all my racist rants and ignorance, you were always there to keep me in check. You always told me I was being ignorant. I am finally happy to admit that you were always right. Thank you for being level-headed, non-judgmental, and politically correct. I've learned a lot from you even though you are my younger brother. I hope I am becoming an older brother you can finally look up to. Love you buddy!

I want to thank my amazing family as a whole! Each and every one of you has supported me throughout this entire process. When I started telling all of you about this project, I wasn't sure what type of reactions I would receive. I must say that the enthusiasm and unbridled support I was given, really gave me a boost. I know you've all been waiting anxiously, yet you've all been patient. I was expecting some of you to come at me sideways and ask what was taking so long! I apologize as the process was more than I expected, but it's finally here!

I want to personally thank my cousin Nikki Pierro. You went above and beyond in helping me. I know you say that's what family should do, but not everyone does. Thank you for rallying others and getting behind me.

I want to thank my closest cousins. The Crisci's were always an integral part of my life. Rosie, Jo-Jo, and Angela Crisci, thank you for always having my back. You three have always been there for me and supported me. They say cousins are your first friends in life and I'm happy that you three were exactly that. Rosie and Ang, you have small parts in the book but thank you for allowing me to include you.

I want to personally thank Jo-Jo Crisci. You were extremely understanding and supportive. I hope that you are not offended by anything written. We were kids and everything that happened was a lifetime ago. I really am trying to help people and I think your story is powerful. Thank you for letting me include that story as a part of mine.

I want to thank my best friends. My very best friend, Pete Pascarella, I could never thank you enough. You've always been there and not just in the process of releasing this book. You've been there for me in life and that means more to me than anything. I could not have done this without your support, so thank you my brother!

One of my other best friends, Scott Jankunas, thank you buddy! You supported this from day one. Your belief in my future success, instilled a belief within myself. Thanks for checking in and having a vested interest in the progress. It's people like you, that made me see this all the way through.

Most people have a top five, the top five people in your life. Besides my family, I am extremely lucky to have a top ten filled with the most amazing friends in the world. To my best friends in life, who have all stood by me and supported me. I want to thank you all. It doesn't matter that some of us have drifted apart and have built lives for ourselves. I know all of you have families and things get hectic. Immediate family should always come first. We, however, are family as well, in a different vein. We have formed a brotherhood that can never be broken. That's why all that really matters are the times that we get to be together. When we get together, it's as if no time has passed and we get along just as well as when we were kids. The times that we need someone, we are there for each other. When one of us falls down, there's always one of us to pick the fallen one up. To my crew, we'll ride together until we die. Thank you, my brothers! In no particular order, here are the ten "kids" who are always there for me:

Pete Pascarella	**Scott Jankunas**
Augie Pugliese	**Ed Rakler**
John Bartley	**Dave Pepe**
Dominick Petracca	**Ralph Giacobbe**
Bill Dillon	**Rich Marino**

Thank you especially to Rich for allowing me to tell my crazy stories about torturing him! You're definitely the star of the show my friend!

I want to personally thank Tony Iovino. Thank you for being understanding. I didn't include you in the crew because you have a special place in my heart. I am sorry for any way I hurt you back when I was bully. I am sorry that I didn't accept you as part of our crew. I want to officially welcome you to the crew, even though you've been a part of it for a while now. I'm glad that you stuck around with us, even when some of us were jerks! You are an extremely funny guy and I am so glad you are in my circle of friends.

I would like to thank my amazing aunts. Aunt Marie, Aunt Martha, and Aunt Pitsy, the three of you have always supported anything I have ever done. You were some of my biggest fans when it came to my writing. Thank you for that!

I would like to thank my Lospinoso cousins, Joey, Donna, and Barbara. The three of you have always had a vested interest in what the "Lospinator" is doing with his life. For that I can't thank you enough. Joey always talks about the Lospinoso legacy. I hope I have made that legacy proud!

Thank you to my dear cousins, Jackie and Noel Fullman. Noel, your story really brought the book together and inspired the back cover quote as well as my mission statement. I can't thank you enough for your courage to tell me your story. Just know I will do everything I can for you in the future. Jackie, thank you for bringing the story to light for me. You also displayed courage by standing tall and telling your daughter's story. I hope you enjoy what I've written. Thank you both again for being amazing!

I would like to thank Maria Cino. Sorry to your husband, who I'm sure is amazing, but I will always know you as that! You may not know it, but you helped light a fire under me. I was down in the dumps and I was bedridden from an injury. You messaged me and encouraged me to write again. You told me how you loved my writing. That's really what jumpstarted this whole process. For that, I will be forever grateful. I hope the book lives up to your lofty expectations.

Thank you, Jessica Reynolds! When I was writing this, I had many memories that flooded back to me. We had an amazing friendship and I'm happy we are starting to rekindle that friendship. Back in high school, you tried to show me how to style my hair and have some semblance of fashion sense; whatever the heck that was back then! I appreciate you, as whether you know it or not, you were the start of me actually gaining some form of confidence. For that, I'll forever be grateful. I'm glad we reconnected old friend. It just goes to show that true friendship can be forged at any time in life and can last the test of time!

Thank you, Jesse Vitale. Almost two years ago, I had a horrible person leave me homeless, broke, and with nowhere to go. You took me in and got me back on my feet. I lost what I thought to be a legitimate book contract. This horrible person really did a number on me. I was devastated and I almost gave up on my dream. With your help, I picked myself back up and I became more determined to publish this book than ever. Without you, this would not have been possible. Thank you so much "Jersey!"

Thank you to my roommate and good friend, Thayer DeMay. After Jesse helped me get back on my feet, I landed in your Air B&B. You didn't know it at the time, but I was a broken man. I know I hid it well. I am so glad we hit it off, as I couldn't ask for a better roommate. Thank you for giving me a place to live and being there for me in general. Oh yeah and the front and back covers ROCK!!! You ROCK brother! OH YEAH!!!

Thank you to Walter Bayless. You just recently came into my life, but you have helped me hone my writing craft. You also inspire me on a daily basis. You cannot quantify the worth of inspiration! Thank you, my new friend.

Speaking of inspiration, I have to thank Christine Rydzik. You have been more than inspiring on my journey. You pushed me to get outside of my comfort zone and to better myself. You sent me a life changing book, <u>Think and Grow Rich</u>, which has had a profound effect on my psyche. I feel enlightened like I never have before. Thank you!

The last friend I would like to thank is my best bud in the world, Clayton Green! You changed me in ways I could never express. You opened my heart and made me realize that when it comes to friendship, age does not matter. We will be #1 Homies for Life, buddy boy! Thank you for being my little brother!

Thank you to my editors:

Maribeth Cassels, you only did some brief work with me, but you inspired me. I did change some of my action sequences because of your suggestions. I wish I was as brilliant as you. Thank you for your input.

Sarah Banks, thank you for the first edit. For the price, you were absolutely amazing. I would definitely recommend you to newer authors and I'll pass your name along if I can.

Liz Delton, what can I say? You were phenomenal. Thank you, as your final edits were fabulous. You really made the book more readable. You were a little above what I wanted to spend, but you were worth every penny. I will obviously, recommend you to anybody looking for a solid editor with tremendous style.

Thank you to the anti-bullying advocates that allowed me to use their materials. First to Jane Clementi of The Tyler Clementi Foundation, thank you so much. The Upstander pledge has a powerful and extremely important message. I will continue to spread that message.

Thank you to Lil and Dustin DeVaney as your story is an immensely emotional one. Thank you for allowing me to include your story as part of mine.

Thank you to Daphen Williams of the organization Bullying Stops Here Inc.! Thank you for promoting my Kickstarter campaign. You are all about the cause and I can't wait to visit your community in the future. You'll be one of my first stops.

Thank you to Marsha Manion and Brady Adams of a publishing company which I will not name. Even though we parted ways, you two were the only ones who believed in my work. Thank you for standing behind me and believing in <u>BULLY COMPLEX</u>!

Thank you to Christine Comoroski. I tried to contact you, but nobody could seem to find you. I wanted to thank you for letting me take you as a partner on the day of our senior class trip. You changed me for the better that day and for the rest of my life. I don't know where you are, but if you are reading this, please contact me. I would love to reconnect with you! Thank you for making me a better man!

Thank you to my late, great uncle, the Kenilworth Legend himself, Uncle Bish. Without you in my life, I may not have had any soft spots in my soul. I may have been a total menace without you. I miss every day without you. Thank you for giving me heart, as you inspired me as you always wore your heart on your sleeve. Rest in peace dear uncle.

To my late grandfather. I know you're looking down and I meant no disrespect to you whatsoever. I know you grew up in a different time. I wish you lived longer because I always wanted to know you better. I will see you in heaven dear grandfather. Rest in peace and thank you for making an amazing family.

To my late, great Uncle Olly, thank you for being there for my father. The day you passed was one of the hardest days of his life. I wish you could have witnessed the release of my book as I know you would be proud. I am carrying on the Lospinoso legacy. Rest in peace dear uncle.

To my recently passed uncle, Joseph Crisci Sr., I'm sorry I didn't get my stuff together sooner. You should've been able to see this with your own eyes. I know you'll be reading it up in heaven, but it's not the same. I think it's amazing how you made amends with your son and I hope our stories make you proud. You were a huge piece of my childhood. Your home was like my second home. Thank you for letting my sister and I feel welcomed all the time. Rest in peace and thank you for being a huge part of my life.

Rest in Peace Miss Logan. When I heard of your passing, it hit me hard. I know you would have been immensely proud of me, because I finally did it! I wrote a book! I always told you that I would write one in the future. I wish you were here to see it. I know you're looking down and smiling upon me. I'm so happy that we grew closer my senior year. I'm sorry I hurt you prior to that. Rest in peace my dear teacher. Rest knowing you taught me so much.

Rest in peace Brian Hirth Sr. You were one of my father's best friends and I wish you were here to read my book. I know you would have enjoyed the parts with my dad. Thank you for being in my life and being my dad's dear friend.

Rest in peace Mike Santangelo. I can still hear your laugh buddy. You were struggling to live towards the end of your life, yet you still helped me out. You said you would do anything to help the success of my book and that meant the world to me.

Rest in peace Michael Rothery. Your passing was sudden and unexpected. I want you to know that I will help as many people that find themselves in a similar position as possible. My next book will go a long way towards helping those in need. I'm already working on it and I wish you were here to help me with helping others.

Rest in peace Bob Jeans. You were taken from us way too soon. When I wrote about wrestling practice and the wrestling team, I couldn't help but think of you. You were an integral part of our team. I'll never forget watching Rocky IV with you on the nights before our meets! You used to get me so fired up. I want you to know that I still have that fire. See you in heaven old friend.

To my fabulous Kickstarter supporters, thank you! Without you, this obviously wouldn't be possible. With your help and financial support, my dream has finally been printed into reality.

A SPECIAL THANK YOU TO MY TOP TIER SUPPORTERS:

Albert and Sonia Lospinoso

Jennifer Lospinoso

Pete and Yolanda Pascarella

Scott and Lauren Jankunas

Pete Ramos

Lou Pascarella

Rose Crisci

Joe and Patty Lospinoso

Chris and Donna Koenig

Ralph and Fiorella Giacobbe

Ed and Iliana Rakler

Justin Roman

Doreen Therese

Ray Mack

Melissa Hilbrandt

And thank you to the rest of you amazing Kickstarter supporters:

Cassandra Taylor and Shane Shather

Steve and Roberta Chmielnik

Brandon Davis of Bravo Delta

Augie and Kara Pugliese

John Bartley and Michelle Panichi

Bill and Karen Dillon

Chris Reino and the Reino family

Jay and Cecilia Pedde

Will and Angela Marrero

Barbara Lospinoso

Nikki Pierro

Larry and Debbie Pierro

Pat and Marie Venice

Karen Venice

Brian and Jacqueline Fullman

Vincent Farro and Ann DiFrancesco

Mike and Maria Lokith

Marie Farro

Anthony Spatola

Joe Chango

Joe Steinau

Chris Toma

Anthony and Annie Basille

Dave Boot

Jessica Borowik

Wayne Hastrup

Jason Bentley

Jonathan Zommer

Lynn Castaldo Pipitone

Phil Drogon

Brendan Spiegel

Michael Keleher and Jessica Redling Keleher

Brian Hart

The Creative Fund by BackerKit

Thank you to everyone who allowed me to include in my story. Especially those who had an unsettling, uncomfortable, embarrassing or painful story in which I shared. Thank you specifically to Dave Goldberg, Fred Clock, Jamie G. and the other Dave who I talked with for hours. Dave I did not share your last name as I am unsure if you want the world to know what was shared. However, I want you know that I appreciate you opening up to me. I am humbled to now call you a friend.

Last but certainly not least, I want to thank God. Most people thank him first. Well, I am in no way, most people. I do acknowledge that without him, none of this would be possible. However, I am not someone who pushes religious beliefs on others. Hence, why I am thanking the almighty Lord last. There have been too many "coincidences" for there not to be a God. He has continuously sent me signs throughout the writing of this book. He has guided me and shown me my path in life. For that, I will be forever grateful. I feel enlightenment like I never have previously in my life. I have found my true calling. I'm finally awake! To the rest of you, you don't need to believe in God. You just need to be aware and be awake. STAY WOKE PEOPLE!

Let's all join together in the fight against the bullying epidemic. Allow me to light the path to peace and unity. Let my book, **BULLY COMPLEX** show us the way.

AUTHOR BIO

Anthony Lospinoso is an American born, first time author. Lospinoso has been writing on and off his entire life, and *Bully Complex* is his first full length book. The book follows the author on an emotional true-life journey, where he undergoes several transformations. *Bully Complex* is a story of pain, victimization, bullying, and ultimately redemption.

Although *Bully Complex* is Lospinoso's debut book, he has been published previously in newspapers and literary magazines. Early on, his aspirations were to be a newspaper writer, but he lost his way. He has worked many different jobs over the years and has been a struggling artist most recently. Lospinoso is hoping to make this book the start of the next chapter of his life. There were several defining moments that changed him for the better. These revelations opened his eyes to the bullying epidemic and made him realize his purpose in life.

With the launch of *Bully Complex*, the new author would like to add advocate to his list of accomplishments. His goal is to help as many kids as possible. He has poured every ounce of his being into this book, and he has spent the past half-decade honing his craft. Now, finally seeing the finished manuscript come to fruition, he hopes sharing his story with the world will initiate change for the better. Lospinoso is making strides in the anti-bullying community; learn more about his story and advocacy at his website bullycomplex.com which is coming soon.

MISSION STATEMENT

To help children who are being bullied. To give kids a voice who are being victimized and tell them it's OK to speak out. To deter bullies from persisting with their harmful actions.

It doesn't matter if you're pretty, you're popular, an athlete or considered an outcast, no kid is immune to the bullying epidemic. I am here to be an advocate for those who have lost their voice . . . to give a voice to the voiceless. It is imperative that adults, bullies, and victims galvanize (come together) and join forces to eradicate bullying once and for all.

If you are thinking about hurting yourself or committing suicide, or are worried about a friend or loved one, then please call the

National Suicide Prevention Lifeline

at:

1-800-273-8355